AFTERNOON LIGHT

AFTERNOON LIGHT

A Memoir

RALPH BEER

Grateful acknowledgement is made for permission to reprint excerpts from:

Tear Stained Eye
Words and Music by Jay Farrar
Copyright © 1995 Grain Elevator Music
All Rights Administered by BMG Rights Management (US) LLC
All Rights Reserved   Used by Permission
Reprinted by Permission of Hal Leonard Corporation

"I am waiting" by Lawrence Ferlinghetti, from A CONEY ISLAND OF THE MIND, copyright ©1958 by Lawrence Ferlinghetti. Reprinted by permission of New Directions Publishing Corp.

Excerpt from CLOSE QUARTERS: A NOVEL by Larry Heinemann, copyright © 1974, 1975, 1976, 1977, and 2005 by Larry Heinemann. Used by permission of Vintage Books, an imprint of the Knopf Doubleday Publishing Group, a division of Penguin Random House LLC. All rights reserved. Any third party use of this material, outside of this publication, is prohibited. Interested parties must apply directly to Penguin Random House LLC for permission.

"Ellie and Lindy" and "Almost Summer" by David E. Thomas, from WATERWORKS HILL, copyright © 2010 by David E. Thomas. Reprinted by permission of the author.

Cover photo AVTG/E+/Getty Images

ISBN-13: 9780997322125
ISBN-10: 0997322128
Library of Congress Control Number: 2016908680

Casey Peak Press, Livermore, CO

Also by Ralph Beer

The Blind Corral
In These Hills
The Jackson Creek Road

It is so small a thing
to have enjoyed the sun,
to have lived light in the spring
to have loved, to have thought,
to have done.

—Mathew Arnold
"Hymn of Empedocles"

PROLOGUE

October in Cottonwood Canyon, up in Montana. Rags of an early snow lay splashed with bright leaves from the trees along the creek, yet the slopes of Doug fir, just a hundred yards to the east, were as dry and warm as September in the early morning sun. It was that time of year when Sam's log house, in the deep shade beside the creek, would have needed a morning fire to drive out the chill. Since Sam's cancer had whittled him down, we kept the wood stove in the living room chuffing along all day. I had been staying with Sam and his wife, Linda, for a week, my second visit in just the past few months. This time I'd brought my big Stihl chainsaws and divided my days between bucking and splitting logs at Sam's woodshed and visiting with him while he rested inside near the stove. Over a span of forty years, Sam's homestead had been close to the center of my life; a place blessed by an enduring friendship and charmed by the sound of cold water in motion.

One afternoon, when I'd finished for the day, I came in with an armload of kindling and stirred the fire awake. I asked Sam how he was doing, and he said, as he usually did, that he felt pretty good. But Sam was growing weaker. Fluid was building in his lungs again, and the hairline cracks in his spine increased his pain each day.

"I've got the shed darned near full," I said. "If I get your coat, could you come outside for a look?"

Sam hesitated. Then he said sure, he'd give it a try.

In 1975, Sam and I had hiked the Gallatin Divide together, an eighty-mile-long series of steep up-and-down ridges and mountain tops that ran south from his place to Yellowstone National Park. Sam had walked each day carrying a thirty-five-pound pack—a mountain goat, tireless, nimble, and quick. I was the one who panted up snow fields and called for breaks. Now Sam got winded as he stood from the sofa to lean on his walker.

I helped him with his coat and stocking hat and draped a wool blanket around his shoulders. We trailed his oxygen line through the house and down off the porch, then one slow step at a time, we crossed a bit of lawn to where the woodshed stood packed with bright sticks of lodgepole pine and fir. Moss grew an inch deep on the cedar shakes of the roof. Cross-country skis, long worn out or broken, were tacked here and there to upright posts and cross beams. We stopped in a patch of sunshine to look at the new rows of split wood that topped out just below the pole rafters.

"Now that's a pretty sight," Sam said. "You're a good man, Ralph."

As I'd worked on the wood during the days, the music of the creek came to me through the cottonwoods. Fast water rushing along a stony bottom, it carried me back through time in that place, then transported me far to the north to another creek, the two streams braiding together in memory, the voices of water in motion, ever changing, always the same.

"Sam," I said. "I've been thinking of writing about the cabin."

The cabin was shorthand for a long-ago time in British Columbia, an experience more than a building, but Sam knew what I meant. We stood without talking for a while—two friends watching afternoon shadows slide toward us across a bit of lawn.

Sam looked over at me. "I think you should," he said.

After a minute or two we turned and made our way back toward the warmth of the fire burning inside.

Sam died a few weeks later. During a storm of grief I hadn't seen coming, I settled into remembering. I scribbled notes and tried to make a beginning, rusty after writing almost nothing for ten years. It was slow going, of course. My concentration wasn't what it had been when I'd written every day, and I found that I tired after just an hour or two. But I made a start, got a page as we used to say, then for five winters I worked to fill my woodshed with rows of words about a bright girl and the joyous months of work and love we shared in the far north woods; about log walls rising and a roof taking shape above our heads, and the friends like Sam Curtis, who had come to help. So many rows of words about learning to love and the discovery of a love that would waiver but not die.

Sometimes memory fails, and sometimes it stays as sharp as a drawknife used to peel logs. I have forgotten most of what that girl and I said to each other in the summer and fall of 1971, while much of what we did remains clear in my mind. Sam Curtis is braided through that story, like one strand in an old rope that will not break. There's the sweet girl with a graceful dip in her stride, who spoke to me and touched me and made me her own. And our other friends, too, people who helped us along the way, who shared our laughter and politics and accepted our behavior as nothing less than natural in those roilsome times.

Looking back, I see victories and discoveries, setbacks and losses. I see things I wish I hadn't done, and I see the faces of those I loved. Maybe enough time has passed to let me enjoy the best and forgive the rest. This book, then, is about an adventure that forever changed my life, and a young woman, who still visits me in the nightlands of sleep, where clear waters make old music under cottonwoods, as they rush along their courses polishing stones.

PART I

I would meet you anywhere
The Western sun meets the air
We'll hit the road
Never looking behind.

—Jay Farrar
"Tear Stained Eye"

ONE

Our hearts know where the best times lie waiting, and sometimes, when we dream, our hearts will take us there. If I close my eyes and become quiet, I can hear a distant white sound coming from where the graduate-student carrels once stood beside the fountains in the Montana State University Library, just as it was in the spring of 1971.

The fountains stood in an open mezzanine that housed the library's botanical area. Ferns the size of trees groped toward skylights far above, as the endless music of water, spilling from various porcelain spouts, created a feeling of serenity in a benign jungle. Hollow metal sculptures leaped up three floors from the fountains' shallow pool to serve as targets for pennies, flung from the upper levels by the listless and the bored. A sophomore's direct hit would make an off-key *kong!* followed by muffled snorts and giggles.

The graduate carrels were tucked away in a dim room behind the fountains, a good place to escape the hoards of damp undergraduates. It was a space reserved for scholars, but there were those among us who didn't take this sanctuary all that seriously. To me it seemed a fine place to read *Evergreen Review*, to think about sex, or to maybe roll a joint. The carrels had a writing desk and single shelf for books on each side, so two people, facing the partition between them, could occupy one carrel at the same time. Grad students reserved these desks for the academic year and used them as much as places to store extra books or to daydream as havens for serious study.

Above the bookshelf in my carrel, where I kept my volumes of Milton and Blake and paperbacks like *Do It* and *The Electric Kool-Aid Acid Test*, I had taped a newspaper photo of Warren Harding and Dean Caldwell, taken with a telephoto lens, as they clung (for twenty-seven days and nights) to the 3,000-foot vertical wall of El Capitan in the first ever "direct" ascent of The Wall of the Early Morning Light. They endured sleepless nights, and they braved all weathers. They refused to be rescued. They seemed like gods to me then, demonstrating as they did, what men might become, when acting out their wildest dreams.

On the other side of the divider I'd taped a photo, torn from a magazine, of Mary Ann Vecchio, crying out in anguish as she knelt above the body of Jeffrey Miller, who had just been killed by a national guardsman's bullet at Kent State University. Those two photos seemed to capture the essence of the America we lived in then in 1970 and '71, an America of heroes and the dizzying heights of unlimited possibility, and a violent, oppressive America at war with itself. While I revered Harding and Caldwell for their courage, I sought refuge in a library from that other world, the one where young men like myself were shipped off every day to a swamp half-way around the world, there to survive pongee stakes and mortar rounds, bullets and various evil forms of clap, in the defense of Democracy in Southeast Asia. One year. More time was available, I knew, for those who grew to love it.

The MSU Library, on the other hand, was a fantasyland of water music and girls, of learning that smelled like old paper, an asylum within a refuge for those like myself who sought not to serve. It was a still place, then, as close to a forest as I could find on the MSU campus, a soft, mossy log of a place, where I could rest my head upon my arms, to nap away the time appointed for the Wordsworth and Coleridge Seminar, for which I had not prepared, and to dream, perhaps, of love.

I had my draft deferment for an extra year, and I made the most of that year by spending half my nights in dim beer joints, by smoking a lot of bad pot, and by luring as many girls as possible into the various trailers and shacks I rented or bummed. I grew my hair and hung a leather stash bag from my belt. I drove a 1947 Chevrolet delivery van painted robin's-eggshell blue. My grades hopped up and down, peaking at the end of an earnest winter quarter, then glissading downward on the March revels of anticipated spring.

Ah, spring . . . a time of twist-top Tokay and firm, nursing-student breasts. So good to be a young man, then, with a copy of *HOWL* in one hip pocket and a dozen tiny barrels of purple mescaline in the other. Without knowing what I was doing, I swung along with increasing momentum, right into the best times of my life.

But *so* much life between now and then. Somewhere along the line we yoked up and took on responsibilities and our lives slipped by. We got steady jobs. We signed mortgages and invented routines. We advanced in our professions and gained weight and became less interesting than we'd once supposed. Time ticked along until colors seemed not quite as sharp, the scent of fresh-cut hay not quite so heady. But sometimes, without warning, we can still catch a taste or scent or sound that strikes flint to steel, sparking a flame that illuminates those minutes, those days, those people who were, and yet remain, so necessary. Once again, sensation stirs recollection, and we journey back in a heartbeat to when the best of it all began.

For me, it is always a Sunday afternoon in April, when water music from the library fountains played on, as I sat alone, failing to read a forgotten book required for a forgotten class that lay open on my desk. It is always the exact moment, when she plopped down her books on the other side of the carrel's divider, and came around to say hello, that is the beginning of this story. Sunlight filtered down from the skylights far above, and the metal sculptures expanded in the warmth, tickity-tick, and the plants and ferns, sensing the end of their Montana winter, screamed with joy.

She was such a sunny girl, small and trim and quick as a chickadee, with dark eyes made even larger by her glasses. There was something about her that always seemed clean, like laundered work shirts fresh from the line. In a quiet way, she had turned out to be the smartest girl in all our classes, and I had come to admire the way she would discover an angle or meaning or connection that the rest of us failed to notice. Mac Watson had once confided to me, in casual conversation, that he thought Sheila was quite beautiful, in spite of the dorsal hump on her nose and the missing bicuspid, which sometimes showed when she smiled.

But it's that moment in the library, when Sheila Malone leaned toward me, smiled, and whispered, "Hi," that I've returned to over the years. A spark in time. A beginning.

As she stood beside me, I noticed the round outlines of her breasts beneath her blouse. I had noticed them before, of course; they were large for a girl with hips like a boy, and so perfectly shaped that in a world of breasts, they were ones a man would remember.

Sheila was usually quick to smile and to laugh, but she seemed especially bright that Sunday afternoon, happy and full of warmth. We were acquaintances more than friends and not quite comfortable alone with each other. We traveled in the same small circle of liberals, surrounded by a campus full of cowboys and conservatives. Sometimes we saw each other at informal social events, where our talk was usually limited to politics or books or people we knew there at school.

Sheila sat down on her side of the carrel's divider to read. She was invisible, yet close enough to touch. I could hear her turning pages. I looked at the metal between us and noticed that my newspaper clipping of Caldwell and Harding's ascent had curled at the edges, as if tired. I'd wanted to scale distant heights, too, but I wasn't a climber. I wanted escape that afternoon, but I didn't want to leave sweet Sheila Malone behind. And that's when I heard those little barrels of purple mescaline calling up to me from my hip pocket. *We are here,* they piped, sounding like wee fairies dancing around a mushroom in a mossy glade. *Come join us, Big Guy, and we'll kick your ass!*

I had no reason whatsoever to think that Sheila used drugs, or, had even—as we used to say—experimented with them. In that regard, she seemed pretty straight, even a little square in a small town sort of way. But that didn't stop me from popping out of my chair like a cartoon figure from *Fritz the Cat*, with a cartoon light bulb glowing in a cartoon bubble above my head, to say, "I've got an idea! You want to get high and catch the movie over at the Union?"

There was no thoughtful pause. Like Molly Bloom, with the rose in her hair at the end of her famous soliloquy, Sheila Malone looked up at me with eyes full of mischief and said, "Yes!"

I showed her what I had in my pocket and tried to explain what she might expect. Then we each swallowed one of those little miracles and went out to sit in front of the Student Union building, where we gazed upon the poor, crumbling hull of Hamilton Hall across the way, that housed our English Department's offices and conference rooms. We basked in the timid sunshine and waited, as full of expectant giggles as children, until the featured film, *2001: A Space Odyssey*, was about to start. Then we went inside to the Student Union theater and found some seats way up front in the empty second row and waited for the lights to dim.

By the time the ape-man flung his bone into the air at the climax of the famous water hole scene, and the bone had turned in its flight to a far-questing space ship, we were both high enough to just step aboard. The hum-drum blockages in our minds and in our lives were gone, and we were freed from ourselves. The *Blue Danube Waltz* had never seemed so buoyant as we found ourselves nearing the great wheeling space station with our milky blue planet turning in the background. Then we lost sight of the Earth and the small concerns of the Earth, until, at some point, we discovered we'd not only sped off toward galaxies beyond all imagining, but that we were holding hands like a couple of high school kids. I think we might have been just as surprised by our interlocked fingers as by a computer singing "A Bicycle Built for Two," as it died. But we did not let go, not once, until the theater lights came on.

After the movie, we walked the back streets of Bozeman until we noticed the full moon lighting our way. Hadn't we just been there and many light-years beyond, in a deep space where moons and planets had aligned so perfectly? Hadn't we understood that alignment and certain secrets of the Universe? It seemed so, yes it did, and we walked on, hand in hand, along silent streets beneath the budding trees, coming down in a gentle glide, holding on to the great distances we'd just traveled and the discovery we had made, because we both knew right then, that after that night, we'd never ever be, either of us, quite the same.

TWO

There are so many beginnings to this story. Although she has been gone many years, lost in time and distance and betrayals on both sides, sometimes even now the scent of a certain woodsmoke or the sound of a distant stream, rushing along through tall timber, will pull me back to a forest, where afternoon light comes down through pines to a shelf of moss-covered rock, a place where the heat and brightness of living was of such sweet intensity that the brief months we spent there burned into me the way a length of iron, drawn from a pitch-pine fire, can burn itself into green wood.

If I close my eyes and let myself drift in that smoke, or on those waters, I can go back to another long-ago beginning, that happened not during an afternoon movie but a couple of years earlier, in the rickety Old Main Hall of Montana State University, on one of those sharp October mornings that can make college students and elk do foolish things. Fall Quarter, 1968: the class was Shakespeare's Tragedies, and she was in her usual place in the front row with the girls who meant to get the best grades. I sat with the lumpy lads against the back wall, where our attention wandered from Doctor Watson's efforts to make *Hamlet* come alive, to those ankles beckoning from beneath the desks up front. I had surveyed each pair, of course, and decided that hers were thick, certainly not ankles to be desired.

That morning our Doctor Watson, who was only twenty-seven years old and right out of graduate school, marched back and forth in his herky-jerky stride, wearing his desperate, three-piece corduroy suit and a scowl, trying to wake us up. He nearly upended his lectern as the ghost of Hamlet's father appeared; then, collecting himself, our good professor floated a question above our becalmed group, and the girl with the heavy ankles rose to it like a trout. She stated her answer, which was actually an opinion, with a crisp certainty that told us she knew what she was talking about. Doctor Watson abruptly came to a halt and turned to face us. He seemed to be waiting for more, sensing an opportunity for disagreement, perhaps, or for the other shoe to drop.

October light poured through the wavy glass of the casement windows in Old Main Hall; elk bugled in frosty meadows within ten miles of us; and I looked up from tamping Cherry Blend into the bowl of my meerschaum to say, "Well, I don't know about that."

She turned halfway around in her desk to look back at me, which struck me as pretty aggressive for a little girl with big glasses. She frowned and waited for me to continue. And right there, memory fails. I can see students sitting in the rows of desks between us, but I cannot recall now the point I meant to argue. What I remember is her dark brown hair, combed down in a straight, Mary Travers do on each side of her face, and her eyes, focused like a hawk's behind her glasses. She seemed darkly surprised when I made my point, and her response, when it came, was delivered with a voice that had taken on a certain edge.

I thought of myself in those days as bold, the way a young man who may not be all that bright is bold, but her posture and her glare and the quickness of her reply gave me pause. I guessed in those first seconds that she might be more interesting than I'd supposed. And I noticed, as she gripped the seatback of her desk with her left hand, that she wore a wedding ring.

Her name was Sheila Marlene Malone. Since she was an English major, too, and because there were so few of us at that land grant college—where hundreds of engineering students carried slide rules in holsters swinging on their belts—we occasionally nodded or said hello as we passed each other on sidewalks and in various hallways. Over time, her ankles seemed to slim down nicely. She was slender and open-faced, and she had freckles. She seemed a little square, to a beer-joint boy like myself, but she shined when she smiled, and she smiled often. She had a brightness and zip that would sometimes pull me around for a second look. Two things a person would notice about her right away: that while she spoke very softly with crisp, perfect diction, she was not afraid to speak up when plain talk was called for. And she suffered from a troublesome hip, which caused her to walk with a swaying, elliptical limp that was somehow quite graceful.

Time passed. I married a girl from the wild-hay country atop the Continental Divide. The war in Vietnam escalated. Campus activism in the Spring Quarter of 1970 brought Sheila and I into contact more often. We took to waving to each other from one sidewalk to another, and we shared rides a few times to meetings and night classes.

One afternoon, I met her as she descended a flight of stairs in the Student Union building, near the University Bookstore in the basement. She was carrying a purse made of woven twigs that looked like a miniature picnic basket, and as we passed each other, she gave me just the brightest smile. I started up the stairs toward the sunlight outside, then I turned to watch her walk away down the hall, swaying gently from side to side as she went.

My father was a blacksmith, my mother worked for the telephone company. We lived in a white stucco house on the east edge of Helena, a little house that my dad built by adding rooms to a couple old farm sheds salvaged from a local dairy. I was a hot-and-cold student in high school, where the best thing that happened to me was music. I played string bass in three city symphony orchestras in the state and ached for a girl with blazing red hair over in the trumpet section. I spent my Saturdays and summers on a little cattle ranch my dad's father owned south of town, a place up in the timbered flanks of the Continental Divide, first homesteaded by my great-grandparents. A thousand acres of pine woods and hillside grassland, surrounded by tens of thousands of open acres just like it, the ranch was a good place for a kid like me—a boy who was awkward and unsure and not all that sharp, a boy who walked more than he drove, and who probably read too many books—to find solace, to regroup, a place to grow some biceps and chase those old mule deer bucks while having the time to ponder girls and the subtle ways of the more polished kids at school.

For some of us, college was a way to recover from the anxieties of high school, an opportunity to try out new identities while groping our way toward the kinds of people we might eventually want to become. Bozeman was an easy drive from Helena, and in-state tuition made college possible. So I took classes and hung out on campus during the week then headed home a couple weekends a month to cut firewood or fix fence or hunt elk. It was a natural, uncomplicated arrangement that opened some unexpected doors. I learned to ski. I learned to drink rotgut wine and to smoke bad weed. I took my first writing class from a fine young instructor from Connecticut named Sam Curtis, and there was something about him personally—a soft spoken direct-ness and a slight unease about his role as teacher—that interested me and made me want to be around people like him.

By my senior year, in 1970, I had traded in my wool slacks and saddle shoes, which had once seemed so collegiate, for a pair of climbing boots made in Garmisch, Germany, and some old jeans patched with bits of red bandana. I grew a beard. I met people who would introduce me to new ideas and new ways of seeing and to other people, who would be at the center of my life for the next forty years. And as I put a little distance between myself and my hometown, I began to feel more comfortable in my own skin.

The Sixties most people think of now, did not make it to Montana until the decade was over. Sure, we listened to the music and thought about the war in Vietnam as something that happened on the evening news, some bad busi-ness far off beyond the horizon, but we came no closer to Woodstock than the screens of our hometown theaters. The Rocky Mountains lay between young people in Montana and the radical politics in far-off Berkeley, and there was just no way the Jefferson Airplane could fly us there.

❖ ❖ ❖

Richard Nixon had already been president far too long by the time my senior year lumbered toward an end. Spring was a cruel season in 1970. Ice thawed and puddles formed on the MSU campus, only to freeze again like polished steel. Nothing much happened that didn't involve muddy skies and slush, until one afternoon, when I stepped into a moment that seems remarkably vivid and of genuine consequence all these years later. On the way to an afternoon class, I left the shelter of the Student Union and turned west into one of those intermittent spring snowstorms that could last for days. A young man with shoulder-length hair was sitting on a bench that divided the currents of passing students the way boulders split a mountain stream. He wore a World War I, U.S. Army greatcoat and held a little cardboard sign on his knees which said: "Stop the War." Snow had accumulated on his shoulders. He didn't move or make any special effort toward eye contact as I passed; he just sat there looking purposeful and calm.

When I came back an hour later, the snow had deepened on his coat and his hair was frozen. Right then my life rose in an unexpected arc. The fella with the sign had not only found a way to cut through all the old arguments on both sides of the war debate, he had the strength to sit there alone—in the center of what was then a depressingly conventional Ag college in a town where Saturday-night cowboys still liked to cut hippie hair—holding his message out for anyone who cared to look. His name was Ray Larson. The coat had belonged to his grandfather, a Montana draftee in The Great War. Ray's one-man demonstration struck me then, as it does now, as remarkably brave and elegant, and it pointed me toward other people on campus who were engaged in odd and interesting enterprises that didn't necessarily lead to a career at Honeywell. I began to seek those people out and found that I enjoyed listening to them and frolicking with them, because they struck me as good people who thought a New World might be heading our way.

The Nixon/Kissinger decision to invade Cambodia in the spring of 1970, and the Kent State killings that followed it, abruptly changed campus neutrality in Montana, at least for groups of students in Missoula and Bozeman. As if overnight, there appeared angry differences of opinion between townspeople and students, conservatives and fledgling leftists. I hit that new barrier in a drugstore near campus after calling bullshit on Paul Harvey, whose noontime radio voice wafted through the store's interior. He'd said that it was widely felt among most Americans that the kids shot down at Kent State deserved what they got. An indignant lady working the cash register blurted out that Mr. Harvey was absolutely right. Her face grew hot when I asked, too loudly, how she'd feel about seeing the college students, who made up the bulk of her business, shot down in the street outside while on their way to classes. We barked at each other, and I heard myself telling her to stop defending the people responsible for all the killing, in Vietnam and now here at home. "Stop the war," I raged at her, and as I stalked off, I told myself that although my lottery number was forty-four, I would not go quietly when my draft notice came.

So even in Bozeman, Montana, we finally woke up and began to take sides. We took sides on the war. We took sides on the footloose freedoms of our youth culture versus the churchy materialism of square people. We took sides on abortion and religion, and we took sides on any other darned thing that seemed vaguely political, including the firing of professors, who, certain deans thought, might lure students off in un-American directions by using leftist books in their classes.

Sure, I'd seen them on television, and it seemed to me that campus radicals had a lot more fun than business majors. Girls in torn bell bottoms and peasant blouses seemed so much more alluring than the young ladies I saw every day clad in the armor of sorority jackets. But I had a wife and a Magnolia mobile home with monthly payments on a rented slab out at Four Corners, and I needed twenty-four credit hours the spring quarter of my senior year to graduate. I would not have had the energy to protest very much if a widely admired young instructor in the English Department had not run afoul of the university administration. A few students and a parent or two objected to Jim Meyers' use of *The Student as Nigger* in one of his classes, and his contract was not renewed. Other students and several young professors joined forces to protest his "firing." Sheila Malone and another troublemaker or two with organizational skills gained access to the English Department office one night, where they cut a stencil and printed flyers announcing a sit-in to support Meyers the following day.

And boy-howdy, did we ever sit in. That snowy afternoon I found myself on the floor in front of the Registrar's office in Old Main Hall, sitting beside Sam Curtis and Richie Furz, another young instructor in the English Department, as they waved a sign that said, "Cut the Crap: Fire Dayton! [a university dean] Rehire Meyers!" Our Doctor Watson, no longer sporting a suit, clumped in wearing jeans and boots. He pumped his fist and growled, and we cheered! Lindy Miller, our "student representative," and number-one smooth talker, went in to see the president of the university, and we sat there grinning at each other, waiting for his return.

We were polite. We moved our legs so people with official business could go on their way. We were all just a little bit scared, too, although the campus policemen who looked in on our sit-in, left without a fuss. It was probably the first ever such demonstration in the history of that little college, and we all got quite a thrill.

A few days later, some of us drove up to Helena to meet with state legislators about the Meyers matter. We wrote letters, we signed petitions, and we went to meetings that sometimes got ugly. But it was spring quarter, and Meyers, who had only a master's degree, was doomed.

At our college graduation, Sheila Malone and I sat together, capped and gowned and wearing MEYERS armbands during the ceremony. I enjoyed her closeness as we sat through the speeches that day, and I was surprised and delighted when that elfin girl with the gold honors lanyard looked the president of the university right in the eye then refused to shake his hand when he presented her diploma. It was her way of saying that administrators should stop firing our best teachers without good cause, a point she made in front of a thousand tax-paying Montanans. That young lady and her gesture seemed heroic to me then, as they do now, all these years later.

THREE

Three days after graduation, a trailer-mover towed my Magnolia mobile home to the Helena Valley, where my wife lived while I spent the summer high in the Elkhorn Mountains, cutting cordwood. Each evening my father arrived with a truck and trailer to haul off what I'd cut during the day, and by late August, we had a small mountain of logs to buzz-saw, split, and sell as firewood. Dad and I came from a line of woodcutters, who had sold cordwood and stove wood in central Montana since the 1890s. In 1901, my mother's grandfather, Fred Bessette, was killed by a runaway team of horses on the Jackson Creek Road while hauling cordwood to Helena. My dad's father and *his* father had cut wood to pay for groceries while proving up on homesteads in Jefferson County. Dad and I might have had chainsaws and trucks, but we were woodhawks, right to the bone.

I hadn't heard the last of Jim Meyers, however. He and Sam Curtis and several other young instructors from MSU bought twenty acres in New Mexico where they'd decided to start up a "new school." I made an effort to keep in touch with the people involved, and from my Elkhorn Mountains wood camp, I exchanged several letters with Sam and his wife Suzie, even agreed to help move their household goods from Bozeman down to New Mexico at the end of the summer.

When we arrived in September, with a U-haul truck loaded down with all their stuff and my motorcycle, the new school seemed more like the commune we'd seen in *Easy Rider*. No one was eating road kill, yet, but things looked none too prosperous. It was sort of a summer camp in the pinyons for college professors who had nowhere else to go. The place was nonetheless called

The Glorieta Finishing School, which gave it a tongue-in-cheek, high-toned elegance that seemed to some of us quite funny. Each morning I worked with Sam Curtis building a stretch of stonewall in what would be the school's main building. In the afternoons a group of us drove to a swimming hole in the Pecos River to splash about and wash off the adobe dust. It was fine summer fun with a bunch of long-hairs, but nothing much moved toward completion at the school during the two weeks I was there.

Sam and Sue had pitched their wall tent in a meadow some distance from the main camp. I slept on the far side of the meadow, out in the open on a borrowed cot. Each morning their golden lab, Lupo, woke me with exuberant barks, galumphing around my cot until I crawled out of my army surplus fart sack to look for my jeans. Once I had my boots on, I wandered over to the Curtis tent for coffee. In the evenings, I adjourned with them to canvas folding chairs beside their tent for bourbon in tin cups. Already Sam and Sue seemed skeptical about some of the principal people there and the prospects of anything like success. There were infidelities and peckish hostilities, even sudden violence when a mustard jar, hurled by an outraged wife, left a wandering husband with a black eye.

I left the Glorieta Finishing School on one of those perfect New Mexico mornings, when the red mesas, and the pinyons and junipers on their flanks, were fired by that crystalline Southwest light. My motorcycle, one of the first four-cylinder, 750cc Hondas sold in Montana, was brand new, purchased from Red Drennon in Helena with a trade-in BSA Victor and a handshake on the balance. I took it easy on the new motor for a while, savoring the country and the empty highway and jacked by the feeling that I was on the verge of something big. Then I rolled the power on and let that motorcycle carry me away.

I rode straight through to Fitzsimons Army Medical Center in Denver. My friend, Tom Crosser, had taken three rounds through the floor of the helicopter he was flying in Vietnam. He'd lost a kidney and some bone in his left leg and was undergoing physical therapy and more operations while still in the early stages of recovery. We'd been best buds our senior year at Helena High, and we'd logged some beer-joint good times together when Tom was home on leave. He was my friend, and it was important to me to drop in to see him as I passed through town.

The staff sergeant at the hospital's front desk took one look at my beard, hair, and sawed-off sweatshirt, and made a decision. "No Warrant Officer Crosser registered here, Sir," he told me with barely concealed malice.

I found a payphone, called Tom's mother in Helena and explained the situation. Tom's mother assured me that he *was* at Fitzsimons, so I went back, tried the desk sergeant again, and got the same results. I could see I'd be talking to MPs if I pushed him, so, at a loss for what to do next, I walked around the grounds outside the main building until I noticed a group of black soldiers—some in wheelchairs, a couple leaning on crutches—smoking cigarettes on the rear loading dock of what turned out to be a ward for amputees. I walked over to them and pulled out my meerschaum.

They were beautiful guys, the kind of young, hard-muscled black men who looked like high school and college athletes or could have been if they hadn't been drafted. They were all missing arms or legs, their various stumps swaddled about in white cloth. They were about my age, but seemed older. They were my first contact with what Vietnam casualties looked like up close, and they took my breath away.

Maybe I was a curiosity to them with my beard and hair, maybe they thought I was selling weed. We stared at each other for a few moments across the vast distances between us, until I regrouped enough to explain that I was looking for a friend who was somewhere in Fitzsimons, but that the lifer at the front desk wouldn't or couldn't tell me how to find him. The soldiers were cool, remote, and silent as they looked me over, but when I described Tom and his wounds, one young trooper in a wheelchair said he knew who Crosser was and on which floor of that very building he could be found.

"Go on up, man. Nobody be hasslin' you. He maybe got a room at the BOQ, too. If you can't find him on Three, check the BOQ over there," and he pointed out a red brick building a little ways off.

Within a few minutes I discovered Chief Warrant Officer Crosser, dressed in hospital coveralls and leaning on his crutches in the hallway near a crowded ward filled with the wounded. Tom stood there looking pale and hurt and maybe a little embarrassed. The wound where he'd lost his left kidney had seeped enough to stain his coveralls, and it seemed to me as I hugged him, that he might be close to tears. We shook hands then, the shaggy college boy civilian and the young warrior pilot, who had narrowly missed death. That handshake was my introduction to the pain and loss of his war and to those thousands of my generation who had lost themselves in it.

I spent three days with Tom, drinking together each night in his room at the Bachelor Officers Quarters until we nodded off, then sleeping late the next day. In the afternoons I lashed his leg in its cast to the side of my bike, tied a pillow to the sissy bar, and gave him my helmet. Then off we went, waving to the MPs at the front gate as we escaped into Denver for movies and pizzas, even a tour of the Coors Brewery in Golden. We went about town at speed, with Tom leaning back against his pillow, sometimes grinning madly while playing imaginary drums, his blue hospital coveralls snapping in the wind. It was foolish and great fun, the kind of heedless risk-taking young men fall into so naturally, when they've discovered that the world will eventually kill them, no matter what they do.

I didn't want to go home, so from Denver I headed east across Nebraska and half of Iowa to visit the small college I'd attended my freshman and sophomore years. The campus in 1970 seemed cloistered, the students in their autumn foliage, so perfect among the red oaks. I lingered in hallways and stairwells, along certain spans of sidewalk, and at benches on lawns that ran off to meet distant fields, places that had become beautiful in memory since I'd once passed through them with a brilliant young woman on one arm, a girl with the black hair and dark good looks of a gypsy princess. She had a husky, wild laugh and a way of bumping me with one hip for emphasis as we walked across campus. Sometimes an expression would cross her face that started with a quick downward twist of her lips—not a smile, but a sign that a good one was on the way. She was beautiful and lithe, true, and she moved with a verve and force that seemed to me as potent as fire.

I walked the campus and watched the students on their way to classes and looked for Suzanne among them, and I was amazed to realize the enormity of my decision to leave her and this strange place behind. It was true I'd run out of cash for the expensive tuition there; that had been my excuse for leaving. But I hadn't made any effort to raise the money needed to stay on. Instead I returned to Montana, started classes in Bozeman, and a year later married a good girl who turned out to be the wrong girl.

How strange it seemed, then, to be back in southern Iowa in 1970, just twenty-three years old and far too young to be overcome by such an unexpected sense of loss. I tracked that gypsy girl down in Omaha, only to find her married, too, and teaching school. I rode on, heading west, her voice alive in my head. I was gut-shot and twitchy, and I discovered, somewhere in the great expanse of South Dakota, that some decisions have consequences.

On what should have been the last day of my ride back to Helena, I hit a cold front at Big Timber, Montana, that was as abrupt as walking into a frozen-meat locker on a July afternoon. I throttled the 750 down, pulled to the side of I-90, put on all the extra clothes in my pack then pulled my Korean War-surplus raincoat over my head. Wet flakes, the size of nickels, were falling in Livingston, but because I was so close to home and almost out of money I decided to go on. I slalomed up the east side of the Bozeman Hill until I was creeping along with both feet down for balance, my boots sliding like outriggers through the freezing slush. I passed eighteen-wheelers as they lost traction and slid to the edge of the road; a little farther on, a truck-and-trailer had jackknifed, blocking one lane. Truckers were pulling over to chain up, but I skidded on, trying to keep my revs as low as possible without stalling the engine.

Any blip of the throttle made the rear tire spin, which whipped the back end of the bike around. I went on, peering through my goggles, having more and more trouble controlling the bike as my hands and face and feet went numb.

Somehow I reached the summit, where a stiff wind had frozen the slush into slabs of ice. When I started down the Bozeman side of the pass, I found that if I rode on the outside shoulder, where there were no tire tracks, I could keep moving in a more-or-less straight line. From the top of the Divide, it took me an hour to reach Bozeman, where several inches of heavy snow covered the subdued streets.

I had trouble getting off the bike at the liquor store, where I loitered long enough to warm up before dropping my last few dollars on a bottle of Canadian Mist blended whiskey. On the sidewalk outside, it was clear I could not go on. But I had no place to stay to wait out the storm and no plan at all beyond the whiskey.

Doctor Watson, called Mac by his friends, his beautiful wife Elena, and their little boy, Toad, had been in Santa Fe while I was visiting Glorieta. I was sure they'd be back in Montana by then, since the academic year at MSU was about to start. I hoped they'd give a wayfarer like me shelter for a night at their place above Spring Hill, maybe ten miles south of town.

It was late afternoon and slow going uphill through several inches of snow to their place at the end of the Spring Hill Road. By the time I arrived, my soaked boots and jeans had frozen, and I was likely in the early stages of hypothermia. I rode the big Honda straight into Mac's open shed, shut it down, and stared dully at the place where Mac's beetle-backed Volvo should have been parked. The shed was as empty as it was dark and cold. There were no tracks in the yard or on the front walk, and it began to sink in that I'd arrived back in Montana ahead of them.

My pack and sleeping bag were wet, I was soaked and chilled through and through, and I'd gone as far as I could go. I checked the doors, then the windows until I found one unlatched in a bedroom. I crawled in and pulled off my boots. The cabin seemed nearly as cold inside as the shed had been outside, and I began to rattle as I was overcome with shivers and shakes. I found some newspapers and kindling and built a fire in the fireplace then stripped down

20

to my shorts. I arranged my clothes on chair backs before the fire, wrapped up in a blanket, poured myself a tall whiskey, and watched the snow skirling past outside. Dusk settled into night and the storm blew on.

I found eggs and butter in the refrigerator and some Krusteaz hotcake mix and syrup in the pantry, so I fixed a cowboy supper and ate right from the frying pan. One wall in the living room was lined with Mac's books, and I read titles as I chewed. When my clothes were dry enough to wear, I brought in my pack and a couple arm-loads of wood from the shed, built up the fire, and settled down on the couch with Turgenev's *Fathers and Sons* and another glass of bourbon. And an odd thing happened. As I relaxed and watched the fire and listened to the storm outside, I found myself thinking again about Suzanne and what had happened in Iowa and Omaha. That misadventure had been aching in me as I'd crossed the northern plains, and I wondered if writing about it, in some oblique way, would help me sort it out and put it to rest. Maybe I could try a poem or two. The idea grew into a notion, and in the months ahead, I made my first attempts at writing, not for school assignments, but as something necessary for myself.

The storm stalled against the Bridger mountains and dropped a foot of snow. Nothing moved the next day. On the third day someone plowed the road; a Chinook wind blew in, and the road turned to mud. I gave up and called my wife in Helena. When she arrived, I put a note on the kitchen table under the remains of the whiskey, explaining what had happened. I left my bike in Mac's shed, and rode back to Helena in our blue VW bug, suspended between a sense of defeat and the feeling that a new horizon was about to be revealed.

When we returned to Bozeman the next weekend for my motorcycle, I took along a cardboard box of elk steaks and deer chops and a case of beer. I'd broken into Mac's house and made myself at home, after all, and although we had become friends that spring, Mac and Elena certainly didn't know me well enough for me to occupy their home without their consent. All these years later, I can't imagine doing such a thing again. Maybe it was those extraordinary times, maybe it just another folly of youth, maybe I'd had no choice; but I was much relieved when Mac and Elena shrugged off my apologies for breaking-and-entering, laughed as I told them about my trip over the Bozeman Hill, accepted the meat we'd brought, and insisted we stay for supper.

When Elena and my wife went to the kitchen, Mac and I wandered out back to share a joint. Mac, with his round, John Lennon eyeglasses and Robert Redford good looks, seemed to be a completely different person than the awkward young professor in the corduroy suit who had flailed away at *Hamlet* and *Macbeth* just two years before. There he was, transformed in jeans and a chambray shirt, looking like a hand who worked in a saw mill. But he was so quick and bright, so fast and focused, so damned smart. He might have been an academic whiz, but he was also a natural mimic with a Zap Comix sense of humor; a man of wit and a delight to be around. That we had become friends, seemed to me then, as it has ever since, to be a great gift to my life. As we passed the roach back and forth and looked out across the Gallatin Valley, which was once again as warm and serene as a late summer day, I told Mac about my visit to Fitzsimons Army Hospital. I told him about the black guys on the loading dock and my wounded friend, Tom.

"What's your draft status?" Mac asked.

"Man, I'm 1-A, all the way, since graduation. Just waiting for the letter, you know?"

Mac opened a warm beer and we passed it back and forth. "You going to go?"

"I don't know what else to do, now that I've finished school."

Mac squinted into the light off west. "How about graduate school?"

"Nah, man. Not with my grades. No way could I get in."

We finished the beer, started another. "If you could park it here in grad school another year, maybe the fucking war would end," Mac said. "You'd try that if you could get another deferment, right? Seems to me that reading Milton beats getting shot."

"You are sure about that?" I asked, and we laughed. But when I saw that Mac was serious about his idea, I said, "Hell, yes, I would. Absolutely! But I don't know if that would get past my draft board in Helena."

Mac looked off toward the Spanish Peaks to the south then squared himself up. "I'll go call John Parker," he said and walked off doing his imitation of Charlie Chaplin.

I turned in a slow circle in the Watsons' yard, looking from the farms on the valley floor below to the foothills of the Bridger Range around me. *I can walk on my own legs. I have both my arms. I am not disfigured, nor gut-shot, nor maimed, nor damaged in my mind. That is what matters right now.* It was so effortless, admitting the truth and making the decision that would change the course of my life forever.

John Parker shuffled papers about on his desk until he found his matches then stoked his briar. "I've spoken with the Dean," he said. "We can admit you immediately on a provisional basis. One quarter of 3.0 or above will convert the provisional status into full acceptance to the Master of Science in Applied Science, Humanities Option/English Literature Degree Program."

John was the Chairman of the English Department, sort of a Harry Truman without the edge. In his fifties, he seemed older, in a tweedy sort of way. He was wool socks and herringbone and always smelled of pipe smoke, but John Parker was the sort of man who would do the right thing without expecting a reward. That afternoon he looked over his glasses at me. "Mac tells me finances are a problem, so we've arranged fee waivers for you and some modest financial aid." After explaining a few details and handing me a sheaf of forms to fill out, John stood, extended his hand across his desk, and I swear he said, "Welcome aboard."

I walked from the English Department in Hamilton Hall to the Student Union across the way, went down to the dimly lit Bobcat Lair in the basement, where the less reputable students drank coffee and lurked about.

You remember that kind of student lounge, where every table had tin ashtrays full of butts, and the floor was littered with crushed paper cups. I went directly to a cigarette machine, plunked in a quarter, and pulled out the knob for a pack of Camel Filters. I bought a Coke from another machine and punched in James Taylor's "Fire and Rain" on the jukebox. Then I sat down at a table, lit the first of the thousands of cigarettes I'd smoke in the next thirty years, and as that world of possibilities I'd sensed earlier began to open before me, I filled out John Parker's paperwork.

My wife and I had several long talks that began about this time. We'd known each other since before high school, and we were friends, so we were able to tell each other, without great difficulty or passion, what was wrong in the marriage. Mostly it came down to this: We did not love each other in the ways we'd expected. Intimacy was awkward at best. She worked for a conservative lobbying outfit and wanted a settled, secure life. I wanted almost anything that did not involve Vietnam and thirty years of eight-to-five jobs like my folks. The truth of it was that we'd damaged each other during our marriage, and we both wanted that to stop.

A week after I met with John Parker, I went in person to speak to my draft board, which was housed on an upper floor in the great stone pile on Helena's Last Chance Gulch known as The Power Block. I had climbed into a black suit and wing-tips left over from high school, put my father's reading glasses on my nose and presented myself as what I imagined a hapless student of literature should look and sound like. I pitched a far-fetched, whimsical story about studying Blake with the well-known scholar Dr. Allen Watson. The members of the board seemed awfully nice about it all, even chatty, and when I walked out of the building into afternoon sunshine, I had the deferment for an additional year in my pocket. Salvaging that year seemed almost too easy, but I've never stopped blessing Mac and John Parker and my draft board for making it possible.

FOUR

There was a certain edge to the days that followed the afternoon Sheila and I spent in deep space. We seemed awkward, felt slightly embarrassed, perhaps. Eye contact was fleeting. We simply didn't know how to act when we bumped into each other, but to our credit, we didn't pretend that nothing had happened. We began to locate each other on campus with unusual ease. We'd pass in a hallway, then leave together for slow walks in the old neighborhoods east of campus, as the spring rains fell. Or we'd sit in an empty classroom without saying much at all. Sometimes, in the evenings, we climbed from a third-story window in Hamilton Hall to sit on the rusting iron fire escape, where we could talk and enjoy the spring light. Once, although neither of us was in any sense religious, we took a King James version of the Bible onto our fire escape and Sheila read aloud the verses of Ecclesiastes 3. "To every thing there is a season and a time to every purpose under Heaven: A time to be born, and a time to die; a time to plant, and a time to pluck up that which is planted; a time to kill and a time to heal; a time to break down and a time to build up."

We knew we had entered a time for breaking, for ending, but we had no idea of how to get on with new beginnings.

We were stiff, oddly formal, almost Victorian. There was no further hand-holding and no secret embraces. What was happening was less a courtship than a time of looking and listening. Neither of us could have explained what we were up to, because we did not know. But it seemed clear to both of us that we were not in control. We saw something new in our lives and in ourselves as the days passed, and that recognition pulled us toward a new beginning. We made no plans, but the germ of a new direction was growing all the time.

The days were harder for Sheila than for me. I'd been separated from my wife for most of a year, and although she was a fine girl, and we continued to like each other at a distance, there was just no going back to the marriage for either of us. For Sheila, things were not so simple. She still shared a moldering trailer, parked under some old cottonwoods beside the Gallatin River, with her husband, Jon, who was finishing up his engineering degree that quarter and very much in love with his wife.

Without discussing it, Sheila and I settled into clandestine meetings. When other people were present, we kept a distance between us. It was probably a bad job of over-acting. We were likely as obvious as sunrise on an ocean, or at least we should have been, considering the attractions we felt. Our meetings were furtive and serious, an hour here, in the campus chapel; an hour there, behind the bobcat cage, where the poor MSU mascot paced away his days alone. Yet we made not one attempt to meet for trysts. There were no whispered endearments. Suddenly as sober and square as the middle-class Americans we sometimes mocked, we met in greening parks to talk about everything but about what we were doing or what we would do. We were unsure of ourselves and of each other, but we made our rounds at the university, going through days when the best thing that would happen was to touch hands as we passed in a stairwell full of students.

We shared our secret with growing enthusiasm. We told no one, enjoying the excitement such secrets create. We discovered contradictions: We tried to be calm, to be subtle, but the moments we spent alone together packed such a kick that we sometimes felt short of breath.

W. S. Merwin came to campus and gave a brilliant reading of his poems one evening, after which, those of us in the know drove out to Mac and Elena Watson's place at Spring Hill for a late evening of marijuana, cheap beer, and laughter. At some point Sheila came through the front door into the living room, where I was sinking, all aglow, into the deep cushions of the Watsons' sway-backed old sofa, a piece of furniture as familiar and warm as a slumbering farm animal. Sheila sat down on the fat haunch of the old beast's armrest and placed her hand gently behind my neck, so that her fingers touched my shoulder. She seemed to me then so centered and aware, so winsome and full of grace. She looked down at me and smiled.

We sat together in the low light, surrounded by people who'd come to enjoy a poet. A fire burned in the river-rock fireplace before us; students and teachers milled about, talking and laughing together. W. S. Merwin had joined a few of us outside for a toke, and I'd become a fan. Later, when John Parker arrived and passed the sofa on his way to the kitchen, he gave Sheila and me a quick second glance.

In memory, there remains an afterglow to those soft moments, which still seems as magical and dreamlike to me as great fires burning at night beyond a distant horizon in an unknown land. Sheila, small and alert beside me, our friends and others we knew only by sight, all so young and confident and smart, so filled with talk and laughter as they passed around us. I remember a sense, then, of great contentment, as if I'd discovered at last a place and time and people I'd been looking for. I could feel her breathing beside me. We'd not held each other before, but a warmth passed back and forth between us during that casual public embrace on the Watsons' sofa, that was the beginning of a great heat.

Of course our secret quickly became gossip. Jon at last found out, and the days and nights thereafter were filled with complications, some more ugly than others. There he was, more than once pounding on the door of my room late at night, a man suspended somewhere between great grief and violence. But what do you say to such a person, twisted by such loss? All I could think to tell Jon was the truth, "Man, we haven't *done* anything. Go home. Talk to Sheila." Did I feel for him in his pain? Yes, I did. Would I try to steal his wife away if I thought I really had a chance? You bet I would.

We had no plan. It was true there'd been no physical contact beyond walking arm in arm or sitting together as we had at Watson's. We had not talked about the future, aside from some verbal daydreaming about alternative ways of living, including, of course, the cliché of cabins in the woods. Days passed and spring advanced until Sheila had enough of Jon and the stresses between them. It happened quickly. She packed her clothes and a few books and drove off in a 1964 Chevrolet El Camino pickup truck, whose engine Jon had overhauled in the kitchen of their trailer. She fled to Denver, where she found an apartment downtown on Lincoln Street and a job in a sweatshop sewing window coverings. Her leaving was sudden, and when she was gone, I found Bozeman suddenly quiet and not as complete as it had seemed.

I dawdled. I did not give a damn about my classes nor my grades nor the degree, not even freshman girls with flowers in their hair. In the absence of the woman with the quiet voice and glide in her walk, what remained in Bozeman seemed oddly out of focus and beside the point. Even my friends, Sam and Suzie Curtis and Lindy Miller and Mac and Elena Watson weren't enough to ease the silence she'd left behind.

I neglected my work until I could see little hope of salvaging my classes. There was always the Draft in the back of my mind, and I knew that at the end of the semester, I'd be out of school and once again 1-A with my draft board. Huge anti-war demonstrations were taking place in Washington, but the generals continued to say we'd soon turn a corner, that they could see light at the end of the tunnel, that someday they'd find a cliché that made all the death and dying worth the effort. But the war and the draft were no longer my first concerns. I wandered around Bozeman and the MSU campus, forgetting appointments, missing classes, and failing utterly at the Introduction to Composition class that Sheila had left behind, a class I was then supposed to teach for the duration of the quarter. My heart wasn't in it, and, because I didn't know what I was doing, I ended up talking about "creativity" and "good writing" until one of the football players in the back row asked me to explain what the heck I meant by creativity and good writing. He wasn't being a wise guy. It was an honest question and a good one. But, since I had no idea what I meant, his question revealed that I had no business in front of that class or any other.

I assigned papers with subjects like, "Describe the instant when you have been most afraid." Twenty-eight out of thirty papers described car crashes that had happened on the way home from keg parties in high school. I'd thought the assignment was creative, but the papers the kids brought in were so similar in their details—the beer, the midnight blacktop twenty miles from some small Montana town, the crying tires and breaking glass—that I would have bet a pre-existing file on that exact assignment could be found on every floor of every dormitory and frat house on campus.

What had I been thinking? Had the American experience become so homogenized, I wondered, that even our most terrifying moments had become car-crash songs? I had not given the class my best shot, but right about then I ran out of ideas. Then I ran out of give-a-shit and started coming to class high. The class went down a toboggan run from there to become what Professor Jack Fulsom would later describe in a faculty memo as, "the Ralph Beer and Sheila Malone fiasco." Jack looked and acted like he worked for the CIA. I couldn't imagine anyone giving a damn about what he thought, although in this one instance he was right.

Sheila had no telephone in Denver. We sent letters back and forth, but the length of time between a letter received, a reply, and the next letter was so long that neither of us could know what the other person was thinking. Everything in our lives was up in the air, and letters were not much help. For me, the uncertainty bred long nights and vague days. A week passed. Another. I stopped attending classes and spent afternoons dozing in the spring sunshine on various campus lawns. The voices of students passing by seemed like birdsong as I drifted off. Beautiful, beautiful birds who would soon depart for their summer breeding grounds.

My baggie of purple barrels had mysteriously run down to but one remaining little fellow, lost and alone in a wrinkled press of foul plastic, so long re-folded and crushed in the hip pocket of my jeans. I hated to see him there, as lonesome as a cowboy song. So one Friday afternoon I took him out and put him on my tongue.

Late that night, in the sad little room I'd rented for a few months from Ma Story, Bozeman's most infamous slumlord, I stretched out on my bunk, and, in the glow of colored lights left over from someone else's Christmas, I read aloud the entire "Rime of the Ancient Mariner," right straight through.

Like the Mariner's ship, I, too, was becalmed, lying dead in the water, waiting for a breeze to lift my sails. In the crazy glow of mescaline and Christmas lights, the poem seemed unusually vivid in all its gruesome details. The poor sailor—whose great sin hangs about his neck, remained wretchedly adrift upon the windless waters, "where slimy things did walk with legs upon a slimy sea." He shared his dying crew's dreadful thirst, and endured the passing of ghost ships, manned by the dead.

I finished the poem, and the night burned on, until, in the hour before dawn, I, too, seemed to catch a breeze, a faint wind rising. And before I knew it, I was on my feet and in motion.

I made coffee then packed shirts and jeans, long johns and socks into my frame pack, stuffed in my duck-down sleeping bag, a sweater, and lastly a copy of *A Coney Island of the Mind*. I pulled a poster advertising a poetry reading off my wall, and painted the word "Denver," on the back with some black and gold paints meant for model airplanes. I found my last few crumpled bills hidden in my copy of *One Flew Over the Cuckoo's Nest*; they amounted to something like twenty dollars, the very last of the money I'd earned the year before, cutting firewood in the Elkhorn Mountains.

By the time I hiked out to I-90, the sky had turned gray and sleet was slicing by on the wind.

FIVE

A couple of bleary cowboys, on their way home from a Bozeman Friday night, took me as far as Livingston, where the Mad Inventor immediately pulled over in his white Cadillac and picked me up. An overweight, pasty guy in his sixties, the Mad Inventor wheeled his Caddy along that great byway of the American West at eighty miles an hour, steering with one hand and lighting cigarettes with the other. He ignored the weather as we rolled across the Montana prairies, all the while talking about machines and describing in great detail, how the square metal object, that he was personally hand-carrying all the way from Seattle to the United States Patent Office in Alexandria, Virginia, was going to revolutionize home plumbing. His masterpiece would do this by replacing the "goose neck" under every kitchen and bathroom sink in the land.

Somewhere between Billings and Sheridan, Wyoming, I began to suspect that he was the kind of crazy person who buried his victims in the crawl space under his mother's house. But the snow whipping past us across the sagebrush flats just outside my window, made the risk of cruising with a cannibal seem quite acceptable. He talked on about metallurgy, patent sharks, the costs of production, while I tried to stay alert.

Later, I would decide that he had been practicing a sales pitch or hallucinating. But during the years since he gave me that ride, I have peeked under a good many sinks, looking for a mysterious, square metal box, chromed and precisely fitted to the pipe where the gooseneck drain resides. But no. The goosenecks have won, and the Mad Inventor's fixture, like those magical, eighty-miles-per-gallon carburetors we heard so much about in the 1960s, has not materialized. And I have wondered, as I have wondered about so many other bits and pieces of this adventure, was it not real? Did the Mad Inventor not speak to me of a marvelous gizmo and how it would reshape our plumbing? Did he not whisk me from Livingston, Montana, to an exit ramp near Midwest, Wyoming, and wave with great enthusiasm as he drove off?

Oh, he was real enough, another goof with a plan, certainly as real as the captain of a ghost ship in a boy's bright mescaline dream. This much I do know: Square drain protectors are at least as rare as the great Albatross.

There I stood, feeling the wind ripping through my jeans and jacket, atop an overpass, looking back to the north for on-coming traffic and the promise of another ride. To the east I could see a narrow blacktop road winding off into the barrens toward Edgerton, Wyoming, which lay several miles beyond the bleak horizon. There was a seedy-looking truck stop behind me, a couple hundred yards from the Interstate. It might have offered warmth and hot food, but I was a wooly lad with a backpack and patches on my jeans carrying more than a little cultural paranoia. Even though I was a farm boy myself, it seemed reasonable to expect no kind welcome from those truck-herding hillbillies therein, when they saw my beard and caveman hair. I had my sleeping bag and the hard-shell army-issue raincoat that at least helped break the wind, and I knew if worse came to worst, I would bed down in a gulch for the night and let the snow drift over me rather than take my chances in the bright lights over yonder.

It was 1971. There was even *less* traffic in Wyoming back then than there is today. Every few minutes a pickup truck or eighteen-wheeler would come wavering out of the white north, and I'd hold up my pathetic little sign: "Denver," in model-airplane paints. The trucks neared without slowing and hurtled by in a fury of slush and fumes, and I understood exactly where I stood in the all-American food chain. The very idea: a hairy dropout like me, lurking in the late afternoon, expecting free transportation to speed him toward the distant arms of true love. Who, in his right mind, could believe in a Kerouacian pipedream like that?

Minutes became an hour. My feet grew cold, even in good rag-wool socks inside my stout German boots. The strange grey hills of the Teapot Dome country loped off toward the east, and I began to wonder about what I was doing. Sheila had no idea that I was on my way. We had no understanding about getting together, and I had no idea what she planned to do about Jon. My beautiful high of the night before was long gone, and as I shivered in the wind, various unknowns gathered around me. All I had was her address on an envelope flattened in my shirt pocket and twenty bucks in my wallet. Still, maybe because my alternatives in Montana seemed to have run their course, I knew this wind-swept four-lane, running south through the grim sagebrush hills of Wyoming, was the trail I needed to follow.

As I stood there with my sign, I realized how much I did not know about this girl in Denver, aside from a few stories she'd told about her past. Her childhood had been anything but conventional. She'd grown up in the back rooms of the Forty-Four Bar outside St. Ignatius, Montana, the kind of road-side saloon near an Indian reservation, where serious afternoon drinking was done by white men—a "No Indians" sign on the door. But the Forty-Four had also been the kind of clean, small-town tavern where Sheila's folks invited old men with no families to share their Thanksgiving and Christmas dinners when they closed the bar early at sunset.

Sheila's beautiful momma came from a pioneer family of fundamentalist Christians there in the Mission Valley. Sheila's daddy, Jesse Roberts, a survivor of the Bataan Death March, was probably a little crazy. He was a gun trader and expert shot, who, on several occasions had stood tin cans on Sheila's head and sent them spinning with well-aimed pistol bullets. This was not a family legend, exaggerated over time. It was, others have assured me, all too true.

Jesse Roberts used to load Sheila and her momma and sister, Marilyn, into whatever jalopy he had running at the time and head off to gun shows around the West without even so much as gas money. Sheila said that some-thing always came through. Her daddy would barter and trade, exchanging a pair of spurs or a six-shooter, perhaps, for gas and groceries. As far as Sheila could tell, when she was growing up, life on the road just seemed to take care of itself. They never went hungry, and when all the trading was done, they'd come home with a different bunch of guns and a little cash to spare. After all the time she'd spent in hospitals, and at home, healing from operations on her hip, Sheila came to love that freedom her daddy showed her, the freedom to just take off and live on whatever came to hand as the miles drifted by. Jesse Roberts died young, but the adventure of going down the road with her folks set a hook in Sheila that would always pull at her from deep in her center. Maybe it was that wanderlust that gave me a chance with her.

Years later, I kept a picture postcard of Jesse Roberts, as he aimed a Colt's dragoon revolver across the bar in his saloon, on the wall above my writing table in Missoula. He looked like a fierce little man, about as solid and direct as a .44 caliber bullet. I liked that photo because it was so easy to see his daughter, Sheila, in the person he had been. He came home from the Philippines with malaria and other health problems that he was able to hold at bay for a few years. Lung cancer killed him while Sheila was still in high school.

I hunkered against the Wyoming wind and tried to imagine Sheila as a kid, swinging along on that leg of pain. Her left femur had lacked the ball of bone that should have fit into the cup of her hip socket. She'd spent a lot of time at the Shodair Children's Hospital in Helena, recovering from operations meant to ease her pain and help her walk without crutches. She spent lonesome months after each operation, healing at home, a bright kid forced to stay indoors, who watched her friends as they played outside in the sun.

A couple miles from where I stood, the narrow highway that the Mad Inventor had taken after dropping me off, ran east across a vast terrain of oil lease country and summer pasture. But it was no place for a ranch kid turned counter-culture wannabe, with his beard and stash bag and meerschaum pipe, to be loitering in the open. I was thinking about the night ahead when I saw, coming my way down that very road from Edgerton, a dark speck that became a car that eventually turned into a 1950 Ford four-door sedan, just like the one my folks drove to church every Sunday morning while I was growing up. I held my breath. Would it swing onto the Interstate and head north? Or would it continue under the four-lane toward my side of the road? The old Ford slowed, and kiss my ass and call me Mildred, if it did not keep coming straight under the overpass, to swing up the southbound on-ramp toward me, and Thank You Jesus, after it had passed me by, it slowed, stopped, and backed up.

They were missionary boys, two lads who'd been doing church work up yonder in the wild outback of Wyoming, who were kind enough to not tell me about their endeavors in great detail. Best of all, they were headed for Denver. Circles within circles it seemed, 1950 Fords and young men preaching the word of the Lamb, those two saved me from a long black night in a cold arroyo. Ever since that dark afternoon in Wyoming, I've tried to go easy on missionaries when they come along doing what they think they must.

They were in their early twenties, and they turned out to be not only a major stroke of hitchhiking luck, but pretty good guys, as well. We exchanged personal histories and our notions on where the country was headed, until they noticed, somewhere out in the great wasteland between Douglas and Cheyenne, that they were running low on gas. They didn't seem to know the road any better than I did, and when their gas gauge showed empty, with no hope of a town in sight, we pulled over.

Off to the west of the highway, across maybe a mile of sagebrush flats, we could see the outline of ranch buildings in the growing dark, but at that distance we could not tell if the place was occupied or just another abandoned line camp. The lads had a five-gallon gas can in the trunk, so we hiked off into the wind in hopes of finding fuel.

Our luck held. The man who opened the door was very decent about selling us some gasoline from his ranch tank, and he seemed mildly amused at the various hapless travelers who occasionally made the trek to his place, just as we had. I paid for the gas, and we took turns lugging the can back out to the highway. When we later pulled up to a diner, I bought dinner, too. "My treat," I told them. "You boys saved my ass out there."

As we drove into night-time Denver, the lights of the city suggested a space-ship metropolis lost in a bottomless void. So bright, surrounded by such darkness. It didn't seem possible that I could have been transported in only a day to this glowing nightscape, which seemed so awfully *big*. Suddenly, the emptiness back at Midwest seemed much safer.

How was I ever going to find Lincoln Street, in all those electrified miles spread out before us? How could I even begin to navigate through it? But I didn't have time to feel overwhelmed before my new friends suggested I camp at the house where they and some other young Christians were staying and wait to find Lincoln Street the next morning. I was fading fast after logging no sleep the night before, and staying with them was among the easiest decisions I've ever made.

There was hot coffee the next morning, and when I showed the boys my envelope with Sheila's address, they gave me directions to the downtown Capitol area and the neighborhood I needed to find. I laced up my boots, shouldered my pack, and shook hands all around. I thank them for their cheerful help and hospitality to this day.

Outside, Sunday morning was running strong: the sun was out, the wind down, and I hit the byways of Denver with my big pack, swinging along in my stout German boots, just eating that sidewalk up. I admit to feeling lucky and quite proud of myself, too; and, in the morning light of that new day, so brave and optimistic: one of Kerouac's Dharma Bums, on the prowl for poems and enlightenment and love, frisky and bold, open to the wisdom of Buddha and the grace of the boxer, Mohammed Ali. I walked several miles as the day warmed around me, and I felt fine, so limber and strong, striding across that vast new city in the American West, which did not seem at all threatening on that particular American morning, as I headed toward a girl I hoped would go with me, on a genuine, all-American adventure of our own.

Six

I walked past the Capitol and Whew! Look at the big-city buildings! There was the Denver Art Museum, which I couldn't imagine entering under any circumstances, let alone while carrying a mountaineering pack and my load of road dust. I crossed Lincoln Street as it headed south, and within a few blocks I found the red-brick bungalow where it stood sandwiched between other houses with the same 1910-to-1920s working-class look that I'd grown up with in Helena. Of course there was no white El Camino parked out front and no answer at the front door when I knocked.

I tried to imagine where she would be on a Sunday morning. Running errands or maybe folding her wash in a laundromat? But I could feel my sails droop, like the old Mariner's, as the wind of my momentum fell away. The house had been split into apartments. The front hall beyond the window in the door was so dark, so still, that it wasn't until after much doorbell pushing, that I raised someone from deep within, who said, Yes, Sheila lived there but the El Camino might have been gone for a day or two.

I didn't have a plan, so I sat on the porch swing for an hour enjoying the sunshine and the quiet neighborhood while reading one or two of Ferlinghetti's poems. After a while, I decided to leave my pack tucked behind the swing and head off to explore. It was still that kind of America, then, a place where you could plunk down on a stranger's porch and not cause a panic inside the house that would lead to a visit by police; a time, even in a strange city, when a hairy lad could leave his possibles unguarded, and expect to find everything as it should be when he returned.

Morning slid into afternoon, and squalls off the mountains pulled a grey chill over the city. Somewhere within sight of the state Capitol I found a diner and splurged on coffee and a bowl of chili. I kept asking for extra crackers until the waitress and I were both embarrassed. As the chili rumbled in my belly, I walked on to look around the Capitol until I found a rundown theater that promised warmth and a place to nap. I dozed through a Western absurdity starring Julie Christie cavorting with Warren Beatty. With each close-up I expected to hear "Lara's Theme." But the movie beat walking cold streets, so, what the hell, I dozed through it again.

When I returned at dusk, there was still no El Camino. I settled down on the porch swing, and the street light down the block came on, and the temperature fell. As I sat in the still darkness, smoking my meerschaum, which I was certain made me look ruggedly elegant, I asked myself again what the hell I was doing. Lines from a Three Dog Night song began to skitter through my head, *"Don't turn on the light, 'cause I don't want to see . . ."* and it occurred to me that not one person knew where I was. Something, something, something about his *girlfriend, who's "passed out on the floor."* I don't think I'd understood until that moment how adventures like this could suddenly turn so lonesome.

The drugs that had been tobogganing through my bloodstream during the past few weeks seemed to have fled my system to the point where I could list on my fingers some of the highlights of my present state of affairs: I was finished at school. Grad school was, like, totally over. I had an unresolved deal involving a wife back in Helena, where there would be some very pissed off parents in a matter of days. Actually, as I thought about it, I saw that I was fleeing those parents as much as the wife. What a mess. All those people were tangled up like a big snarl of barbed wire that had somehow wrapped itself around me. And there was the Draft. In a matter of weeks I'd be eligible again, and this time I would be on my way to what was still a hot war in Vietnam. I had maybe ten dollars in my pocket, which was all the money I had in the world. And here I was, waiting on the doorstep of a different girl, also married, who had no idea that I was not still in Bozeman pretending to be a student, but was instead sitting on her front porch shivering in the growing dark.

I took out my Sail and tamped some of that fine tobacco into the bowl of my pipe, struck a wooden match on my thigh, and took a few puffs. Sail, a nice soft Cavendish, seldom failed to soothe me, but when I touched fire to bowl that evening, my situation snapped into focus, BAM, like the jolt off a spark plug. I was not a Jack Kerouac *Lonesome Traveler*. I was a guy from Montana, who was most comfortable in the woods and fields of an old ranch in the hills south of Helena, where I'd spent summers and weekends, cutting wood and picking field stones behind a plow, stacking hay, and working cattle with my dad and his father. Hell, I'd never hitch-hiked *anywhere* until *yesterday*, yet here I was, suddenly seven-hundred miles from Bozeman, lurking about on the front porch of a house, where people I did not know might be peeking through curtains at that very moment, whispering, "Is he still there?"

My future, including how I'd get through this night, seemed lost in the approaching dark. What came beyond the next hour I could not begin to guess.

Minutes ticked by. The evening chill worked its way through my jeans. And finally it hit me that Sheila might not be coming back here at all. *Oh, fuck me!* Had she left Denver for good? Was there some news, as yet unknown to me, a turn of events more recent than her last letter, that might involve her heading back to Montana and Jon? Was it possible that we had passed each other at some point on the highway just yesterday? I noticed a new cramp in my empty belly and wondered if I should try to talk to someone inside the house.

I knew I'd soon have to take off my boots and slip into my sleeping bag to stay warm. And I knew that I was spooked. The rising energy that had carried me this far was quickly bleeding away.

I also realized that for quite some time I'd felt the increasing need to take a long-overdue piss. Except for trees along the street there wasn't much natural cover. But a man does what a man has to do. When I couldn't wait any longer, I slipped off the porch as quietly as I could, eased into the shadows along the side of the house, and unzipped. This is how things go wrong, I thought, imagining a silent patrol car easing down the street to hit me with its spotlight as I sent a loud stream into the weeds. The people in the lighted rooms of the neighboring house just beside me would certainly think I was a peeping tom if they looked out and saw me! I had to be silent, invisible, stealthy! But as the stench of hot urine rose in the night air, I couldn't seem to slow it down much less stop. It went on and on in a roaring, steaming cascade, and I stood with my faithful Johnson in my hand, waiting for porch lights to flash on and outraged voices to cut the night, until at last a few sad drops fell onto my boots. It was quiet at last as I zipped my jeans and slunk off like *Aqualung* on the prowl.

Back on the porch, I pulled on a sweater and dug out my duck-down bag, then unzipped it and fluffed it over my legs like a quilt. Headlights came down the street and passed, lighting the houses and sidewalks along the way, then retreating into red dots that flared at the stop sign at the end of the block. Except for distant sirens, the silence returned. My pipe lay cold in my hand, and it seemed awfully lonesome, out there in the vast night of Denver.

I had scraped the stone bowl of my pipe and refilled it by touch when a vehicle slowed and pulled over to the curb in front of the house where I sat. To my great relief, it was not the Denver Metro Police, but a white, 1964 El Camino, and the person who stepped out and locked the truck's door and started toward me along the sidewalk was sweet Sheila Malone. I felt like I could breathe again, and without thinking, I struck the wooden match in my hand with my thumbnail and touched the fire to the tobacco in my pipe. The flash and flare of the match stopped Sheila cold, and I realized that she had no way of knowing who it was, lurking there in the dark. From the shadows, I said, "Sheila, it's me. It's Ralph."

She laughed and gave a little skip as she started toward me. "Oh, hi!" she said.

We met on the sidewalk and put our arms around each other and hugged for a long quiet time. She was warm, and she seemed quite small. And as I leaned down to kiss her hair, I felt a quick little pain pass through me. I felt her warmth and her arms around my waist, and as I felt myself open to her, I began to shiver.

"You're cold," Sheila said. Then, with the surprise that had hung suspended while we held each other, she said, "My, God! What are you *doing* here?"

I felt a clarity that surprised me, and I felt a certain calmness about what I was doing. "I've come to get you," I said.

"Oh, yes!" she answered. "Of course you have."

Then we walked together up the porch steps, our arms around each other, as if this was the most natural thing we could imagine. I gathered up my sleeping bag, stuffed it in my pack, and we went inside.

We remember such events, when so much else in our lives is forgotten. The dust left by our average days is carried off on the winds of daily life, but if we are lucky, we have these sparks in time, these bright moments when we come awake to a blessed turn and sweet acceleration that lift us from ourselves and let us feel like movie stars. Such memories come from an instant of clarity, a convergence, when people and place and event have joined to make light, the way a flaring match in darkness makes light. We remember these best times because we then had the courage to claim prizes of great importance that our lives had been pulling us toward. A hope was realized, a great yearning satisfied, a new beginning discovered. Years later, we see in such events how we found a person we'd wanted all along to discover. We love the people who share such moments, and we carry them with us forever, like fire in a horn.

SEVEN

I woke Monday morning to find Sheila up and dressed and putting together a sack lunch. The day was already bright, with sweet spring sunshine pouring through the dark casement windows. I'd relaxed during the night, and when I got out of bed, I felt completely used up. I could feel the accumulated hours and miles of the previous days and nights sitting like sandbags on my shoulders. Coffee didn't help, and I was relieved when Sheila put me back to bed before heading off to her job at the drapery shop. When I woke again, the sun had traveled around to a different set of windows. I took a quick shower and was dripping puddles on the front porch when Sheila parked out front. She came across the lawn with a bag of groceries, walking with that graceful dip and swing of hers. Then she stopped and smiled at me. "You look so fierce in this light," she said. "A man-child of the forest come to town."

I liked the sound of that, so I took the groceries from her and held the screen door open as she passed through to the dim hallway within.

Since we had no plan, we had to invent one. That evening we diagrammed our options on a brown paper grocery sack. We could go "underground," that is, stay in Denver to work and keep a low profile. I would avoid the draft by becoming invisible. We could head off and do the underground thing in some other city, say, in California where winters were easier and life might be more fun. Or we could cross the border into Canada, where Sheila had family, and where I'd be safe from Uncle Sam if I could get Landed Immigrant status. It all seemed quite vague and distant.

"I want to find a place out in the woods and build a log cabin." It sounded silly, when I said it aloud, almost simple-minded.

Sheila and I had made no commitment to each other, and we hadn't asked for any long-term promises. We were still harnessed to our Montana lives, but none of our options included going our separate ways. Until that evening we had not attempted to plan a future together, yet there we were, as dusk fell again in the great city, trying to invent one.

All around us, America was wallowing in VW buses, rock concerts, and Free Love. Yet Sheila and I had not become intimate, nor had we spoken of love. It seemed we were little more than acquaintances who were fond of each other. That night, as during the night before, we shared the sagging bed that had come with the apartment, an antique iron affair with its ancient mattress and groaning springs that slumped toward the middle, so that much to my delight, we were pulled by gravity toward each other's warmth. We lay in the dark and whispered like two kids enjoying a sleep over. Sheila's husky voice in the darkness was a balm that relaxed me, as if a safe harbor resided in her voice, a sheltered place that I had not known existed before.

Like most of our generation, Sheila and I had wanted a love story. Not a big cinematic production, but at least one with our own theme song and enough action to put wind in our hair. We often didn't know how to act with each other, but we must have sensed that such a love was right there in front of us, if only we didn't spoil it. We were sometimes clumsy or too formal with each other. But in the sweetness of lying together and whispering in the dark, all the uncertainties fell away, until we drifted off and the murmuring gradually stopped.

The next day, I dropped Sheila at her place of work then drove the El Camino downtown to an employment agency, where I got a job moving pianos. The good people in the employment office, who would take a hefty chunk of my first check as payment for their services, had apparently been waiting for someone with my qualifications, that is a young male with heavy arms and sloped shoulders, not too much ambition, and a current driver's license. Within a few minutes I was lined up to deliver a piano to Kansas for the Denver music store that would be my employer.

That afternoon, on a whim, I swung into the parking lot at the Gates Rubber Company. Gates Rubber was located right in town but had the grim look of a walled city out of our dark past, a fortress complete with conical-roofed water towers and grimy buildings that faced the street like battlements, blocking any view of the inner works. Gates Rubber had been a Denver institution since the early 1900s, but it looked like a workhouse right out of Charles Dickens. Flushed with my success earlier in the day, I bopped in, all bright and frisky and confident, to fill out some application forms. I met with an interviewer, and before I knew it, I'd been hired and assigned to begin work, just like my piano-toting job, the next day. Gates paid better wages than the music store, there would be no employment-service cut from my check, and Gates promised a steady forty-hour workweek. But if Gates Rubber looked like a hell hole from the outside, just how bad, I wondered, would it be on the inside? Probably, I guessed, every bit as bad as the American Smelting and Refining lead smelter in East Helena, where my father ran the blacksmith shop, and where I'd worked three summers to help pay for college. The smelter was so poisonous and filthy that it made Vietnam seem like a reasonable alternative. Gates Rubber had that same "Land of Mordor, where the shadows lie" look about it. But that was America in 1971—a country where a young guy with no skills could blow into a strange town and by sundown the next day, have two jobs.

That evening, Sheila and I sat on the porch swing and listened to the sirens of the city. Sheila listed the various expenses of living in Denver: Rent, gas, utilities, and groceries alone came to a number very close to the combined wages from two low-paying jobs. I brought almost nothing to the pot, and it looked like we'd use up what little cash we had just trying to last until I got my first paycheck. If no unexpected expenses came along, like car trouble, we might be able to save a few dollars a week. Putting together a wad of get-away cash would take all summer. About then it dawned on us that if I were hiding from Uncle Sam, I wouldn't be able to use my Social Security number or have anything listed or registered in my name.

Sirens flamed toward us down Lincoln Street. We held hands, and watched the week-day traffic go by, until Sheila said: "Hauling pianos to Kansas? What the heck is that?" She crossed her eyes and tipped her head back so that her mouth fell open in an attitude of massive blankness. She pretended to snore.

"I know, I know," I answered. "What was I thinking?"

Sheila put her hand on my thigh. "I want to find some big woods far away and build a log cabin, too," she said. In her voice, my idea didn't sound quite so simple-minded, not at all like the kind of utterance that's usually followed by an embarrassed silence.

Just then a middle-aged woman wearing an apron over her dress opened the screen door and said she'd like to speak with Sheila. They stepped inside together, but I could make out some of what the landlady said. She and her husband had noticed that Sheila had a male visitor. "But in your rental agreement, you said you were single."

"Yes," Sheila answered. "That's true."

The lady didn't seem especially upset or hostile but simply very matter-of-fact when she said, "I'm afraid we can't allow such an arrangement in our house. You may stay if your gentleman friend goes. But he will not be able to live here with you."

"I see," Sheila said. The screen door groaned as Sheila came back to the porch.

"I heard," I said. "The plot thickens."

We sat there feeling lost and numb, and the traffic on Lincoln Street went by, trailing tail lights and fumes as darkness fell.

"Tell me more about the log cabin," Sheila said, her hand once again on my thigh.

The next morning we had breakfast, then we began to pack. At eight-thirty, Sheila left to get her pay at the drapery shop. I carried our things outside, then swept and mopped and dusted the apartment.

I knew I was a foolish and craven young man. I knew I was leaving my family and my life in Montana in wreckage behind me. I knew I had sometimes been lazy, and that I'd made mistakes that had led me to the edge of a vast darkness that could have grown until it covered everything from one horizon of my life to the other. But I could see a light out there in all that darkness that was worth walking toward.

I had few notions about my future, just daydreams about becoming some kind of beatnik poet who'd risen from the sweating classes to write an as-yet-unimaginably good novel about life and love in America. Fantasies, of course. Monumental silliness. Cabins in the air.

We packed our things in the El Camino and drove away without looking back. As we headed out of town, we stopped at a neighborhood market, where we stocked up on road food. Some apples, a bag of crunchy granola, and a sack of red beans for supper that Sheila got soaking right away in a big Kerr canning jar filled with water.

Sheila had been able to get her apartment deposit back, and that put some folding money in our jeans. Our last stop was an old mom-and-pop service station, where I checked oil and tires, topped off the gas tank and picked up a free Texaco road map. Just as the noon traffic started, we took Colfax Avenue west out of town, and, in the spirit of living off the land, we decided to swing by the Coors Brewery in Golden for the tour and free beer. An hour of bright copper kettles and heady fumes and foaming glasses of Coors' finest, and we were back outside in the sunshine, all smiles as we turned off Highway 40 onto Interstate 70 and "motored stately" up that first long grade west of town, heading for the mountains and all that life might give us, in a land as yet undiscovered, far beyond those mountains.

There's an old joke out West that says: "The most beautiful sight in Montana is Butte in your rearview mirror." We might have thought that of Denver, too, if we hadn't felt so good. Sheila peeled an orange while I ran the four-speed Hurst through the gears. The El Camino pulled us up those hills like a great locomotive, while a song, that would become our road anthem, played on the Chevy's radio. It had been written just for us, and for all those like us, who were hitting highways all across America, and it started off like this: "I remember to this day, the bright red Georgia clay, and how it stuck to the tires after the summer rain . . . ."

We passed the first pines in the foothills, and glanced at each other and laughed with great happiness in the sunshine. Lobo's song played on. And we were back on the road again.

If there had been a barrier between us and the freedom to just light out for territory, we drove through it that afternoon, on a stretch of winding road that climbed the eastern flanks of the Colorado Rockies. It was the spring of 1971, and there was no traffic, no cars at all on that great rising highway. We had it all to ourselves, road and mountains and world. We sang along with the radio and watched the countryside flash by as we found ourselves together at last.

People who have found intense happiness in new love, when that love had joined a sense of limitless horizons, will remember their own feelings and know what lifted us and let us soar, as we climbed the Divide and crossed the summit of Berthoud Pass, headed north toward Winter Park and all the country roads that lay beyond. The afternoon sun fired the snowy peaks all around us. Spring touched the high country, and we touched each other, laughing with the pure joy of sweeping with such ease through forests of aspen and fir.

During the brief time in our lives that this book tries to touch, there were several of those If-I-could-relive-the-ten-best-times-of-my-life-again-type days. This was one such afternoon: the dark forests below us, a fiercely blue sky above; Sheila's low voice and our laughter, a counterpoint between us, as we swung along a road that rose then dropped away down sharp grades, only to turn and climb and wheel again and again around the flanks of mountains; and our happiness seemed then, as it does now, to have been more than we had ever expected or hoped that happiness could be.

Somewhere, far to the west of the Great Plains, shadows lengthened across the road, and we began to look for a spot to pull off for the night. Within a few miles we found a dirt two-track that turned off the highway to our left. We bumped down the trail for a couple hundred yards to a mossy log cabin that was still boarded up for the winter. A mad stream filled with melt water flashed off through the pines below the cabin, and we walked down to it and listened to the music of mountain water as it rushed away toward big rivers and the sea. A sagging rail fence seemed to mark the boundary of the cabin property, and we decided that it would be all right to leave the truck at the cabin and make our camp beside the creek.

I built a little squaw fire. Sheila got her red beans boiling in a tin pot. We spread a blanket over a nest of grass and pine needles we'd gathered and arranged against a sheltering bank. We had two blankets, my duck down sleeping bag, and our coats for a bed. Evening came down around us, carrying a mountain chill. Stars glittered in the growing darkness above the encircling trees. We made coffee with water from the stream and ate apples and waited on the beans, which, after boiling a couple hours, were still as hard as marbles. We pulled on sweaters and shared a blanket draped around our shoulders and watched the fire. I lit my meerschaum and let the sweet smoke climb the night as we talked and shared our warmth.

We eventually gnawed on those half-cooked beans then spread our blankets, pulled off our boots and jeans, and wedged ourselves into my down bag. There was not much room for two people, but we piled on our coats, and got as comfortable as we could. We lay with our arms around each other and whispered in the light of the dying coals. I felt the heat of that girl nestled in the crook of my arm as we watched the great wheel of stars turn overhead, and I could not have imagined anywhere I'd rather be. We were a young man and a young woman, filled with light and the force of youth, not yet savvied up and hardened by years. We believed life was full of good things and good people, and that those good things and good people would always win and be there for us. The day had been long, the hours full, and we dozed together there, safe with each other in the vast night, as the embers of our campfire collapsed on themselves and grew dark.

EIGHT

We traveled as if time was ours, then and forever. For the next two days we drove those narrow back roads across Wyoming, heading generally toward Yellowstone National Park and Montana. To our great good luck, the bright skies and warm weather held. We pitched our little camps in the evenings and took squaw baths in icy creeks and made meals of macaroni and cheese, canned stew, and fresh fruit. In the mornings we'd shake the frost off our gear, scramble half a dozen eggs in Sheila's cast iron frying pan, and throw the egg shells into our coffee pot, adding new grounds on top of old.

We were mountain men. We posed beside our fires leaning on sticks like fur trappers on their Hawken rifles. We looked off toward distant mountains and talked in dialect straight from Bud Guthrie's *The Big Sky*. "Stretch our plews and raise some har, Hoss," Sheila said, while waving a spoon.

"This child aims to eat beaucoup hump fat and kitch the clap!"

"Whiskey heap good!" Sheila laughed as she poured coffee into our tin cups.

And I thumped my chest and said: "Take many beaver. Steal ponies. Find squaw, you betcha."

We played at being carefree and literary. But the truth was, we were spooked by what we were doing and by what lay waiting for us in the days ahead. We were going back to Bozeman, where our friends were still involved with classes and final exams as if nothing had happened. There would have been gossip, and we would have to face that. More important, we needed to deal with possessions, to sell what we could for ready cash and to say good-bye to our closest friends. We still weren't sure of each other, or that we would actually do what we'd set out to do. We didn't know how to act as a couple. And I think we worried that the familiar Bozeman scene, where we'd been friends, would pull us back from where we were, toward being graduate student buddies again. Although we didn't talk about them, those many uncertainties kept at us, worrying us, like mosquitoes circling a campfire late at night.

One evening, somewhere south of Jackson, we followed a logging road away from the highway to a meadow at the edge of an old clear cut, one that was coming back into scattered, second-growth pine. Below us, in a slough where beaver dams glinted in the evening light, a few frogs began to call to each other in high, eager voices. As we made camp and cooked our meal, more and more frogs joined the singing until great numbers of them were trilling and chirring in ever increasing volume. After supper, we walked down among the beaver ponds, where we came upon dozens of the little fellows, bright green and about the size of my thumb, all wailing away as if their hearts were breaking. As it grew dark, their music swelled in volume until the air in our little valley seemed to vibrate with insane urgency.

This, we thought, must be a sign. But what could it portend? Surely it had something to do with sex. Sex, and lots of it. The frogs sang, and their anthem filled the evening air with a thrumming so insistent and loud we might have moved our camp if it hadn't already grown dark. So we banked our little fire and crawled into our nest of coats and blankets and the ever-inadequate sleeping bag, then held each other and watched the heavens turn out there in the dark celestial void.

"They sing but once each fifty years," Sheila said, her soft voice nearly overwhelmed by the great chorus of frogs, "or, when true hearts do pass them by."

"The lady knows not the frogs."

"Oh, but I do," she said, no longer quite so playful. "I understand them well enough."

She fit in the crook of my arm as she lay folded on her side with her back against my chest. I could feel her warmth filling the space between the sleeping bag and our bodies, and her welcome heat seemed to me like a shield against all that cold and dark and lonely distance out there beyond us. She was small and brave, and I liked her very much. I touched her perfect breast with my fingertips, and after a bit, I brushed her hair back and touched her cheek. And I understood that she was turning the course of my life, as if I were a compass in her hand. And that was all right with me, because I knew I needed what waited for us in that new direction, and that I was ready to go off with her to find it.

"My good lad," she said, "If I could be the Fairy-Queen of frogs, I'd claim you as my Prince."

"And I'd be yours, sweet girl," I said, "tomorrow and for evermore."

In the morning, a great silence lay upon the meadow. A mist hid the beaver ponds as we built a fire and made our coffee, and not one sound came up to us from the slough.

By 1971 the "Summer of Love" was long gone in California; Woodstock's mud had dried; and even those of us in the backlands of the American West had discovered free love by the time Sheila and I crossed into Yellowstone Park that morning. But she and I had been holding back, still quite shy with each other, even while jammed together in that fetid duck-down bag. We acted as if we were both innocent of sex and the desire for sex with each other. There wasn't even any real necking. We curled up together and enjoyed each other's warmth at night. We held hands during the days and sometimes Sheila would rest her hand on my leg as I drove. But there was no hard breathing, nothing like the hot and heavy sex that drove our green age.

The park hadn't opened yet for the season, but the road was clear of snow, so we drove in and proceeded on like the tourists we were, eating oranges and looking about for bears and bison and other wonders. Except for the National

Park Service vehicles that we passed here and there, we seemed to have the whole place to ourselves. We saw so few cars that from time to time we wondered if we would be caught and expelled.

But no one stopped us. We drove on, going past retreating snow drifts that marked the courses of the streams they covered and dense swaths, too, of aspen and lodgepole forest, until, by the time we passed Yellowstone Lake, the day had grown so warm that I pulled off my shirt and drove bare-chested with my elbow at a jaunty angle out the El Camino's window. We stopped often to get out and stretch. We took little walks, going hand-in-hand across open parks to look at the paradise of timberlands and streams that lay all about us. Once, at the edge of a vast meadow, I walked among a dozen grazing elk, my bare chest and arms as white as the winter that had just passed. Sheila called to me, and when I turned to look, she snapped a photograph.

Near the headwaters of the Yellowstone River, where it empties north from Yellowstone Lake, we took soap, towels, and a blanket and waded across shallow water to an island in the stream. We pulled off our clothes and soaped up and rinsed the lather from our bodies with water that had been snow only a couple days before. We were screened from the road by brush and scattered trees, so we spread our clothes on the river rocks, and leaned back to dry ourselves like otters in the sun. Neither of us had had a full night's sleep since Denver, and we were drowsy, there on the sun-warmed gravel.

I looked with great pleasure at Sheila's breasts, which were as round and perfectly formed as God's own fruit. Her nipples lay hidden in each breast, as if too shy to come out and call attention to themselves. Her personal beauty seemed to me to be centered there, in her breasts, and they sometimes made me a little crazy.

Sheila stood, and there came a moment when her smile and her breasts and her calm voice merged with the music of the river, as it rushed past all around us. She was not bashful in her nakedness. As she stood above me, I could see, on the inside swale of her left hip, two heavy ridges of scar tissue that ran from the bone of her pelvis down her thigh, a map of old wounds where surgeons had cut her when she was a child. I reached out and traced the scars with my fingers, following them on their courses.

Sheila looked at me, then spread our blanket on a bit of sand beside the water and reached out to me. "Come here," she said.

We were new to each other and awkward early on, as we made love for the first time on that gravel bar near the headwaters of a great American river. But as we fell into a rhythm and found each other, I discovered that Sheila was as eager in her passion as I was, and during our sprint toward climax, she stayed with me, stride for stride, as we ran.

When we had finished and lay panting on the sand, Sheila laughed. "That was swell," she said. She brushed her fingers lightly down my back and over my rump so that sparks fired through me, causing my scalp to tingle and my legs to quiver and twitch. The sun warmed us, and the sounds of water in motion played on around us, and fool that I was, I began to doze.

"Can I trust you?" Sheila asked, pulling me back from sleep.

I sat up and looked at her, and at the water shimmering with light as it swept past beyond her. "I . . . What a question. I think so. Yes, yes, of course you can."

Sheila knelt facing me and looked into my eyes. "So tell me then, why me?"

Her question caught me completely off guard. After a silence that seemed too long I said, "Because you like to laugh. Because you're curious about so many things. Because you're smart. And because you're beautiful and friendly and brave."

I took her hands in mine. "Yes, brave. That's *it*! Do you remember the big meeting of students and faculty about Jim Meyers, when Dean Dayton claimed the administration was shaping MSU into the kind of university he'd want his own children to someday attend, and you stood up and interrupted him and said that if his future university was going to be created by firing our best instructors, it sure wasn't the kind of school you'd want *your* children to attend. Do you remember?"

Sheila nodded. "Sure," she said

"I can't tell you how much I admired you that night. You were fierce and quick, thinking on your feet, and by God, you showed more courage than all the men in that room. Since Mac's Shakespeare class I've known you were quick, and I thought you were sexy, too, in an unusual way, but that moment, when you stuffed Irving Dayton, that set the hook in me."

I put my hands on her knees, and decided to tell her everything. "And there's another moment. One afternoon, early in our senior year, we passed each other at the bottom of those stairs in the Student Union—the ones that go down from street level to the bookstore in the basement. You were carrying a goofy little purse that looked like a picnic basket, and you smiled at me and said, "Hi," as we passed. You were swaying away from your weak leg the way you do, and you seemed so . . . so open and bright. There was a radiance in your smile that touched me and made me happy. Does any of this make sense?"

Sheila smiled. "Oh, yes," she said. "Of course you're making sense. We've been looking at each other all this time, and we've each seen things that have resonated."

"Then let me ask you the same question, Sheila. Why me?"

"I need a new start," Sheila said. "I don't want to be an engineer's wife or anybody's wife. I want to jump into life and splash around and stir things up. Maybe building a cabin is a way of beginning all that. The attractions I've felt for you are both animal and intellectual. Since we've known each other I've thought that you were sparky, something of a bad boy—you know, the motorcycles, the girls, the dope. But I've always liked your looks, your smell, and the way you could make me laugh."

"My goodness. I might fall for a guy like that."

"Let's not get carried away," Sheila said and smiled. "I do have another question. If we run off and build a cabin, what then? What will we do once the building is done?"

"I'd like to try to write a novel." It sounded a little silly, even as I said it, but I'd been writing in secret for the past year and felt the work, slight as it was, showed some promise.

"I didn't realize you were so ambitious. Can you write a novel?"

"I like good stories," I said. "I've know some interesting people, who might be springboards for characters. Maybe I could write a book about you some day."

"Hmmm," Sheila murmured. "Make me beautiful and brilliant and wanton." Then she pointed downstream. "Look!" she said.

I turned toward where she pointed. At a bend in the river, just where it went out of sight, a blue heron stood motionless as an alder snag in shallows near the edge of the water.

"If we had a cabin, Sheila, what would *you* do?"

"That's easy. I'd read all the literature we were supposed to read these past five years. I could study, finally. Really focus on the plays and the best books and the criticism. Wouldn't that be fine?"

"Yes, I think it would. You're the smart one. You can figure it all out and tell me what I need to know in order to write top-shelf stuff."

We watched the heron for a while, as the great bird waited for the unwary.

Sheila took my hands in hers. "It's settled then," she said. "Now if you can stay awake, we should get dressed and go build our cabin in the woods."

NINE

L ess than a week after I'd hitched out of Bozeman in a snow storm, Sheila and I headed north on Highway 89 from Mammoth Hot Springs toward Livingston, enjoying a blissful afternoon under Montana's great pleasure-dome of sky. We picked up Interstate 90 at Livingston and climbed the east side of the Bozeman Hill, soaring upward in the El Camino, hawks riding a thermal. Just west of the summit, the highway passed through sunny upland meadows bordered by dark bands of forest. New grass and a few wildflowers touched south-facing slopes, and the beauty we passed through reminded us of what we were planning to leave behind. The day had been the rising crest of our time together on the road, but as we coasted down the hill toward Bozeman, we could feel the town rushing up to meet us.

Shelia pulled over to the curb on East Main. I shouldered my pack as she waved and swung back into traffic. I passed through the lengthening shadow of the old Bozeman Hotel, headed for my room in Ma Story's student ghetto, and a sudden uncertainty went through me like a good punch. I stopped and turned in a slow circle, looking from the familiar fire station on the other side of Rouse, then south toward Main Street. Just as quickly as I had stepped into that shadow, I felt my confidence slip away. I walked a bit farther north then stopped again and stood looking around me.

Had it not been real? Hadn't we camped, that girl and I, beside mountain streams where we lay in each others' arms and watched the stars overhead scribe parabolas across the sky? Hadn't we that very day, stretched naked on warm sand in the encircling flow of a holy river, and hadn't we joined ourselves together then in an act of love? The few days we'd stolen now seemed as miraculous and unreal as a dream.

We had known each other on those Bozeman streets, during lives that now seemed far away. Could a new life together be possible? Would we really leave this little town, where our separate lives had grown slowly toward each other? Could we cut ourselves loose from this place and marriages that had not worked? Could the days and nights of this past week sustain us in the days and nights ahead? Or would we lose our momentum and return to the safety of lives that had already failed us?

I set off down the broken sidewalk, shrugging the weight of my pack onto my shoulders. And as I snugged the pack's hip belt, I faltered. My God, I thought, what could I ever do if she changed her mind?

Jon Malone and my wife were bystanders in what was happening now. Sheila and I had not talked about the details of our marriages, and I didn't know what was missing in hers, except that for Sheila, the marriage wasn't enough. I knew we would hurt some people; I didn't know how Sheila felt about that, but I didn't like it. As the years have passed, I've wondered if I already knew, absolutely knew right then, that Sheila would be so important to the map and meaning of my life that I'd had no choice.

I was not the only person responsible for two marriages hitting the wall. People change. They inflict damage on each other to get what they want. Sheila and I were young and selfish. We were willing to leave wounds behind us that would be slow to heal, if they healed at all

Sheila found Jon at their trailer beside the river. She did the best she could to end the marriage right then. I'd seen how she could act calmly and with

a certain quiet grace under stress. She was quietly aware of other people's feelings, and she could be direct without being aggressive or hurtful. She could get difficult things done with a minimum of fuss. And she did. Sheila signed away her half of the trailer and got the El Camino's title changed into her name and packed some books and clothes, and told Jon—just as I later arranged with my wife—that whatever property remained, after she went out the door, belonged to him.

That evening, I used up my spare change at the neighborhood laundromat. The road dust and campfire smoke, it seemed to me, washed away all too easily. Back in my room I boxed my books and was folding rag socks, long johns, and wool shirts into a haversack when Sheila pulled in with milkshakes and a bag of burgers and fries. It was the first hot, completely filling meal we'd had in days, and it might have been awful greasy fast food, but it was as good a supper as could be had on this planet, then, for under two dollars. We wiped mustard and mayo from each other's chins and grinned like it was the last day of school. The burgers and fries were hot and good, we were together, and that was enough.

While undressing in the light from a candle stub that night, Sheila sat down on the ancient metal bed that had come with my room. Someone, years before, had painted its frame the color of custard gone wrong. Sheila noticed that some of the dozen or so vertical rods forming the headpiece were painted different garish colors. She also noticed the little bottles of high-gloss paint, intended for model cars and planes, that rested on a shelf above my bed. "Okay," she said, holding a bottle of metal-flake "hot-tamale tangerine" to a bed rod of the same color, "what's this all about?"

"Well, you see . . ." I tried, then stopped. How to explain to this perfect young woman—who was just then removing her blouse to reveal her lovely breasts in a white cotton brassiere, which moved me then as the moon pulls tides—that each time I'd bedded a strange girl in my poor hovel, I'd later tallied the score by painting another rod a new color. "It was a like a hobby, you see . . ."

"Uh-huh?" Sheila said, smiling at me as she shook the little bottle.

And I saw that she was way ahead of me. " . . . and to commemorate certain successful occasions . . ." I said.

Sheila tilted her head to one side. "You painted one of these rods every time you scored with some poor unsuspecting girl?" she said, breaking into a soft, wicked laugh. "But there are only, let's see . . ." and she counted the painted rods, touching each one softly with her fingers, then glancing back at me, "seven? But you have eight bottles of paint. Did you forget someone?"

The next morning, after Sheila and her friend Vickie had gone off to outfit our expedition, I painted the eighth rod in the old bedstead with the overwrought, metallic "Sunburst Lemondrop" that I'd been saving for last.

Midmorning. I staggered across campus with a box of books to sell at the Buy-back Window in the Student Union. It was Finals Week, and students were milling around outside, showing acres of white skin in the blinding spring light. After standing in line for an hour and receiving a pittance for my books, I found Mac Watson striding down the sidewalk from old Montana Hall with a stack of blue books he'd just collected. I tagged along as he hustled up the stairs in Hamilton Hall and headed to his office, his laughter echoing up and down the hallways as I described hitching to Denver. Mac was in full Waldo Pepper mode, the sleeves of a Clover Leaf Dairy work shirt rolled above his elbows, the name Glenn embroidered over the left breast pocket. He might have looked like he drove a milk truck in Hollywood, but thank God, the corduroy suit was gone. Mac was by then our favorite, our rabble rouser, our resident wit, our grown-up bad boy. That morning, I realized how much I liked him; how much I respected him; how much I admired him. And, damn it all, I hated to say good-by.

Mac dumped the blue books onto his desk and pointed at them. "The 'Age of Reason' Final," he said, "God help me. I think I'll just give everyone an A."

He stepped to his window and looked down at the crowded sidewalks below. "Sheila is the best student I had here," he said. "She could get into a first-class graduate program anywhere. She could have her PhD and be teaching at a good university within three years. I hope she knows what she's doing, running off with you."

When I didn't say anything, Mac turned from the window and squinted at me. "Oh, Jesus," he said, beaming through those round, wire-framed glasses and barking out his great laugh, "I'm sorry. Ralph, you done got the prize! You do *know* that?"

I didn't have a ready answer. I just wanted to thank him for the many kindnesses he'd shown me and for all he'd done to keep the MSU English Department awake. I wanted to thank him for giving us confidence and for generating some fun. I wanted to thank him for being my friend. But students kept peeking in, needing to see Mac about grades or final papers, and I could see it was time to go. I gave him a big hug and said, "Thank you. We're going to miss you and Elena and the Toad, Doctor Watson. We are going to miss you a lot."

"We love you both," Mackie said. "Just because you're running off with our star won't change that a bit."

In the hall outside Mac's office, I ran into Bob Figgins, the Department's Anglo-Saxon scholar, who, after less than a minute of intense negotiations, bought my crazy old Chevrolet panel truck. Bob gave me a hundred bucks, and we transferred the Chevy's title at the Student Union, where I handed him the keys. When we shook hands he said: "You two are the big news around here, you know. You've gone and got famous."

Bob and his brother Bill had both taught classes I'd enjoyed. Two local boys from Livingston, they had burrowed into the mysteries of *Sir Gawain and the Green Knight* and *Paradise Lost*, as I sat in the back of their classes smoking Camels and gazing out the windows. "I guess so, Bob," I told him. "I know Sheila and I have made a hash of it here. Right now we're saying our good-byes and trying to get out of town. We should be gone by tomorrow."

Bob lit his pipe and smiled at me as if he wouldn't mind going off on an adventure all his own. But he had long ago dropped anchor in the academic life. I could see he wished us well, but there would be no sailing away for him.

When I got back to the student ghetto, Sheila and Vickie were sorting a heap of goods in my room.

"We ran into Lawrence," Sheila said. "And he lent us his Gulf card." She held up the famous credit card that our friend had received one day in the mail after finishing his master's in political science. He hadn't asked for a credit card; it had come unbidden from an oil company busy cultivating future customers. So, for the past couple months, Lawrence had turned the card into gold. He bought sets of tires, auto parts, sporting goods, even furniture, then sold the stuff to friends for cash at steep discount prices. Lawrence had no intention of paying Gulf for anything. Yes, Siree, he was making a political statement. The card was a one-hundred-percent pure rip-off of the System. It would soon be as hot as a Roman candle, but for now it was a cash cow that Lawrence hoped would give chocolate milk until he got out of town.

"No charge," Sheila said. "Lawrence said to keep to it a few days. We're all gassed up and ready to go."

To my amazement I saw a fluffy new sleeping bag (that looked like it just might zip together with mine), new blankets, groceries, a case of motor oil, and some cold imported beer, all the necessities young revolutionaries would need for an invasion of Canada.

TEN

The next morning Sheila and I left Bozeman and drove to Helena. I wanted to get it over as fast as possible and was relieved to find no one home at my folks' house on Butte Avenue. I couldn't imagine how I'd face my parents, or what I could have said to them that would have made sense of what Sheila and I were doing. I took some old work clothes and my logger boots from the basement and packed them into a steamer trunk. We put the trunk in the El Camino along with some axes, saws, and other hand tools that I knew we'd need. Lastly, I slid my .25-35 Winchester deer rifle behind the El Camino's seats and chucked a couple boxes of shells into the glove box. When I went back inside, I checked the firewood kitty for cash, but it was empty.

I felt I was running out of breath every minute that Sheila and I were there in the familiar rooms of the house where I'd grown up. I had crawled about on those linoleum floors before I'd learned to walk, had stood in my crib there and jabbered before I'd learned to talk. I had watched icicles three feet long grow outside its windows when I was a boy, had studied all those evenings at the desk in my room during high school. A little stucco house on the edge of town, filled with so much power, so much pull.

My father had built it himself, finishing one or two rooms at a time, working weekends and evenings, while going through an apprenticeship in the blacksmith shop at the American Smelting and Refining lead smelter in East Helena. My mom had gone back to her job at Bell Telephone when I was three years old. They were honest people who went to work five days a week, paid their bills on time, and wore their finest clothes to church on Sundays. They didn't borrow money. They paid cash for what they needed and saved a little as they went along. They loved Franklin Roosevelt and voted a straight Democratic Party ticket, and they didn't complain about the taxes they paid. My folks were decent people who had grown up poor during the Depression, people who spent most of their lives trying to claw their way into the Middle Class.

I was their only child, and they had been good to me. But there I stood in their silent house, planning to cross the border into Canada that very day and never come back. During the hour or so Sheila and I were there, I thought I was saying good-bye to all my life that had come before, to the rooms Dad made from start to finish, and to every familiar object in them; good-bye to my parents and all my friends; good-bye to the countryside off south, where my grandfather's ranch lay tucked away in the foothills I loved.

My wife and I had talked about ending our marriage, although nothing had been settled. I didn't want to see my wife or anyone else in Helena, so Sheila and I drove south from town and took the Jackson Creek Road at Montana City to a lane that dropped east off the Cutler Grade toward the grasslands and timbered gulches of the Howard Beer Ranch. We parked in a sheltered spot among some pines where a homestead cabin once stood, before my grandfather moved it, with log rollers and six horses, to join the rest of the ranch buildings down by the creek. From the El Camino, we took off on foot, following deer trails through stands of dog-hair fir to a granite headwall that overlooked Jackson Creek and the cluster of buildings that stood on Robert Beer's original homestead. We sat on a granite outcrop, and looked at the tors and cliffs beyond the creek, and at Sheep Mountain's granite fist rising against the sky, off to the southwest. We could see hayfields beyond the canyon the creek had cut, fields that my great-grandfather and his son had cleared from actual forest. A few of my grandfather's cows were crossing an alfalfa field over there, heading down to water.

From where we sat, we could hear a spaced, low sound, like a muffled bass drum in a slow, faltering march, its beat halting then beginning again, the dull blows coming up to us from the ranch buildings in the distance: Pumm, it went. Pummmm. Pummmmm.

It was my grandfather, in the back room of the log cabin he and his father had built from logs cut with two-man cross-cut saws, logs they'd skidded into place with Percheron horses. He was splitting stove wood. He lived in the front room and kept a couple cords of dry wood in back, where the kids had slept when my father was a boy. The old man had a big fir chopping block back there, that rested on tongue-and-groove floor boards, which were nailed to the pole joists he and his dad had notched into the walls' bottom logs. There was a foot of air between the flooring and the native dirt below it, creating something like the space inside a drum. Each time he brought his ax down on a block of wood standing on the chopping block, the flooring boomed under him with a sound that was both ancient and sad. As Sheila and I listened, a man in his seventies, who had once been stringy and quick and driven by the same fires in his blood that now burned in mine, was down there, alone in the cabin where he'd once loved a woman and made children; the shack where he and my grandma Mabel had raised those kids and made good times out of almost nothing at all, during the hardest of hard times.

Pumm. Pummmm. The sound of his blows rose to us. Near the end of his life, almost as worn as the floor he stood on, that hard old man worked up a jag of kitchen wood for the next few days. Sheila and I sat on lichen-covered stones and listened with a growing sense of wonder to music from another time, when a man's skills resided in his hands and his power in his heart. I'd wanted her to see this place before we quit the country. I had wanted her to see or feel something like this music that would tell her who my people had been. I'd wanted to say good-bye to the grandfather I'd never see again, but when the time came, I found I wasn't man enough to face him.

As we looked across the timbered ridges above the meadows, it occurred to me that if the old-timers could build log cabins that lasted sixty years and more, then so could I. What didn't seem possible was that I could leave this place on Jackson Creek for good, because it was alive and booming in my blood, and it always would be, no matter where I was.

As we walked back to the El Camino past boulders and old firs that shaded grassy little parks, Sheila knelt and ran her hand across the dark green leaves of a plant I hadn't noticed before. "Oh, look," she said, touching red lumps among the leaves. "Strawberries."

Maybe it was all the time I'd spent reading books instead of boning up on how to deal with the real world. Maybe it was related to all that grade-D dope I'd smoked and the dopey dreams I'd conjured up about becoming a Gypsy-rover-lover poet like the Beat Generation madmen I so admired. And maybe it was just in the nature of a spur-of-the-moment escape to distant territory with a girl I didn't know. But it wasn't until we headed north across the Helena Valley on I-15 that I realized I had no idea how to go about being a draft dodger, or how to enter Canada to stay, or how to make a living up there if we did get in.

Had I done any preparation for this adventure? Had I written ahead for information on Canada's immigration procedures, the way any sane, grown-up person would have done? Had I filled out and sent off paperwork in advance to be sure I could qualify as a "Landed Immigrant?" Had I compiled a folder of high school and college transcripts, letters of reference, and copies of a resume, which would surely all be required to become "landed" and to find work?

Why, hell no I hadn't. That kind of preparation, had it occurred to me at all, was exactly the sort of squaresville chicken-shit I would have blown off, the kind of anxious, nit-picking attention to detail that high school chemistry teachers and bookkeepers and bankers probably loved. But as we passed Great Falls and loped off into the vast wheat country north of town, heading toward the border crossing at Sweet Grass/Coutts, I didn't feel like that hipster outlaw at all. I was spooked about crossing the border and the guards at the border, who would be asking all sorts of tricky questions; evil cats in bellhop uniforms, who would likely probe deeper and deeper until they found soft spots in my craven, wife-stealing soul.

I had never been out of the country and had no idea what to expect, yet there I was with a steamer trunk full of work clothes and hand tools in the back of a vehicle that didn't belong to me, traveling with a beautiful young woman who was married to someone else. How could I explain my reasons for wanting to enter their country? *A little sightseeing, Officer. Some fishing? Heading up to visit friends, Sir. Their names . . . yes, yes . . . their names would be . . . absolutely . . . and . . . and why do I have a rifle behind the seat in the truck but no fishing poles?*

Good grief. Neither of us had any identification papers other than our Montana Drivers' licenses. No birth certificates, no passports, not even recent mail to establish a Montana address.

Within fifty miles of my hometown my guts were roiling, and there was the stink of fear on my skin. Of all the questions I could imagine border officials asking, I seemed awfully short on good answers. Already feeling like a jailbird on the run, while we were still a hundred miles south of the border, I was sure I'd get tangled up and give answers that were so unconvincing the nice people at the border station would say, "No. No, you cannot enter our Dominion. We know your kind, you immoral Americans, with your Spiro Agnews and Yippies and war. We have no room up here for any more shirkers and wastrels and draft dodgers, thank you very much!"

Then what would we do?

I didn't want Sheila to see me getting nervous, so I tried to conceal my fear with scowls and gruff talk and non-stop pipe smoking. But I didn't fool her any more than I fooled myself. We had gone beyond brave talk and were smack up against the deep belly-burn of doing.

By the time we stopped for gas in Sunburst, I was rattled. Sunburst, back then, was the kind of little prairie town where the sky came right down to crush the land, where grain silos outnumbered people, where the wind never stopped. Enough oil had been discovered to bring in a major producer like Texaco, but the town looked hunkered down and raw. The Sweetgrass Hills broke the horizon to the east, and last fall's winter wheat was up and green in the drill rows. But the sky was overcast to the north, and in the fading light, the buildings along Main Street seemed lonesome and mean.

As I washed the El Camino's windshield, lost in speculation about the trickery of border officials, the door of a tavern across the street banged open, a man flew out, hit a light pole, then collapsed onto the sidewalk in a heap. A prairie primate in a dingy white T-shirt emerged from the greater darkness within, bent down, and proceeded to rain blows on his fallen comrade. I could hear his workman-like grunts and the steady thudding impact of fists on bone from where I stood. It seemed to go on a long time.

America. It could be so sweet, that land of plenty, then suddenly turn insanely violent, from the low-life, redneck rage of its small towns, to the police brutality in the streets of Chicago, to the carpet bombing of Vietnam. Somehow our country had lost its way. How could it be the same country our fathers had fought to defend? How could it be, that in just twenty-five years, the home of the brave had come to the point where its sons and its daughters fled in order to live in peace?

When I climbed back into the El Camino, the man across the street lay on his back as if taking a little nap. Sunburst had grown tranquil again.

Sheila had family in British Columbia and had crossed the border several times. She knew the drill. She made a short list of questions we might be asked, so I could respond with brief, confident answers. To avoid all sorts of complications we'd need to keep our story simple. Clearly, we would have to postpone any thoughts of legal immigration until later. That, or face a bureaucratic snarl we couldn't begin to imagine, but which might send us packing right back to Montana.

Sheila said the border people would want to know how much money we had, how long we planned to stay, and if we had any firearms. Sheila said, "Don't sweat it. They do the same thing over and over all day long. They're not looking to bust anyone. They're just putting in their eight hours, doing their jobs."

Paranoia was an overused word in our generation's lexicon of drug-related psycho-babble, but in the miles from Great Falls to the Canadian line, a little key materialized in the region of my medulla oblongata that unlocked doors to hallways where FBI agents were already hot on my trail; to rooms where the borrowed credit card we'd used for gas and supplies would lead to havoc for our Bozeman friends; to closets that looked a lot like jail cells.

I felt as exposed as the raw nerve in a broken tooth. It was a condition that would come and go over the next few months, and if it wasn't paranoia, it's as close as I ever want to get. Neither of us was a practiced liar. Our notion was to keep our story simple, then to stick to it. But we knew our load of axes, cross-cut saws, and carpenter tools, would look suspicious since we were also loaded down with an array of camping gear, books, dishes, bedding and winter clothes. Although our story was that we were going to do some camping and sightseeing, and to help Sheila's sister, Marilyn, with a log addition to her house, much of our cargo just didn't make sense.

Low clouds were coming in from the west, and the parking lot lights were on at the border station when we pulled in. There it was, marked by a flag with the big red maple leaf: A land at peace, a place of sanctuary where we thought we might find a new life. I don't know what I'd expected on the other side of that magical line, but from what we could see, the Promised Land looked mostly like a whole lot more prairie.

A pleasant, apple-cheeked gent in a dark blue uniform sauntered over to the El Camino, bent down, and gave us a quick look. Just as Sheila had said, he asked where we were planning to go, how long we planned to stay, how much money we had, and if we had any firearms. The four hundred dollars we had between us seemed to strike a positive note, and when I stepped out of the El Camino and showed him my rifle, he didn't even blink. Actually, the border official seemed congenial, although maybe a little tired, until he noticed the steamer trunk and the mound of gear in the truck bed behind the cab. He asked what was in the trunk, and when I tried to explain, my voice seemed ragged and loud. He raised his eyebrows then directed me to pull the El Camino into a parking lot off to one side.

I tried to stay calm as another border official, this one wearing a sea captain's hat with gold braid, walked over to the truck and wrote down our license plate number. Together they opened the trunk and commenced pawing around in it. Our rosy-cheeked friend pulled out my pair of WW II bombardier pants and looked at me as if he'd just uncovered a trove of latex rubber fetish wear. Luckily, I had no idea what to say and just stood there with my mouth open.

The tone of the questions became stern if not quite accusatory, and we soon found ourselves at a counter in the brightly lighted interior, where we answered questions about our cargo and our intentions again, to even more officials. I floated up to a muted place near the ceiling, where I could hear a deep, far-off roar. Yellowstone Falls, perhaps.

I couldn't focus on what was being said, until Sheila stepped in and saved us. Her soothing voice and dead-straight demeanor likely did the trick, although her sentences seemed disjointed and far away. "Yes," she said again, "we want to see the parks, do some camping, maybe a little fishing, too. Sure we brought some warm clothes, we'll be in the Rockies. The tools are for helping my sister and her husband for a few days with an addition to their house in Kaslo. No, we will not accept any payment."

Sheila's level gaze must have seemed as convincing to them as to me, because pretty soon one of the men was talking to Sheila about the lingcod fishing between Kaslo and Balfour, and it was all I could do to hold off a major fit of giggles.

We must have seemed flakey at worst, a couple more goofy American kids off on a spur-of-the-moment, half-assed adventure, but I was surprised at how Sheila's confident manner had turned the official tone back toward something like friendly banter. And it began to sink in, again, as it had in Mac Watson's Shakespeare class, that there was more to this Sheila Malone person than I suspected. Soon enough we found ourselves climbing back into the El Camino, and proceeding grandly off, following our yellow brick road into an enchanted land of prairie grass and winter wheat. I could not have been much more relieved if I'd suddenly found my draft status re-classified 4-F.

Sheila found the lyrics to the Canadian national anthem in one of the handouts she'd picked up at the border station. A half-mile north of the line we tried singing "Oh, Canada" to the tune of "Oh Tannenbaum."

"True patriot love in all thy sons command," we yodeled, "with growing hearts we see thee rise. The True North, strong and free!"

Nothing rhymed; the words didn't make sense; and we sang poorly, but when our song staggered to a halt, I said, "I just don't get national anthems. Why not sing "of things that matter, with words that must be said?"

"We are not a 'dangling conversation' my friend," Sheila said.

"Good catch," I said. "I'm impressed."

Then, as dusk collapsed into night, our adrenaline high faded away, the darkness became complete, and it started to rain.

ELEVEN

We drove on into the night, listening to Canadian radio from Lethbridge play the same Top Forty hits we listened to in Montana. We talked about our route the next day from Calgary, as the wipers swung back and forth, back and forth, taking us gently in the direction of sleep. Finally, talked out and too tired to be good company, we parked at the edge of a field just off a ranch road near Calgary. We threw an old army tarp over our gear in back then slept for several hours, waking every few minutes, cramped and twisted and chilled in the little cab. During the night, from the edge of sleep, I saw Sheila talking our way past border guards. A bass drum sounded a long ways off, and Mac Watson roared, "You got the prize!" And as we slept and woke and slept again, the rain danced on the roof above us, a comforting white noise, there in the dark night of Canada.

We woke under chilly wet skies, found old Highway 1A, and followed it west from Calgary into the mountains, which hid their secrets from us behind big-bellied clouds. We'd been together nearly a week, most of it on the road, camping out along the way. We had managed to do laundry in Bozeman, and we'd showered at my student hovel. But we were rumpled and wrinkled that morning, bleary from lack of sleep, disoriented among the clouds.

It was a tight fit inside the El Camino. Two bucket seats—which could not be reclined—separated from each other by a low console and the chromed knob of the Hurst four-on-the-floor shifter. We had no room to spare for anything beyond our jackets, a thermos, the ever-present bag of apples, and, naturally, a few books. The intermittent rain and mountain chill kept us inside the truck and moving for longer stretches than we liked. We treated each other with a self-conscious courtesy that sometimes became awkward and strained. But on that chilly grey morning, as we wound through the mountains, we shared a feeling that we'd crossed a line of no return. And we discovered that all we needed to keep us going, as we drove in and out of clouds, was hot coffee and a decent road song on the radio.

My mother and a girl friend had driven my mom's 1937 Chevrolet coupe to the parks in the Canadian Rockies before she married my father and settled into a life of routines. She came home from Canada with souvenirs that became familiar objects in our little house on Butte Avenue: A pair of bronze, cowboys-on-horseback bookends, a white, six-point Hudson Bay blanket, and some tourist-shop knick-knacks. While I was growing up, Mom would get a little dreamy when talking about the country she and her friend had seen at places like Banff and Lake Louise, her tone suggesting a wonderland of peaks and glaciers reflected in cold lakes, a kind of car-park Eden filled with strolling black bears and Mounties in red. In one of the photos from that trip, my mother stands smiling in a new cowboy hat and Hudson Bay coat, beside the front bumper of the little Chevrolet she called her Bluebird.

Her trip to Canada had been one of the high points of her life, those few days disconnected for the first time from family and hometown, when she caught a glimpse of a larger world and its possibilities.

I hadn't thought much about my mother's trip, I suppose, until it occurred to me that rainy morning west of Calgary, that there I was, at almost the same age, driving the same byways, toward the same magical places she had traveled through and later remembered with genuine fondness. It was a great circle that had taken over thirty years to complete. My mother was by then fifty-two years old in 1971. She had touched something and let it go. I did not intend to make the same choice.

We went through Banff with the heater on, then followed the Continental Divide north, low mists beading on the windshield as we drove. Near Lake Louise we turned west on Highway 1 toward Golden. As we dropped down the Divide, the overcast began to break up, with patches of sunshine chasing shadows across the road ahead. Sheila opened a book I didn't know and began to read aloud a story that seemed to mirror our own sense of airy unreality. It turned out to be exactly the book we needed for our journey, since we were feeling the power of a similar strangeness in the beauty all around us.

Sheila read, articulating each syllable precisely in that crisp way of hers, the first sentence, which described a man, a colonel no less, remembering, as he faced a firing squad, an afternoon in his boyhood when his father had taken him to see ice. She read beautifully, modulating each phrase, pronouncing the Spanish names correctly and without hesitation, letting each sentence roll forward in a soft, certain cadence, until the words, flowing along on her musical voice, took us into a remote land of wonder. As the sky cleared ahead, and the mountains reared above us, two new countries were revealed, as if blended together, the one just beyond our windshield, and the other, which Garcia Marquez called Macondo.

Golden was a small town that seemed to maintain its own feel while catering to tourists for a few months each year. The sky had turned a deep, snappy blue, so we parked and walked the main drag arm-in-arm, enjoying the sunshine and surprised to find some of the shops closed; a tradition shared in many Canadian towns, we discovered, when merchants locked their doors one afternoon a week to take a few hours off for themselves.

We switched our American money for Canadian currency at a local bank, and discovered that we were a few dollars short of four hundred dollars Canadian, which was all the money we had between us in the world. We put Lawrence's credit card in the mail and found a grocery store where I bought my first pack of Player's "Navy Cut" cigarettes, which came in a flat blue box. I opened the pack and turned back the foil, slipped out a cigarette, and turned it in my fingers, a man of international tastes, indeed.

We climbed into the El Camino and pulled out into the nearly deserted street. Without thinking about it, I lit the cigarette. Sheila rolled her window down and fanned the air with her hand. "Enough! Could you please not smoke in the car, please?" she said.

When I faked a puzzled look, Sheila craned her neck toward me, crossed her eyes, laced her fingers about her throat and held her breath. She gurgled and gasped for air. She turned pink.

I had a bad nicotine habit by then and normally smoked most of a pack of Camel Filters a day in addition to my pipe. I had been smoking as we drove along, since we'd left Denver, but by the time we reached Golden, Sheila had enough. I hated to waste a fine smoke like my first Player's, and I didn't want to give in, so I stopped in the middle of the street, got out, and smoked. A car behind us honked politely. I took a last couple of hits before letting the butt fall, still burning, into the street. It was our first open disagreement, and while I pretended to not take it seriously, I understood that we'd crossed a line and moved on to another level.

We were tourists, of course, stopping often as we drove through Canada's Glacier Park. Still ahead of the season, as in Yellowstone, we had the park to ourselves. Every few miles we pulled off the road to scramble onto boulders, there to gape at the near-vertical masses of rock and snow and ice in the distance.

Between stops, Sheila read. Through our windshield, the South American jungles surrounding Macondo merged with the great conifer forests of North America. The book's characters sprang to life and traveled with us as we drove those easy, dream-like miles of twisting asphalt. The day passed in its own time, a time when clocks meant nothing at all.

In 1971, it was still possible to find camping spots near main roads in Canada and the western United States, even near national parks. During our travels that spring, it did not occur to us to look for campgrounds any more than it would have entered our minds to stay in motels. In the late afternoons we would put up our camping-spot antennae, and pretty soon we'd see a forest road or tracks in the grass leading off to some private spot beyond the sounds of passing traffic. Maybe it was a run of pure dumb luck, but again and again we seemed to find ourselves in beautiful, secluded spots with a creek, a river, or a lake close at hand.

The evening of the day when Sheila began to read *One Hundred Years of Solitude*, we found a wondrous spot beside a lake near Revelstoke. We strung our tarp on a line between two trees near the edge of the water, built a campfire, and cooked our supper, so caught up in the story, that Sheila read on by firelight after we'd crawled into our joined bedrolls. It was such a haunting tale, that account of a people in an enchanted forest, a story that invited itself into my dreams that night as the sound of Sheila's voice carried me off into sleep.

I woke to a muffled, gray light at dawn. Small waves lapped against rocks along the shore just a few feet away. I turned onto my side and looked at Sheila. Her face, relaxed in sleep, was as open and perfect as a child's. Again, something about her struck me, something clean, the way cats are clean. Her dark hair lay coiled across the nylon of her sleeping bag, and I stroked it with the backs of my fingers without waking her.

When I rolled onto my belly to look out at the lake, I discovered fog hovering a few feet above the water. From my low vantage point I could see a good distance out across the lake in the clear air beneath the fog. The morning was still, with no sound other than waves, and nothing to be seen except fog and lake.

Then, flying just above the water, a gang of Canada geese rocketed past following the shoreline. They called to each other with great urgency, their wing tips touching the water, leaving ripples in their wake. I could see their eyes. A jolt passed through me, as if a switch had been thrown, and I found myself standing naked in the wet grass, looking out into a world turned white. The hoots and wing beats of the geese faded off, and as I stood with my head in the mists, I lost track of where I was. My life seemed then as fresh and intriguing as if it had just begun. I stood in that sweet wetness, reborn and newly anointed.

"What is it?" Sheila asked. "What happened?"

"There were geese!" I said. "Right here, flying under the fog. They went by so fast, I didn't have time to wake you."

"Geese?" she said, as she sat up. "Fog? Oh, my!"

Then, with that enthusiasm of hers, as if this was the best dawn she could ever imagine, she spread her arms, laughed, and said, "Good morning!"

There was an eagerness for life in her voice that caught me up then, as it so often did, an eagerness to embrace of the world and all the good things in it. A shiver ran through me as she climbed from her sleeping bag to put her arms around my waist. "This *must* be Macondo," She said. "Are you a colonel?"

"Only if I don't have to be a private first," I said, before bending to kiss her full on the mouth. I kissed her eyes and her forehead and her hair, and I felt like a colonel, indeed.

I pulled on my damp jeans and boots and built our morning fire, then dipped water from the lake into our coffee pot and set it on stones to heat at the edge of the flames. The wood we'd gathered the night before was damp and slow to catch, and as I prodded it into flames, I watched as Sheila stood on her sleeping bag to dress. She had the kind of naturally lean body that young women work so hard to create in gyms today, and she knew it had power where men were concerned. At a hundred and ten pounds, her body had unusual definition, narrowing from her shapely rump to a slim waist and flat belly then swelling again to her perfect breasts. The fire hissed and popped, but I couldn't look away from her. The fire smoked, and the smoke drifted past me to braid itself around her. Sheila pulled a sweater over her head, swept her hair back into a pony tail, and noticed that I was watching. And I saw something register in her eyes as she looked at me, an understanding of her beauty's power, perhaps. Then she smiled and said, "Hi." It was a greeting that never failed to touch me, with its soft warmth and genuine sense of welcome.

When young people find the person they were born to search for and find, time can be pulled and stretched and folded back on itself like a mysterious confection. Time thickens and stops and starts again, so that memory becomes a series of still-life portraits. Looking back across the years, I can see that girl, suspended in smoke and morning light, as if captured in amber.

While Sheila started breakfast, I folded our tarp and hung our sleeping bags on the rope between the trees, hoping they would dry. I broke dead limbs from the trees around us to spark up the fire and dipped a pan of water to heat so we could wash up.

For breakfast we had steaming bowls of cornmeal mush, lightly salted, with big pats of butter melting on top. What more could anyone want?

We ate and walked along the shore as the sun tried to burn through the fog. "I wish you could have seen them," I said. "They were just off shore and really cracking on. I had no idea they could fly that fast."

"Mmmm? I saw you, though," Sheila said. "I saw you standing there carved from marble. A statue in fog, with no fig leaf whatsoever."

The mists opened and closed around us, and a strange yellow light filtered down through the trees as we cleaned our dishes. We built up our little fire and made fresh coffee and decided to wait for the fog to lift before driving on. We filled our cups, sat down facing the lake, and Sheila opened *One Hundred Years of Solitude*. As the fog drifted like smoke across burning water, she read a scene of incredible loveliness about an innocent girl named Remedios, who had gone out one day to hang up her laundry, and, while the village folk watched in helpless wonder, Remedios the Beauty left the earth, rising amid a flapping of linens, on a wind of light.

Remedios ascending into the heavens was so unexpected that we glanced at each other, then looked up into the clearing sky, as if we might see her there, rising still and waving down to us. And we gasped and laughed at the wonder of it. Already that morning, I'd been shot through by geese winging past at eye level, I'd been stunned into stillness by the beauty of a girl dressing in the smoke of our campfire, and I'd been blessed by Remedios the Beauty, as she rose above all earthly cares with her laundry. I drank my coffee and looked out across the clearing lake and listened to Sheila read. And I knew this was it. I had entered into the adventure of my life, and if not completely ready, I was as ready as I would ever be.

We kept on west toward Kamloops, and in the early afternoon we found ourselves entering the open grasslands and orchard country of the Okanagan Valley. Sheila had family to the south around Vernon, and she had been as far north as Kamloops once or twice. Still, we knew next to nothing about the geography of central British Columbia, and as we pulled into Kamloops, we had no idea which direction we should go.

Our plan, of course, had been more notion than plan. We wanted to build a log cabin, somewhere in the woods near a cold stream of clear water with a few miles of privacy in all directions. It would be in a place of tranquil beauty, lush with moss and deep forest duff, a place where we would settle into a perfect daily routine to write great poems and stirring prose. Big game would amble by through aspen and birch; friends would visit often; and the fishing would always be good.

We had pictures of such a place in our heads, but our Shell Oil Company road map was not much help in locating it. Why hadn't it sunk in that a search for the actual location might be difficult? Perhaps it seemed reasonable to assume that cheap available land would be in abundance in all that largely unsettled, unmapped land that stretched from Idaho to Alaska. Surely we could poke about a bit and bango, there it would be! But as we drove into the afternoon traffic in Kamloops, we felt like we were right back in the states.

The first real sun of the summer was out in force that afternoon, the streets of Kamloops hot and crowded. We weren't in town five minutes before a bread truck cut in ahead of us on a busy street, and I had to slam on the brakes to avoid a fender-bender. The town reminded us of Billings, Montana, another boomtown in open country, with plenty of new construction and too many cars. Like eastern Montana, the Kamloops area was clearly not log cabin country. After our slow, happy meander north from Denver, Kamloops, with its suburbs and four-lane streets and motels, reminded us that we still inhabited the world we were trying to leave behind. Wherever we were headed, Kamloops sure wasn't it.

We stopped at a supermarket, where the asphalt was getting tacky in the afternoon heat and went in to stock up on fruit and oatmeal, eggs and juice. Then I walked across the street and bought an oil filter for the El Camino. In a city park we spread our sleeping bags to dry on the grass, unfolded our map on a picnic table, and tried to decide which way to go.

Sheila described the land to the southeast, down around Vernon, as beautiful grassy country. Two of her mother's brothers owned ranches near Lumby. The winters were open, Sheila said, and there was some forested country scattered throughout the foothills. But the area had long been settled. Free, or even cheap land, was a thing of the past. Besides, Sheila said she wouldn't be very comfortable near her Bible-loving uncles, Gideon and Waldo, who clung to their fundamentalist Christian roots. They were good, honest country people, Sheila said, but they practiced their religion and would take a very dim view, indeed, of her adultery with a bearded heathen who refused to fight for his country.

We discounted the country we'd already passed through to the east as a tourist route, although we hadn't explored at all off the blacktop. And here we were, suddenly discarding the entire Okanagan, including all the country to the south of us. Who knows what we might have found if we'd explored for a few days down around Merritt? Kamloops likely would have worked well as a base to deal with problems like immigration and employment. But that afternoon, we couldn't seem to get out of there fast enough.

The area to the west seemed interesting, although we had no idea what was out there in all that vastness, other than, at some point, the coastal ranges. Since we would have to head west to pick up the main north/south highway, we decided that continuing west was our only choice.

From Cache Creek, Highway 97, called "the Cariboo Highway," ran through the interior towards the big woods of the north. The North, as in those words in the national anthem: "The true North, strong and free." We *liked* the sound of that, so we packed up our gear, topped off the Chevy's tank, and without a backward glance, were on Highway 1, headed for Cache Creek. From there we planned to swing north on Highway 97, the road that would take us into the famous Cariboo District, where I'd be strong, Sheila free, and the two of us forever comely and brave.

In the early evening, we low-geared our way down an abandoned logging road until we found a dozed-over area where logs had once been sorted and decked. I was as thoughtless then, about environmental concerns—like diesel spills and toxic engine sludge—as the loggers who preceded us. Certainly heedlessness was part of our Western heritage. In central Montana in the Fifties and Sixties, it was hard to find a gulch back in the hills that didn't have a tin can dump, or a creek without old car bodies used to rip-rap cutbanks.

Without a second thought I parked the Chevy at the edge of the deck-site, where the loggers had serviced their machines. Used motor oil had soaked the ground, leaving a black, tar-like crud an inch or two deep. I crawled under the El Camino, unthreaded the crankcase plug, and drained our dirty engine oil right out onto the ground just like the loggers had done. I pulled the dirty filter and threw it, trailing a kite-string of oil, onto a pile of half-burnt slash, then screwed on the new filter and filled the engine with clean oil. Young blockhead that I was, I scrubbed my hands with sand and congratulated myself on a job well done.

We drove across the clearing and down to the edge of some woods that stood near a brushy little creek. Sheila pulled everything from the cab of the El Camino and began sorting, cleaning, and repacking those things we needed to keep close at hand or out of the weather. I gathered armfuls of small wood and kindling, crumpled up a newspaper, and laid our evening fire. We had already entered the first stage of a my-job/your-job routine, which speeded things up and gave us some alone-time when we could regroup after all the hours together in the El Camino. I was water carrier, fire-starter and dishwasher, while Sheila prepared our hot meals each morning and evening, took care of our bedding and laundry, and kept the grocery list.

That evening, it seemed to us that we'd camped awfully early in the day. The sun was still well up in the sky, but my wristwatch said eight o'clock. Finally it dawned on us that we were far enough north to see a difference between the length of our nights here and those in Colorado and even Montana.

"Sheila," I said. "Your attention, please." Sheila walked over to our fire pit, and I pulled my draft card from my wallet and handed it to her. She hadn't seen a Selective Service card before, since her husband had been exempted from the draft for health reasons. Sheila read both sides of the card aloud, beginning with its full title, "Selective Service System Registration Certificate," then going line-by-line through my personal information and the warnings of severe penalties, including fine and imprisonment, that could result from the loss or disfigurement of the card itself. "The law requires you to have this card in your possession at all times . . ." she read aloud, ". . . for identification or to advise your Board of any change of address." Sheila handed the card back to me and cocked her head to one side looking puzzled. I gave my draft card one last look, then knelt and lit it with a farmer's match. The much-worn little piece of paper flared up for a moment as I used it to spread flame along the crumpled newspaper under the kindling of our evening fire. In a moment the card turned to ash and was gone. "Free at last," I said. "Thank God Almighty, we're free at last."

Sheila put her arms around my waist and squeezed. "Yes." she said. "I am so proud of you," and from the intensity of her hug and edge on her voice, I could tell she meant it.

It seemed like a brave gesture, and I felt good about it as we held each other. But burning my draft card sent little flares of uncertainty through me, anxieties that would come and go over the weeks and months ahead. I had just committed a felony. Hadn't the card said a ten-thousand-dollar fine? And how many years in prison was it, for the card's "willful destruction?"

My anti-war declarations back in Bozeman seemed awfully feeble to me then. Actually resisting the draft—as opposed to talking about resisting the draft—was a serious thing, one that might have consequences. That much was suddenly clear to me.

TWELVE

For the next few days we drove gradually north, turning off the Cariboo Highway to explore what few side-roads there were. Settlements along the highway, we learned, were named for the original roadhouses, built to shelter road gangs in the 1860s, along what was then called the Old Cariboo Wagon Road. The early boarding houses were expanded to include livery stables and stores to serve early travelers and settlers when the road was improved and became known as "The Queen's Highway." So, as we traveled north, we stopped at places with a gas pump, a store, and half a dozen cabins for rent, that still bore names from another century: 70 Mile House, 100 Mile House, 150 Mile House.

Shifting gears to actually search for a place to build our cabin took effort, the way going back to work after a honeymoon takes effort. At first, the act of looking for a bit of land seemed vague and unreal. Where to begin? And how? The country went on and on and there were woods aplenty, but so much of what we saw was swampy, overgrown, or hill country far off in the distance with no roads whatsoever. We spent most of each day on the highway speeding up and slowing down. The weather turned cool, the skies grey with drizzle during the evenings. At night we woke to rain tapping on the poor tarp above us.

One evening, as we lay in our sleeping bags, Sheila said, "I'm going to call home tomorrow and let Mom and Jim and Marilyn know I'm okay. They won't bother us, but they'll be worried about me by now."

"Sure," I said. "Good idea."

"Will you call your wife or your folks?"

"I don't think so. That's probably not necessary right now."

We lay quiet, propped on our elbows, looking out across a valley littered with slash and stumps left behind by loggers. I didn't see how talking to my family in Helena would do any good. What could I say that would make sense to them about why I was here?

As I looked from the ravaged landscape beyond our little camp back to Sheila, I saw how my desire for her pulled me along toward wherever we were going. *Look at her*, I thought. *Look at her*. And when I did, all I cared about was the warmth of that young woman breathing there beside me, and the sounds she made when we loved each other during the night. She transported me to regions beyond this world. And I wanted to go with her to those secret places, that she seemed to create with such ease.

Day after day we lived on oatmeal and eggs, beans and rice. Then one afternoon, after backtracking south to Cache Creek, we went into a truck-stop diner and ordered up pie à la mode. Maybe because of the rain; maybe because we didn't have any idea how to search for cabin sites, our days had become a herky-jerky, stop-and-go, in-the-truck, out-of-the-truck affair that burned a lot of energy, didn't produce results, and left us rattled. Our little hoard of cash was trickling away with each gas stop and every bag of groceries. But the pie at Cache Creek was home-made, and the vanilla ice cream melting on top so extravagant, that by the time we were dodging puddles in the parking lot, we were again ready to find a camping spot for the night, a sheltered place where we could build a smudge, stretch our tarp, crawl into our sacks, and enjoy each other.

"I like pie!" I said.

"I'm for ice cream," Sheila answered, and we skipped toward the El Camino, swinging our arms back and forth, in high spirits once again.

Like so many other times when we were together, it seemed possible to be playful the way children are playful. We were and weren't all grown up, and, although we didn't talk about it, we were scared about what we were doing.

What saved us, we discovered, was focusing on the Right Now, on trout we saw darting across a creek or on a slice of pie at the end of a rainy day. We couldn't admit it to each other yet, but we were afraid we'd fail, afraid that in the end our dream would prove to be nothing more than half-baked foolishness. Yet sometimes, all it took to turn things around was apple pie and ice cream or two sleeping bags zipped together.

We were twenty-three years old, and for the first time in our lives, parents and grand-parents, aunts and uncles weren't looking over our shoulders; for the first time, spouses and best friends weren't there to tell us what we should or shouldn't do. We had broken free of hometowns, relatives, and friends. But now that we were on our own, all that freedom felt like its own kind of trap. We needed to get out of the truck, pick up some tools, and go to work. We just didn't know how to make that happen.

At Williams Lake Sheila called home. When I asked how the conversation with her mother had gone, Sheila shook her head and looked away. Then she said, "A girl we knew when I started college was kidnapped, held at gunpoint in a seedy motel and sexually abused until she managed to get hold of her abductor's Colt .45, with which she promptly shot him in the belly. Mom and my step-dad, Jim, are worried the same thing has happened to me, and it's pretty hard to convince them on the phone that I've run off with you under my own power, because I want to."

"What should we do?"

"I'll stay in touch with them. Beyond that, I don't know."

The area around Williams Lake was ranch country, where we saw some popping fine saddle horses. But we were surprised at how few roads left the main, north-south blacktop. The few backroads we followed turned into bogs and four-wheel-drive-only cow trails. Clouds traveled low in the sky. Sheila remained unusually quiet as we moved on.

We saw more poplar, aspen, and birch in the woods surrounding little settlements named for creeks and lakes, the kind of one-gas-station towns that catered to highway travelers and so often seemed shabby and sad. Without knowing exactly when, we had entered the Cariboo, a vast wet land of heavily forested hills, tall-grass valleys and swamps, where the mighty Fraser River cut its way south, through a countryside the locals called "the bush."

By the time we reached Quesnel, British Columbia, it was clear that I couldn't keep indulging in expensive Canadian tailor-mades, so I bought a pouch of Dominion long-cut tobacco and several packs of Zig-Zag papers and tried to roll my own. I'd grown up around old-timers like my dad's father, who rolled their own smokes with effortless grace, but hand-rolling was, I discovered, harder than it looked. I'd rolled little joints in college, of course, but my first attempts at making actual cigarettes resulted in torn papers and tobacco spilled in my lap or on the ground. The few smokes that I could lick off and light, resembled the classic bell-shaped curve—a pregnant bulge in the center and nothing but paper at each end.

In the evenings, beside our squaw fires, I'd take my failures apart, discard the ruined papers, and try again until I wore the tobacco out. Things sometimes got a little tense in the El Camino as rain pattered on the roof, while I ripped papers and spilled tobacco on the seat and entered the first stages of nicotine withdrawal. When I actually managed to light one up, Sheila chased me out into the rain where I growled, smoked, and kicked pine cones across the road. After a few days, I was able to shape, roll, lick, and light what looked like a cigarette with hair growing from both ends. These ugly little units would hold together long enough for me to drag some smoke into my lungs, but they required much spitting to clear away the bits of tobacco that stuck to my tongue. The only good thing about hand-rolling was the bearded Zouave soldier who served as the Zig-Zag logo. He seemed heroic, like some kind of French-Canadian lumberjack, bold with women, much loved by his friends. He also looked like the kind of man who could roll perfect cigarettes in a high wind, using just one hand.

Quesnel was a mill town where pulp and plywood plants gobbled up whole forests of softwood trees. It reminded us of Missoula, another pretty river town of sawmills and paper-making plants. The Fraser ran through Quesnel the way the Clark Fork ran through Missoula, and when the wind was right, the tainted air tasted almost the same. We stopped for gas and splurged on ice cream cones. Quesnel was busy, an actual town, a likely place to find work if we needed wages in between writing projects and trout fishing. The mills could be, we thought, with great if unintentional condescension, interesting places to research the Canadian working class. Such was the extent of our naiveté that we assumed money wouldn't be a problem once I started writing.

By the time we arrived in Prince George, we felt—for reasons we couldn't explain—that we were getting too far north. Prince George was a busy sawmill town with teepee burners and smoke, pawnshops, and pickup trucks with flapping fenders; the kind of place where men with sloped shoulders walked the streets in hard hats and torn mackinaws. There were some rough-lookers, both Indian and white, who'd obviously been wrecked by accidents in the woods or alcohol. These Canadians loitered outside the pawnshops and taverns, often seated on curbs, their arms around their knees, as if waiting for an idea or inspiration that could save them.

As we walked the streets, we discovered second-hand stores with goods that told us about the frontier life being lived out there in the bush. In each of these dusty joints, shelves bowed downward under the weight of small engines, pumps, and generators; chain saws, jacks, and rope block hoists; there were hand-powered kitchen appliances, canning jars, and kerosene lamps; and for footwear, patched gum boots, slope-heeled White's loggers, and old fashioned, knee-high lace-up boots. Rifles and fishing poles stood in racks behind counters. All the necessities for life in the north country and more.

We haunted one store in particular—a place that bought and sold used books, in addition to the regular stock of rough goods—where we could see all the tools and gear we would need. So many things, and so distant, since we had no surplus cash. After much looking and some moderate haggling, which

Sheila handled with humor and good sense, we bought an old-fashioned, galvanized laundry tub that looked like it might hold water, a corrugated washboard, a Bear oilstone, and some worn paperbacks.

Like Kamloops, Prince George was a crossroads town, and, as in Kamloops, we didn't know which direction to go. For several days, we used Prince George as a base, taking short trips east and west and north, only to turn around and return to town late each afternoon. In the evenings we camped in a not-so-private spot where a two-track road petered out in a stand of snowbrush near the edge of town. We washed our hair and took standing baths in the washtub, but we felt increasingly ratty, like lost hippies on the bum. Yet it was there, in our little hobo camp in the weeds outside Prince George, that our sense of being way up north was confirmed. We lay in our sleeping bags one evening, dozing in broad daylight, until almost ten PM.

Sheila, I think, would have explored all the way to Alaska if we'd had the money. Without knowing why, I felt Prince George was about as far as we should go. One day we set off to the north to explore the country between Prince George and Dawson Creek, but by the time we got to Mackenzie it seemed we were fighting against a force like gravity that increased in power with each mile. Finally we stopped, looked at the cut-over country that lay ahead, and turned around.

The next day we decided to go as far northwest as Prince Rupert on the coast, but again we couldn't seem to overcome the strange inertia that slowed us until we stopped and turned back toward Prince George. We were afraid of spending all our cash on gasoline, true, and it might have been that we were running low on stamina after so much time on the road. Mostly, though, I was running out of guts. I felt as if we'd climbed too high on a dangerous mountain, and I was afraid of falling.

One night, as we lay in our sleeping bags watching the green swoops of northern lights flare and sizzle across the sky, I was reminded of a long-forgotten yearning from my boyhood. As the aurora borealis swayed in sheets of shimmering green above us, I told Sheila how I had often come home from Bryant School, down by the railroad tracks in Helena's tough Sixth Ward, and turned on my mother's brown Bakelite radio and listened to "Sergeant Preston of the Yukon." Sergeant Preston, of the Royal Canadian Mounted Police, maintained law and order in the far north with his wonder dog, Yukon King.

By just clicking that one knob I could forget the gloom of Miss Westveldt's classroom and enter a land of frozen rivers and vast spruce forests where bad characters like Lucky Pierre the Trapper needed to be tracked down and brought to justice. By God, I remembered telling my seven-year-old self, a man and his dog could do things in country like that.

I told Sheila how the show's theme music, an overture called "Donna Diana," had lifted me out of myself and carried me off to those snowy expanses in such a way that I could feel the thrill of riding a sled pulled by eager huskies. It felt like flying. And I knew that someday I'd mush my own huskies through dark woods, on trails that only prospectors and Indians and trappers knew, racing to music that only Yukon King and I could hear.

But in that sticker patch outside Prince George, British Columbia, with the North of my boyhood dreams right up there in those swirling green streaks of light, I felt our momentum slipping away, our sense of adventure turning into a meandering routine of disappointment. So much land had been clear-cut, so much posted with red No Trespassing signs, that there didn't seem to be much possibility left in any of it.

Up 'til then we had been looking for extra-sweet, ice-cream country. After a few days near Prince George, we understood that we needed to look for actual places with dirt and rocks and trees where we could build our cabin.

So, we resolved to do no more aimless driving. I didn't want to identify myself to anyone, giving in to an unreasonable feeling that authorities of some stripe might already be on the lookout for me. So Sheila visited several real estate offices in Prince George, hoping to get a lead on a cheap piece of land. She described to agents what we were looking for and what we could hope to afford. And, since we had almost nothing to spend, our options quickly narrowed down to one raw possibility.

A realtor sent us off with directions and a couple maps to find a place called Campbell Lake. Eventually we discovered a dirt two-track off the highway that took us through a mile of bush to a beautiful body of icy, tea-colored water. At one end of the lake we found an old sawmill and a huge pile of rotting sawdust that spilled right out into the water itself. We climbed to the top of the sawdust and looked at our map, which turned out to be the plat of a town-site that had been laid out, surveyed, and recorded during a period of frontier optimism around 1910. Streets and city blocks were squared off and drawn to scale. Actual lots had been surveyed and staked out when the plat was drawn up, and a notation at the top of the plat declared in fancy script that the place was henceforth to be known as "Campbell Lake, the Denver of the North."

In the snappy afternoon sunshine, we felt a surge of optimism as we gazed across the water. It was a beautiful, secluded spot with fishing right out the front door! But when we oriented the plat map toward the location of the entrance road, it seemed the lot marked "for sale" lay somewhere under the sawdust heap beneath our feet, and might even run out into the lake itself. Apparently, just a lot or two in the town-site had been sold, ones where the mill was built before the lake had filled up. We turned the map this way and that, but it was true. The future Denver of the North lay out there at the bottom of the lake.

We looked at each other in disbelief. "Why, hell yes. We'll take it," I said. "Would cash be all right?"

"Oh, dear," Sheila said, sitting down on her coat to dump sawdust from her shoes, "this won't do at all."

"And just look at all this great sawdust we'll get for free," I said.

It must have been a joke Prince George realtors played on dreamers and fools like us, the wanderers and tourists and hipsters who passed through town asking about cheap land. Maybe the realtors thought a big enough fool might come along one day and buy the lot, no matter where it was. As we scrambled down from the sawdust pile, we admitted that for the moment at least, we were lost. I boosted Sheila onto a punky log—which must have once been five feet in diameter when it was still a tree—then climbed up next to her. We sat there at the edge of the lake and dangled our feet down toward the water that lapped against the shore just below us.

There, at the edge of the great north woods, on a radiant afternoon in early June, we watched fish jump and talked things over.

"Yes," Sheila said, "we've been naïve and goofy, thinking we could come all this way from Colorado, and find, with hardly any effort at all, a perfect spot in a virgin forest, a site just waiting for us to claim."

"You don't have to sugar-coat it," I said.

"Love, we don't even know *how* to look for a place."

"We can forget real estate offices, that's for sure," I said. "We can't buy spit."

We drove back toward the highway, each of us lost in our own blues. As we turned onto the blacktop, a radio announcer, sounding very Canadian, reported that Simon and Garfunkel, whose songs had been like anthems to us in college, had confirmed that, yes, it was true. Their break-up was final.

THIRTEEN

Back in our hobo camp on the outskirts of Prince George, we lay in our sleeping bags and looked up at the swaying trees in the lingering daylight. Sighs followed long silences, both of us talking to ourselves in our heads, asking what the hell we'd got ourselves into.

I thought Sheila had fallen asleep when she said, "Hey, Leroy. Do you remember that country we liked back toward Quesnel?"

"Yeah?" I answered. "I'm not sure . . ." The truth was that we'd seen so much country that it now flowed together in a swirling collage of landscapes opening and closing around a black ribbon of highway.

"Let's go south tomorrow and take another look," Sheila said. "If we *are* too far north, it won't hurt to backtrack."

We could hear big trucks running though their gears out on the highway. Stars winked on overhead. And, since we had no other plan, I said, "Sure. Let's take a look."

We spent the next two days wandering on and off the fifty miles of Highway 97 south of Prince George. The bush grew almost to the edge of the pavement in places, then the country opened out into grassy pastureland. In some spots we could see the Frazier River winding its way around sandbars and oxbows just west of the road. Off in the distance, beyond wild hay meadows, the log buildings and corrals of established ranches stood in the shadows of distant woods.

The overgrown feel of the bush appealed to me, land where the aspen and poplar, alder and birch created a mysterious understory beneath taller pine and spruce. Old cottonwoods of great girth shaded creeks that ran down to the Frazier from distant hills. It looked to be a wet country and a big one, a place where secret valleys could wait undiscovered forever.

We were so green, Sheila and I, that although the rivers and streams we saw were running full to their banks, we never once thought to wonder how deep the snow got in winter. Maybe it was just a couple of sunny days, maybe it was the country, but as we drove back and forth, exploring the side roads and little towns along Highway 97, we began to play. Once, while Sheila rode on my shoulders on a trail, her thighs pressing against my ears, she said, "I knew him, Horatio, a fellow of infinite jest, of most excellent fancy. He hath bore me on his back a thousand times . . . ."

And there we were for a few seconds, back in Doctor Watson's Shakespeare class, arguing some forgotten point as the morning light streamed in through old casement windows.

"Oh, but the Queen," I answered, grunting like an over-burdened horse. "I knew her, too, Horatio, a lady of vast good cheer and monumental weight. Didn't she just tickle my fancy and wear me out?"

One afternoon, we pulled off the highway and parked in front of a little country store in the village of Hixon. The town's post office was attached to the store, and after we'd gassed up, filled our water jug, and bought one of those quarter-pound Cadbury fruit and nut bars, we loitered at the community bulletin board in the store's vestibule. There were hand-written notices for lost dogs, free kittens, a saddle horse for sale, and a kitchen wood stove, cheap. And, written on an envelope, in carpenter pencil, was a notice for some land for sale.

We went outside, walked around the parking lot to stretch our legs, and looked at what we could see of the town. There was a big sawmill, partially hidden by trees, belching steam or smoke off west of the highway, and a few houses and trailers scattered around in some trees behind the store. Like sawmill towns in Montana, Hixon was blue-collar funky, the kind of place where, in winter, when the air was just right, everybody breathed someone else's woodsmoke. Clearly it was not the kind of town that concerned itself with tourism, and in the mid-day sunlight, the place had a good feel to it.

"Let's check it out," Sheila said, "The land for sale."

I looked at her standing there in the sunshine. When I reached out and touched her hair with my fingers, she covered my hand with one of hers and gave it a squeeze. A logging truck loaded with pine turned off the highway toward the mill, and the dust it raised drifted across the blacktop toward us. "You bet," I answered. "Let's take a look."

The people in the Hixon General Store couldn't have been nicer. The lady behind the counter even drew us a little map. We thanked her and headed north out of town. After a few miles we found the turnoff she'd described and followed Coldbanks Road east toward some heavily wooded foothills. We passed a rundown homestead on our left, then swung north at a fork in the road. Within a quarter-mile we saw the place we were looking for, the buildings standing on a slope beyond a little meadow.

The driveway ended at some low sheds, a barn, and for a house, a great gothic pile of wooden beams that looked to have once been ancient bridge timbers. A faded and much dented Case tractor stood in front of the house, but there were no automobiles in sight. As we climbed out of the El Camino, a thick-set man with several days of white whiskers stepped from the barn and looked us over.

Sheila said hello and explained that we'd seen his land-for-sale notice at the store and were curious about what he had to sell. The old fella looked at us with a practiced eye, the way a cattleman might look at orphan calves with ringworm.

His name was Ken Glaze, he said. He was probably seventy, maybe older. He walked like some of his parts had been broken and badly reassembled. I guessed he'd once been taller. I could see he'd used himself hard for a good many years, and that hard use had made him as twisted and tough as a pitch pine stump.

Ken wasn't very clear about the land he wanted to sell, or even in which direction it might be located, although he indicated that if the right party came along, he'd consider selling the whole place, which was several hundred acres. He might have had some rough miles on him, but Ken Glaze also struck me as a shrewd old boy. I could see he knew people, and I suspected he could be circumspect and calculating, the way country people sometimes have to be in order to survive. Within a few minutes he'd most likely pegged us, and could have guessed, within a hundred dollars, how much money we had. As we stood and blue-skied about this and that, Ken certainly knew we couldn't afford to buy land. But that didn't stop him from looking to part us from a few dollars in some other way. When I mentioned that I'd grown up living part of each year on a ranch in Montana, Ken insisted that I take a look at his horses.

One was a sorrel Belgian stud with the flax mane and tail typical of the breed, although he was shorter and closer coupled than the rangy Belgian horses that would later become so popular. The other horse was a tall, apple-assed Appaloosa mare, dappled grey with good spots. She took one look at me and laid her ears back.

Ken's wife, Lila, joined us in the yard and we chatted about their place and the surrounding country and available land in the area. Lila was a big-boned woman whose hair had turned iron gray. She seemed happy to have some company.

Ken mentioned that he'd lost his driver's license because he could no longer pass the eye test, and told us how, these days, he had to backroad it into Hixon for mail and groceries on his tractor, which was by then their only form of transportation. Ken added that he hadn't been able to start the tractor for a week and sure wished he could get to town for his mail. Then he launched into how his mare needed work, or she'd barn-sour on him, sure as the devil, and would I mind helping him out?

Before I knew it, I was throwing a saddle blanket over the mare's back and cinching down a good-looking western stock saddle, while Ken told me how to find the back road to Hixon.

I'd thought I was a cowboy when I was fifteen, although I wasn't even close. I was just another big dumb kid who'd grown up riding well-broke ranch horses. I'd never been around horses that had been spoiled or abused. But when the mare tried to cow-kick me as I tightened the cinch, I got an idea of what I was in for. I swung up, and we made a couple of quick circles in the driveway, as Sheila and Lila and Glaze got out of the way. And I had that peculiar feeling that can clinch up a man's guts before a bad wreck. Ken yelled, "Git a loaf of bread, while you're there," and the mare and I headed off traveling sideways down the ranch lane back toward Coldbanks Road.

I don't remember much about the ride to Hixon, except covering a lot more country than was necessary in the brush beside the road. Each time the Appy tried to duck her head to buck, I pulled her around in a tight circle, then booted her into a trot when we found ourselves pointed in the right direction. The mare wasn't a bronc by any means, but she was big and stout and jug-headed. She acted like she was used to doing whatever she wanted with a rider on her back, and she excelled at sudden stops, before exploding sideways for no other reason than a shiny bottle in the barrow ditch, and she enjoyed trying to scrape me off on trees whenever we got off the road into the poplars. If that mare had had any real action, she would have piled me on the hardpan and gone home trailing her reins. As it was, I eventually found myself at the Hixon Store and Post Office, where I dismounted, snubbed her up short to a telephone pole with her halter rope, and went in for the Glazes' mail. I bought a loaf of white sandwich bread at the store, then rolled and smoked a cigarette. I was rattled and a little shaky after all the fun, but when I settled down, I stuffed the mail and bread under my shirt, flipped the halter rope over her neck, and got a deep seat as quick as I could. We dodged around a pickup then cut in front of a logging truck, the mare trying to buck when the logger's air horn bellowed behind us. I found the dirt lane again, and we headed back north out of town.

When I stepped down in Glaze's yard, after what seemed like hours, the mare had foam around her breast collar and headstall, and I'd had enough of her for one day. Ken seemed surprised to see the mare and I arrive together, and he grinned as I pulled off her bridle.

"Well, what do you think about her?" the old fox asked.

"That's a nice horse, Sir. But I believe she could use a little work."

"Oh?" he said, mischief in his eyes. "Well, you see," Ken confided, "she belonged to a doctor's wife up in Prince George. The lady liked to ride in the evenings, but this little mare would dump her off, then stay just out of the lady's reach all the way home. She didn't give *you* any trouble, did she?"

"Nah," I lied. "She lined out real good. She just needs some wet saddle blankets is all." I was surprised to find myself smiling as I handed Ken the mashed loaf of bread and his mail. I could see that there was more to him than met the eye, and I doubted that he was just another old coot living out his remaining years in isolation and rural poverty. Like the famous onion, it seemed to me, some outer layers would have to be removed before the actual man could be revealed.

That evening we stayed for supper with Ken and Lila. It was dark as a cave inside the timbered house, which, it turned out, Ken and his boys had built using timbers from a railway trestle that had been replaced with steel. It seemed to me like a real treat to have a meal cooked on a wood stove. But, after the home-canned moose meat and spuds, when Lila served canned peaches for dessert, there was a sudden, almost involuntary, Tourette-Syndrome-like explosion from Ken, who barked: "Where's the cream?"

Sheila and I jumped and looked at each other, as Lila calmly punched holes in the top of a can of condensed milk with a butcher knife and put the can on the table. We dug into the peaches as if nothing had happened, but during the weeks ahead, at the least appropriate times possible, Sheila would demand, "Where's the cream!" It didn't matter if we were sharing a can of sardines or changing a flat tire. Sheila and I would jump, rare back and look at each other with wild, startled eyes, then laugh madly at our little joke.

A kerosene Aladdin lamp, with it's elegant slender chimney, stood in the center of the table. When I mentioned that I'd sometimes done my school work in the light of a lamp much like it at the ranch in Montana, Ken launched off into a monologue about the wonders of kerosene as a medicine.

"You got lice or bedbugs?" Ken asked. "Use kerosene! Say you get ax-cut real bad? Before it starts to stink, wash out that cut with kerosene twice a day and she'll heal up lickety-split and not even scar over. I swear to Christ! How about himrongs? Kerosene will shrink 'em right down to nubbins. Cancer? Why, Hell, all the old-timers used kerosene to treat cancers. Worked real good, too. Most of the time."

Lila winked at Sheila, who sat holding her spoon halfway to her mouth. After a bit Ken wound down about kerosene, and we finished up our peaches in silence.

After Sheila and Lila had cleared the table, Sheila asked again about the land Ken had listed for sale at the post office.

"Oh, we could cut you off a little chunk somewhere," Ken said. "Make you out a deed right here at the supper table."

Sheila and I glanced at each other. We might have been college kids, but we weren't quite *that* green. Sheila rolled her eyes.

"Or," Ken said, as if he'd just thought of it, "if you decide to stick around and do something else, we've got a nice cabin over on the Douglas place you could rent for as long as you want."

Ken lit the Aladdin lamp, put an ancient scrapbook on the table, and paged through it, showing us the photos and newspaper accounts of his youthful adventures. He'd been a working cowboy in his native Colorado in the Twenties. He'd saved his wages, built a nice little saddle and harness shop in Silver City, and rode broncs at local rodeos for fun and sometimes a little prize money. Postcards, made from actual photographs, showed a lean, ax-handle-hard Ken Glaze aboard some frightful bucking horses. In one photo, the bronc had gone so high that you could see the top rail on the far side of the corral, under the horse's belly. Glaze had been a genuine peeler, no question. As we looked at his postcards, I felt a little foolish about my breathless ride that afternoon.

A collection of yellowed newspaper articles in the old scrapbook told a bizarre story of youthful romance and foolishness that would have been hard to invent.

Ken had placed in the money at a rodeo in Denver, and, once the dust cleared, he was introduced to a young lady who wanted to meet him. Ken, of course, was a handsome specimen of Western manhood in his big hat and chaps, and the young lady, who was actually a rich girl out on a lark from back east, took a shine to him. The girl's daddy had invented and patented a process for nickel-plating everything from kitchen utensils to pistols, and it had made him millions. There followed a whirlwind courtship and hasty marriage, and newspapers all across the United States and Europe covered the story: "Colorado Cowboy Marries Nickel Heiress," read one headline. Young Ken Glaze was suddenly not only famous, he was also expected to keep his bride in the manner to which she'd been accustomed while drawing on her daddy's considerable resources. She was wild. She had needs. And she used her name to run up bills that Ken had to pay. Within a couple months, Ken Glaze was broke and in debt, his saddle shop and the nickel heiress long gone.

Ken told us the story with practiced ease, adding that he had continued to get letters from strangers—one from as far away as Switzerland and written in German—asking for money. The letters still rested unanswered in their musty envelopes, tucked between blank pages in the middle of the scrapbook.

Lila was Ken's fourth wife. Other women had certainly come and gone during the course of Ken's adventures. The nickel heiress story, however, was clearly a cautionary tale about an unsuspecting young man on the rise who had been waylaid and ruined by a frivolous girl right out of the Gilded Age. Although the fable ended badly, his quicksilver courtship and marriage to that nickel-plated princess seemed to have been *the* event in Ken Glaze's life, the one he returned to and retold again and again, as if he needed to remind himself, and anyone who would listen, of who he'd been when he and the West were young.

In the days that followed, the Colorado Cowboy's story bothered me. Had Glaze loved that fast girl? Had he mourned her when she was gone, or was there only his bright anger at what she'd done to his life? Was the story about a girl who broke his heart or about the brief taste of notoriety she'd brought into his life? Did Glaze yet wonder what had become of her? Did he dream of her still? The questions seemed more interesting than answers. I would never have those answers, of course, but I sensed Ken's memory of this distant wild time was what he had that told him who he was. Maybe that's why it was so important, all those many years later, for Ken Glaze to drag out his scrapbook and tell the story again.

We camped that night and the next off side roads south of Prince George, and, as if our field of vision had narrowed, we continued to explore the country east and west of the Quesnel-to-Prince George highway. On a bright Sunday afternoon, we took Coldbanks Road again, driving on past the Glaze place, following the poorly maintained Government Lake Road as it wandered north. We poked along, looking at the country, enjoying the day and each other. Above a switchback, we passed several beaver ponds and entered a steeper, more heavily wooded country where white birch grew among dense stands of arrow-straight lodgepole pine.

Half a mile above the beaver ponds, we entered a clearing where a sawdust pile marked another old mill site. The Government Lake Road continued north up a steep pitch that was washed out and too rough for the low-slung El Camino, so we parked at the sawdust pile and got out to stretch our legs and explore on foot. Below us, to the east, we could hear running water.

Not much timber had been taken out of the area it seemed, except right around the old mill itself. I rolled a smoke and we wandered around until we noticed the twin tracks of an abandoned skid trail going downhill beyond a very sharp little gulch that had once been spanned by a log bridge. The bridge had collapsed and lay in a jumble of rotting wood in the bottom of the gulch, so the skid trail below was inaccessible by vehicle from the mill site. We looked down the abandoned road, where it headed east through heavy, overhanging snowbrush, and decided to check it out. Once we started down, the snowbrush bending above us created a sunlit tunnel of leaves. We could hear a good-sized stream rushing along out of sight below us.

After a couple hundred yards, we discovered a big creek, fifteen or twenty feet wide, that narrowed farther upstream. The water was clear as daylight and cold; and it roared, as it ran down toward us from the north, through a cut between two steep hillsides, that amplified the stream's voice like a megaphone.

At the water's edge we had to shout to make ourselves understood, but there was, in that bright water, a pure energy of sunlight and motion and music that woke us up. Suddenly we were laughing, kneeling to splash water on our faces where the abandoned logging trail had once forded the creek. Great blocks of sharp-edged granite lay in the riverbed upstream, where they had come to rest, apparently after falling some years before, from the slopes above. Uprooted pines had tipped across the creek, making bridges every ten or twenty yards. We stepped out on a big lodgepole, found the wet bark too slippery to cross on foot, then shinnied over on our butts. Once on the east side, we bushwhacked upstream along a heavily forested hillside, but it was very steep, and the moss that carpeted the boulders slipped and skidded away underfoot, making for slow, treacherous going. Finally, we scooted out on a log across the stream, where we rested, watching ouzels dart through rainbows just above the water, to land and dip on stones surrounded by flashing spray. The ouzels trilled and flirted, ducking under the water to feed, then surfacing to resume their songs as sunlight glanced off the waters and lit rainbows in the air.

Gone was the feeling of emptiness that had grown as we drove so many aimless miles. We both felt it, a sense of unexpected welcome that came from the place and the water, from the light and from the birds. And a gladness rose up in us. We gripped the log with our thighs as if riding a pony, and we raised our arms, as if to receive a blessing.

After a few minutes, we scooted across to the west bank, then began to climb a steep hillside, at times going hand-over-hand, using small trees and roots and fallen logs for purchase. We stopped often to catch our breath then went on again, up through tall timber and rock outcrops until we'd climbed high enough that we could talk and be heard without much raising our voices. We rested, then contoured through the timber toward the southwest, heading back in the general direction of the old mill and the El Camino.

The slope eased off and within a few steps we found ourselves at the edge of a shelf—a level place, maybe a hundred feet by a hundred feet, that seemed to have been scooped or cut from the hillside in some long ago accident of geologic slump or slide. The cut had softened and healed over time as moss and trees and ferns did their work. The level spot stood in sunlight that streamed down through a cathedral of pines, trees that grew close together and straight as javelins as they rose from the shelf to pierce the vault of sky above.

We stood there, looking at that space, carpeted with emerald moss, bathed in holy light, with the echoing, enduring sound of water rushing below us like a distant wind. Somewhere on the slope, which continued on above the shelf, a squirrel chirred. We turned to each other, as if suspended in childlike wonder, and we said, almost in unison, "This is it!"

We looked at each other and looked back at the place we'd discovered, and we laughed.

"This is it," we whispered, as we stood there arm-in-arm, lost in a story-book glade in the big north woods. Then we stepped out onto the actual floor of the place and turned round and round in slow circles, letting our arms rise like wings. "This is it!" we said, as we circled each other. Looking into the light streaming down through the trees around us, we felt ourselves caught up and lifted, and we rose like Remedios the Beauty. We moved among the trees, turning in slow circles like hawks riding a thermal, peregrine spirits laughing as we rose, telling each other again and again, "This is it, this is it!"

And it was.

PART II

"I am glad I don't have to trouble myself about why there is always that iridescent green flash of surprise when our thoughts mesh."

—Sheila Malone
in a letter to Ralph Beer

"Limb 'em close!"

—Howard Beer, Senior
in conversation

FOURTEEN

We found ourselves bushwhacking through heavy timber toward the abandoned mill and the El Camino, but when we paused to rest, language failed us. We could only look at each other and shake our heads and laugh.

"The light," Sheila said after a bit. "It was the light."

"It was the light," I whispered.

We put our foreheads together until they touched, then closed our eyes as we tried to see again the radiant shafts of color slanting down through the tree tops on the hill above the shelf, lighting the moss on the forest floor into otherworldly greens and golds.

"Oh," Sheila said. "I want to go back there, right now. Let's go back!"

"Let's come at it from above," I said, so we climbed north up the hill, and after a couple hundred yards contoured around the slope, back toward the place we'd found.

When we saw it again, we stood on the hillside looking down at the shelf, and the power and beauty of the place drew us in once more.

"I don't think I've ever seen anything like this in the woods in Montana," I said. "Not even close. And my God, we just blundered into it."

We could hear the distant wind-sounds of the creek. Beyond the creek, the timbered slope opposite us leaped up to meet the blue sky above. On the north side of the shelf, a mysterious ledge of broken rock, mostly covered by moss, jutted from the slope, adding to the sense of an enchanted forest. It seemed that just out of sight beyond the ledge, there might be a gingerbread house where little people lived.

But there was more to the spot than a storybook scene of great beauty, one which kindled an almost spiritual sense of well-being in us. At some point, I noticed that the logs needed for a cabin were growing right there, on and around the shelf.

The spot was tucked away out of sight, about a hundred yards from the abandoned skid trail and at least a quarter mile from the Government Creek road, far enough to ensure privacy, yet close enough that we could carry in supplies from the old sawdust pile on foot. There was plenty of fast, clean water down below, and no neighbors for at least a couple of miles. And where we stood was almost certainly government Crown Land.

By 1971, homesteading in British Columbia was a thing of the past, and it seemed doubtful to us that such a small piece of ground could be surveyed and bought outright from the provincial government. And, of course, we had no money to buy *anything*. If there was a way to go at acquiring land like this, there would have to be an unconventional solution. And that's when Sheila mentioned Marilyn.

Ah, Marilyn. Sheila's sister had lived in British Columbia for a number of years, and she'd lived an alternative lifestyle that included being married to an American draft dodger. I gathered that Marilyn was some kind of self-educated savant who understood all sorts of advanced scientific and mathematical theories, but otherwise, was a more or less normal person.

Sheila's call to her folks back in Montana had been difficult, although she thought she'd managed to bank the home fires for the moment. We were both still a little concerned that a posse of Christians might be sent to look for us once we were a stationary target, so Sheila hadn't gone into details about where we were.

As soon as we got back to the El Camino that magical Sunday afternoon, we drove to Hixon, where Sheila called her sister in Kaslo, BC, from the pay phone outside Thorp's General Store. After some explaining about who I was and what we were doing in Canada, Sheila described the spot we'd found and asked her sister for ideas. Marilyn suggested that we check into mining claims. Certain mining claims, she said, allowed for permanent structures, and since the Canadian government wanted to encourage individuals as well as mining companies to get out into the bush to look for minerals, even non-Canadians could file for mineral claims. Marilyn knew this, she said, because there were bush-hippie-type folks who had taken up placer mining claims way back in the woods around Kaslo to use as hunting camps and cabin sites and such. She suggested we go to a provincial government office in Prince George or Quesnel to find out if our spot was on government land, then obtain all the information required to file a mining claim, if a claim would work to secure our secret spot as a cabin site.

As Sheila and I talked about Marilyn's idea later that evening in our sleeping bags, the whole mining claim thing sounded like a too-obvious scam to me, or at least an unrealistic long shot. Hell, we didn't know anything about mining or geology, and we couldn't afford equipment beyond a pick and shovel. "Geology," I said. "Geology is for dudes who carry loupe magnifiers and a rock hammer whenever they venture from their momma's basement. Just building a cabin will be a handful," I added. "I don't think we can swing a gold mine, too."

Sheila squeezed my hand. "Let's check it out," she said, with the subtle decisiveness I'd noticed recently. "If this idea doesn't work, it might lead to something else that we *can* use. And, you know, I think you're wrong about geologists. I sorta like rocks and such. I think geology would be a cool thing to study some day."

The next morning we ran down a street in Prince George through a hard rain, then waited in a crowded government office behind a gang of steaming Canadians already queued up at the counter. Just being in a government building made me uneasy, but we shuffled ahead until our turn came. We asked the nice lady for all the printed information she had about filing mining claims, as well as any other ways of acquiring government land that she might know about. We left with a stack of brochures, maps, regulations, and application forms, as well as instructions on how to locate and file for both hard rock and placer mining claims.

In the El Camino, during one of those spring downpours, when a morning gets darker and darker as a storm settles in, we read the leaflets we'd collected. I had expected all sorts of government-style complications and Catch-22s, but as we read, the process for staking out and filing a placer claim seemed pretty simple, and if anything, too easy. As far as we could tell, it was possible to file a placer mining claim without having produced any gold or even evidence that gold had been found at the claim site.

The first step was to obtain a "Free Miner's Certificate," which had to be purchased and recorded at a provincial government office. There was a $5.00 fee for the certificate.

Then the physical claim had to be measured and staked out on the ground. A twenty-acre, rectangular placer mining claim required only two posts, with a metal claim tag attached to each one. The posts were to be located at the claim's two ends and would show where an invisible line ran from post to post lengthwise through the claim, from which x-number of feet left and x-number of feet to the right of that line, would locate the claim's total width as it lay on the actual ground. The distance between the stakes showed the total physical length of the claim.

The claim had to be located on a stream or have access to running water.

Once the claim had been staked out and measured, a Placer Claim Lease Application form had to be completed and submitted to the nearest Gold Commissioner's office along with a twenty-dollar application fee. Each year after the lease was granted, some "development" work or an annual $250 fee in lieu of that work, had to be paid before the first of January each year. And sure enough, claimants didn't have to be Canadian citizens or even landed immigrants.

I thought it sounded too easy. My radar was up and turning, trying to locate a hidden catch. So we went back through the instructions and requirements for filing a claim again and wrote out a list. But we could still find no hidden bureaucratic trickery.

"This is all there is to it, Cowboy," Sheila said. "We can make this work if our spot is close enough to the creek." Although I still wasn't convinced that anything flowing from a government agency could be this straightforward—except being drafted—we went back upstairs to the government office, where we confirmed on a big wall map that our spot was located on Crown Land. Then we purchased a Free Miner's Certificate in my name. It was Monday, the 14th of June, 1971. My certificate's number was 61745.

That afternoon we returned to Ken Glaze's place. We told him we liked the area and that we'd been out exploring. We asked him if he knew anything about placer claims in the area. Ken said he thought there were some, but he'd never been interested in "that mining stuff," which, he seemed to think, was unfit work for full-sized white men.

Sheila and I looked at each other. I probably wouldn't have said anything to Glaze about the spot we'd found or even about mining claims, but Sheila came right out with it. She told Ken that we were thinking of filing a placer claim or two, and she wondered if he'd still be interested in renting the cabin he'd mentioned to us earlier. Ken, of course, knew by then that we couldn't afford to buy land, but he seemed willing enough to pluck whatever low-hanging fruit from us might come within his reach.

Sure we could rent the cabin on the Douglas place, Ken said. How did twenty dollars a month sound? Then he added, "About that mining stuff, go see Harry. He knows all about it." And Ken gave us directions to Harry Schmaltz's homestead.

Harry Schmaltz lived in an immaculate little cabin on the road I'd taken the day I rode Ken's mare to Hixon to get the mail. When Harry opened his door, we explained that Ken Glaze had sent us and that we'd like to ask him some questions about staking out a placer claim.

Harry was a small, compact man who dressed in matching green work shirt and pants that had probably come from a Montgomery Ward catalogue.

Harry was a retired mill worker with a strong German-sounding accent who liked to wear his hat indoors. He invited us in and put the coffee pot on his wood range to heat. He seemed glad for some company, and, when I asked where he was from, he poured the coffee and told us his story.

Harry was, without question, one of the world's great draft dodgers. Born in German-speaking Switzerland, Harry went to France when his compulsory Swiss military service was about to begin. This was in the late Thirties, when World War II was knocking at Europe's door. When Harry was about to be drafted into the French army, he crossed the channel to England and found work. But after some time in England, he was up for conscription into the English army. Harry said, "I was just too darn close to that damn war." So he found work on a merchant marine ship, disembarked in Canada, immigrated, and went about as far west as he could, to put as much distance between him and the war in Europe as possible. Harry found work in sawmills and logging camps as a millwright and followed that work from one logged-out patch to another. He liked the Cariboo country, so when he retired, he settled in to live out his days on the back-road to Hixon. Gold mining was his hobby, and he was passionate about it.

As Harry described his single-minded avoidance of military service and all the maneuvers he'd made to escape a war, Sheila and I kept glancing at each other. After a bit, we couldn't help laughing, and Sheila pointed at me and told Harry, "This guy, too. He's doing the same thing, only with fewer countries in between."

Harry looked at me then slapped his leg. "Yeah?" he said.

"No Vietnam for me, Sir," I told him. "I'm not going to go."

Harry stood up and, with a big grin, shook my hand again, "Oh, *sehr gut!*" he beamed. "*Sehr gut!*"

Harry had several placer claims of his own, so he knew the procedures for locating and filing a claim. He explained the claim-staking process, how to shoot a compass bearing from one claim-post to a post at the far end of the claim to establish a centerline and its orientation in degrees magnetic north. But first, Harry said, shoot a compass bearing for a temporary centerline from one end of the claim to the other end, then to pace off or measure the distance to the creek, to be sure at least part of the claim crossed running water. "You got to locate your claim on water for a placer," he said, "'cause you need water to work your sand and gravel."

Harry explained that the "centerline" didn't have to be located in the center of a claim's width. He drew a couple sketches to show us how more ground could lie on one side of the centerline than on the other. Then Harry showed us how we could "tilt" a claim, to orient it at, say, two-hundred-forty-degrees magnetic north, so at least a corner of the claim crossed the creek.

"Shoor, shoor," Harry said, when we asked. "You can build a cabin on your claim. Do the placer work every year or send in the money. "Joost pan a little color. Shovel some gravel. Or, some years, pay the government for the claim work. It's a couple hundred bucks. That's all you got to do."

Before we knew it, Harry had us in his back yard with a tub of water, a couple gold pans, and a bucket of black sand that he'd high-graded from one of his claims with a sluice box. He got us started sloshing the water around in slow circles in our pans then showed us how to let a little black sand slide over the downward lip of the pan as the water circled and swirled the material away. When only the heaviest material remained along the bottom edges, Harry pointed at tiny gleaming flecks in Sheila's pan. "Gold," Harry said. "You betcha, that's gold!"

Harry showed us a small bottle of nuggets and another of colors he'd collected. If a man was working for wages, he explained, the man would take all the black sand he could collect at his claim in the summer then high-grade it down later by panning at home in the winter. He could then use heat and mercury to catch even gold that wasn't visible to the human eye. I liked the part about gold. The mercury fumes, not so much. But Harry's enthusiasm was infectious.

When we got ready to go, Harry Schmaltz lent me his compass, an elaborate brass model with a wire sight. It looked like an expensive, high-quality instrument. He also lent us a one-hundred-foot metal measuring tape. I told Harry we'd return them as soon as we'd filed our paperwork, and we did.

We returned to our cabin site that afternoon. A fine rain fell as we paced off the distance up the old skid trail from the creek to get a rough idea of where our claim's centerline needed to be, to include both the cabin site and the creek. Then we ran compass lines north from different beginning points along the old skid trail to help us zero in on the best centerline for our claim. Working our way through the wet trees, we marked our final line with bits of rag tied to tree branches. We measured the distance to the creek at both ends of this centerline with Harry's tape, gutting it up and down the hillside from the creek to the shelf, just to be sure our claim lay across water all the way.

We drew the claim out on the "sketch" page of the application form, trying to shield the paper from the rain with my jacket. We had five-hundred feet on the creek-side (to the east) of the centerline and one-hundred feet above it (to the west), which put the centerline of our claim right through the middle of the shelf where the cabin would stand. As luck had it, both the creek and the centerline of our claim ran almost exactly three-hundred-sixty degrees magnetic north. That simplified everything, but we called our center line "three degrees north," just to seem detail oriented. The overall length, from the south center-post to the north center-post was 1,200 feet, which brought us in under twenty acres by a good margin.

We had to nail up a red tin tag on each of our two centerline posts. The tags required the claim's name as well as the locator's name and the date. As we stood at the north post, soaked to our waists from walking through dripping undergrowth, we thought of our former teacher, Mac Watson, who had been such a good friend to us in Bozeman.

"We could call our claim, "The Hamlet," I said, thinking of that first class Sheila and I had taken from Doctor Watson in '68.

"How about, 'The Mac'?" Sheila said.

"Hell, yes!" I said. "This is all Watson's fault, one way or another."

And we laughed, maybe because Mac was one of those rare people who knew how to laugh. I mean, to *really* laugh, to laugh in such a way that was full of fun, yet wise to the craziness of the world we lived in. In some important ways, Mac Watson had helped us learn to relish the absurdities that swirled around us every day during those Nixon years and to laugh at them. In Bozeman, we had needed laughter almost as much as we'd needed love.

So the claim's name, once said aloud, seemed as obvious as it was short. The tags came with the pre-stamped number 13615 at the top. Just below the claim's number was the line for the claim's name. As we scratched *The Mac* on the red tin with my pocketknife, we knew Mac's spirit—and the memory of his laughter—would help sustain us in the weeks ahead.

❖ ❖ ❖

On Wednesday, the 16th of June, 1971, we were back in the provisional government offices in Prince George, where the lady at the counter took our $20.00 deposit along with our Application for Placer Mining Lease, made out a receipt, and handed it to us with a flourish. "Thank you," she smiled. "You're all set and good luck."

On the street we looked at each other. How could something like acquiring twenty acres of land for a cabin site, that included running water and the timber we would need to build a cabin, have been so easy? How could it have even been possible? I wasn't convinced that what we thought we'd just done was true, but as we walked along I let myself begin to believe.

"Hot dog!" Sheila said, waving our paperwork. "Here's to our cabin in the woods and to all the great sex we're going to have there."

We were giddy, feeling again, almost lighter than air. For a block or two we might have been clouds.

"Let's go shopping." Sheila said.

"Yeah, shopping!" I said.

Our first stop was the one big supermarket in Prince George, where we stocked up on peanut butter, dozens of cans of sardines, and corn meal; oats, powdered milk, and jelly; flour and corn starch and hotcake mix; eggs, margarine, and syrup; canned meat and canned milk; dish, laundry, and hand soap; two pounds of lard and a five pound bag of ginger snaps.

At a hardware store we bought kerosene and two small kerosene lamps with tin reflectors on one side, a good quality bow saw with extra blades, two five-gallon water cans, a dozen new Kerr canning jars with screw-on metal lids, and two big aluminum dish pans. We also picked up a couple gold pans, three buckets, and OFF bug spray.

Since it was time to celebrate, we stopped at one of Prince George's taverns, and went in through the "ladies with escorts" door to a big room full of tables lined up end-to-end. Waiters, wearing white towels as aprons, squired big trays of schooners filled with the Canadian beers of the day. Sheila thought a Moosehead ale sounded good, and I went for the Labatt lager. Our waiter, a harried French Canadian with arms like a pulpwood cutter, informed us that we each needed to order at least two schooners, minimum. Who were we to argue with a reasonable proposition like that? Soon we were wiping foam from each other's upper lip and grinning like bandits. As we worked on our second schooners, we began to understand that the Canadian notion of pub life was to sit at these tables like Vikings, to order pilsners by the pair as fast as possible, and to gun them while shouting at each other above the din. It was almost as if Canadians thought of drinking beer as a job with quotas. In this setting, having a cold one seemed to require almost as much energy as toting 2x10s off the green chain in a sawmill. Still, the beer was cold and mellow, and we drank ours with relish. Then we left a small tip for our waiter and got the heck out of there.

That afternoon we rented the cabin Ken Glaze had told us about. Ken and his sons had built the cabin sometime during the Sixties from cull 2x4s they got for almost nothing at a local mill. They'd stacked the 2x4s one atop the other to make walls of solid wood, three-and-a-half inches thick. Clear plastic sheeting served as windows. In the kitchen/front room we had a wood cookstove, a teetery table, two chairs, and a couple apple crates nailed to one wall for shelves. A small porch with an overhanging roof fronted the kitchen and overlooked a meadow and distant tree line.

An ancient sand-cast iron bed with a lumpy mattress was the only furniture in the dim back room.

Just outside, a woodshed was partly filled with blocks of pine and poplar and aspen. Twenty paces to the east, a tidy log barn, with a nifty little hay mow, stood at the edge of the meadow, and further east yet, a hand-dug well. This was what remained of the original homestead known as the old Douglas place. After Ken had shown us around, he said, "Oh, yeah, Mrs. Douglas. She's out there in the meadow someplace."

"Say, who?" Sheila asked.

"Mrs. Douglas," Ken answered. "Her and her old man came to this country in the Forties. Might as well have been the 1840s here in the Cariboo. They took up this land and lived rough out here by themselves. Then, one winter, she died. I heard the old fella couldn't get her to town or in the ground until spring, when he dug a hole out away from the tree roots and rolled her in."

I could see from the gleam in his eye that Ken enjoyed trying to spook Sheila with his ghost story. "See, after the original house burned down, old Douglas quit the country, and the grave grassed over. But she's around."

Mrs. Douglas was there. Of course she was. We never discovered her grave, although several depressions lay around the edges of the meadow, once cleared by hand but already reclaimed by saplings. We didn't bother Mrs. Douglas, and she didn't bother us. But we were always conscious, during the time we lived there, that like us, she had come there with her man to work and put down roots in a new country. We felt like accidental guests on a place that was still hers, and we thought about her often in our abstract ways.

Sometimes, during the long evenings of that summer, we wondered aloud about her and her life there, as we sat resting on the front porch looking out at the beauty she'd once known. At first we'd assumed she was an old lady, used up by life, worn out by cutting wood and toting water from the well they'd dug and rocked up by hand. Perhaps she was. But during that summer, as I discovered feelings for a young woman that I hadn't known were possible, it occurred to me that maybe the two people who once cleared this land had been as young as us, convinced that life would be happy and full in this sweet country. Maybe this had been the sacred spot of their own accidental discovery, one that turned their lives in a new, irrevocable direction. Why had Sheila and I assumed that Mr. and Mrs. Douglas lived lives of solitary struggle and despair, when they might, at least at first, have been full of hope, believing that an Eden of their own making in this place would bear fruit for them and theirs forever?

We never learned more about Mr. and Mrs. Douglas as far as factual information was concerned, but as we lived where they had lived and worked, we felt that in some important ways, we'd come to know them.

FIFTEEN

Sheila called her sister again to reassure Marilyn that while our Canadian adventure might seem sordid and strange, Sheila herself was a willing co-conspirator. She also told Marilyn that we'd filed for a placer claim and had rented a cabin just off Coldbanks Road, three miles north of Hixon.

Maybe because the old tale of kidnapping and rape still seemed to hang in the air between Sheila and her sister, we weren't terribly surprised when Marilyn appeared at our cabin door as we prepared to leave, in a steady, soaking drizzle, for our first day's work at the Mac. Marilyn had driven most of the night, and was in full elder-sister mode that morning as she insisted Sheila ride along in her rig while I drove the El Camino up to the old mill site, where I surrendered my plastic raincoat to Marilyn. The sisters hiked off to hash things out between them in private. I touched up my double-bitted Kelly ax with our two-sided Bear oil stone, then followed the old skid trail toward the creek, listening to the grumble of water get louder as I went along. The rain was no more than a mist on my face and hands; the morning as soft and fresh as new leaves and wet moss.

The skid trail's ruts cut through a muddy conglomerate of small river rocks suspended in gray clay. The twin tracks were getting slick, and the way the sky had settled down on the timbered hills told me I'd be wet for the rest of the day.

To mark the south end of the claim, we had climbed a steep claybank above the skid trail, cut off a small pine five feet above the ground, squared the top six inches of the standing trunk with a handsaw and axe, and nailed our red "centerline" tag to it. Since the trees on the slope between the claim marker and our building site were so close together, I decided to take out trees here and there to open up a trail. I blazed pines that needed to be cut then picked one a few yards north of our claim marker. It was about fourteen inches through at the butt and like most of the trees on that mountainside, it grew straight and plumb for fifty feet or more. Like the other pines, there were almost no limbs for the first twenty-five feet, and few big limbs for another ten or fifteen. I picked a fall line for that first tree, got down on my knees in the wet duff, and, because I wanted my stumps to be as low as possible, set the saw's teeth against the trunk just three or four inches above the mossy ground. I began to push and pull the bow saw back-and-forth in a more-or-less horizontal line, the saw's blade hissing in the green wood.

I worked bent at the waist facing the ground. Within a minute I was panting. Sweat popped out on my forehead, as raindrops fell onto my neck and shoulders from the canopy of interlaced branches far above, and I soon had to stop to rest. When I pulled the saw's narrow blade from its kerf, I was surprised to see that I'd only cut in three or four inches.

When I was just a boy, I had started cutting poles for stove wood using a sawbuck and Swede saw at the ranch, so I had some idea of what a good bow saw should do. This new saw weighed almost nothing. The blade was only an inch-and-a-half deep and forty inches long, the saw's frame nothing more than a bright yellow length of light-weight tubing bent down on both ends at forty-five-degree angles, with a lever on one end to release or tighten the blade.

I sat back on my heels and looked up at the tree's boughs high above me, and I felt a dull oh-no moment creep up on me. *Are Canadian pines tougher than evergreens in Montana? No. Is it the saw? Hell, it's new. It's not the saw, it's me.* The insight did not gladden my day.

When I finally had the bottom of the undercut finished, I took my Kelly ax, and, by cutting down at a forty-five-degree angle, I chopped out the open mouth of the undercut. The undercut would let the tree's weight pull it in that direction once I'd made a backcut, a couple inches higher, on the opposite side of the tree. When I had scooted around on my knees to face the tree from the other side, I concentrated on keeping the blade level so it wouldn't pinch.

My arms burned as I sawed the backcut, going almost as deep as where the bottom of the undercut stopped. There was no wind, but high up among the falling raindrops, I could see the tree twitch. When only a thin, upright hinge of wood remained between undercut and backcut, the tree began to lean. The butt of the tree at the stump made soft little cracking noises. I got to my feet and watched the top of my tree scribe a slow arc for a few feet, then stop as it embraced the limbs of trees growing next to it. Sure as hell, it hung up.

I sawed my backcut all the way through. I pushed sideways on the trunk, but the tree wouldn't budge. With a cant hook I might have rotated the tree, limbs and all, until it worked itself loose. But, we had no cant hook. I lifted and pushed some more until I was winded, then I stood steaming in the sweet rain that filled the air around me with the spirits of pine and duff and sap. I wished I had a good 6-10 McCullough chainsaw and wondered, vaguely, where the sisters might be. Small branches far above me cracked and a few clusters of pine needles spun down to land around me, but the tree was stuck.

I stood there, bent forward at the waist, breathing hard. And it began to sink in *just* how out of shape I was. Sure, I was young, and I'd been a tough kid, used to ranch work that included lots of time in the woods cutting rails and fir staves and fence posts, as well as cord after cord of firewood each year. But I had spent a long Montana winter smoking cigarettes and pot, drinking Tokay and Buckhorn beer—the official beverages of the Revolution—and ingesting every sort of drug I could get my hands on. I was as soft as an old horse that had stood in a barn all winter.

I looked up at the tree, black against the pale gray sky and realized I was about to be sick. I walked off a ways into the dripping woods, went down on my knees, and pitched up what was left of my breakfast. Acid burned my nose, and a nasty gall filled my mouth. I rested my forehead against a tree and was overcome by a bitter sense of how great my foolishness had been. I had conjured up this silliness and sold it to a decent girl who was probably—thanks to me—making the mistake of her life. As I sat back on my heels, I felt an overwhelming sense of regret wash through me. *Oh, you rash and stupid fucker,* I thought. *Look at what you've done. Behold your folly and your weakness.*

It seemed that Sheila and Marilyn had settled in for a long sister-to-sister conference, so I picked up the bow saw and my fine, two-faced Kelly, which had belonged to Robert Beer, my great-grandfather. I found the next tree along my imaginary footpath, went back down again on my knees, and made the undercut in a direction that I hoped would let this tree fall into the small space where the top of the first tree had been. I slowed down, sawing a bit then resting, sawing and resting. Again, the tree tipped in the right direction when I made the backcut. Again, it settled into the branches of its cousins. Like the first tree, it leaned at a slight angle, with no inclination whatsoever to come down. I remembered Wallace Stegner's great novel, and I decided to think of the slope at which the trees leaned as their "angle of repose." And I thought that if I couldn't handle the job in front of me, I could at least fake being literary. I looked around, picked the next tree, and went back to work.

By the time Sheila and Marilyn came down the skid trail and hiked up the hill past me to look at the building site, I had four trees cut, all hung up. I was soaked through and pretty much done for the day. Blisters on my fingers had broken, and the skin in places had peeled off, leaving raw meat covered with pitch that was black with dirt and particles of tree bark. Marilyn, short-waisted and stringy, looked at my hanging trees, then at me with an expression that told me I was about the most pitiful thing she'd seen in a while. Although she seemed abrupt and nervous, Marilyn didn't say anything about what Sheila and I were doing. She didn't have to. When Marilyn left to drive back to Kaslo that afternoon, I knew she was thinking our big project wouldn't last a week, and I figured she might be right.

The next morning I couldn't stand up straight. I had trouble bending down to tie my bootlaces. My arms and shoulders felt as if someone, whose wife I'd stolen, had caught up with me and gone at me in my sleep with an ax handle. I had trouble just walking outside to make water. But we packed a lunch and drove back to the old mill site, then hiked down the skid trail under a dripping arch of bowed snowbrush to our claim marker, just like we knew what we were doing. There had been no wind, and the trees I'd cut the day before had not budged.

I looked at Sheila and said, "Oh, man, Pal. I don't know about this . . ."

"Let's just get something done today and enjoy this spot," she said. "What should I be doing?"

We walked up to the cabin site and took a look. The stand of trees on the shelf wasn't as thick as on the slope up from the skid trail. A few rotten logs and broken treetops lay scattered around in the area we wanted to clear. Sheila got busy carrying chunks of rotten wood and fallen limbs out of the way, lugging them from the shelf and part way down the steep slope that dropped off toward Government Creek. I went back to my agony of leaning trees, to work on our trail.

That day, more blisters tore open on my fingers and palms as I worked with the ax and saw. Pitch worked in where the skin had rubbed away, and it stuck there like contact cement. I thought about Ken Glaze and his love of kerosene when I had to use it to wash away the pitch that evening. I splashed on the oily stuff, and my hands felt like they'd had been dipped in liquid fire. I'd never been a big believer in gloves, except in winter or for certain ranch jobs like fixing barbed-wire fence. Gloves were for sissies. Only now I wasn't such a tough guy anymore. On our next trip to the Hixon store, we bought lightweight leather work gloves and some yellow rag gloves, because they were cheap, and we wore them until our hands hardened up.

The next few days felt just like the first ones, only not as much fun. We left the Douglas homestead in intermittent rain, and I spent the mornings trying to clear trail. I kept tipping trees to lean into others that I'd cut, and finally a windy night brought down a dozen or more. I managed to cut five or six trees a day, and by tipping them back into spaces opened by trees that had already come down, I began to make some progress. I bucked the straightest trees into short logs twelve to fifteen feet long then limbed them out. Sheila cleared away and scattered the limbs to make our work less visible to anyone who might walk by on the way to the creek. We didn't want to make our path obvious from the old skid trail, so we took out only enough trees to open a path wide enough to let us carry in lumber and supplies. I went back and sawed off all the stumps as flush with the ground as I could, so we wouldn't stumble on them when we used our trail. At the end of the first week, it was possible to see that someone had been at work in the timber there, although from a distance, a casual observer wouldn't have noticed anything at all.

One day, when I had punched the trail almost to the edge of our building site, I hit an invisible wall. I flat ran out of go-power the way a motor stalls when it runs out of fuel. With a chainsaw, I could have taken off four-foot lengths from the butts of leaning trees, letting them step down until they unhooked from the limbs of the trees holding them up. With a chainsaw, I could have easily flush-cut the stumps in seconds. But we couldn't afford a chainsaw, and it seemed beyond belief that it hadn't occurred to me we'd need one. Building the cabin with hand tools had been part of my dream, since I'd wanted to do it the way old-timers had built their cabins and barns. But after just clearing the trail, it seemed obvious that with the tools we had, the physical effort would be far beyond our strength and endurance. As my energy bled away, it seemed my body hurt more all the time. And it was now clear to both of us that at such a slow pace we'd run out of cash before we had our logs down and peeled.

When I'd carried my tools into the little opening Sheila had cleared, I said, "Let's sit for a spell." We hunkered down against a fallen log and looked at the lichen-covered trees around us. "We can't do this," I said. "It's just too damned much." There was a long silence, broken only by the occasional hum of a mosquito.

"No," Sheila said. "We can. We just need to keep coming back every day to peck at it until we figure out better ways of doing what we need to do to make progress. We have to harden up some more and find our stride. We don't have much choice, Pard. If we can't do this thing right here in this perfect place, with the benefit of a roof over our heads like we have at the Douglas place, then where *could* we do it?"

I looked back through the accursed woods toward my nearly invisible trail, overcome by doubts and anger at my own weakness. I didn't want to waste the last of the money we had on this doomed venture, then be so broke we couldn't even get back to Montana. Mostly, I just wanted to cave in and quit. But I could see that Sheila was right. We were down to a couple hundred dollars cash, and we had nowhere else to go. Sheila hooked her arm through mine, and we sat there in the deep gloom of those woods, resting against a mossy log and listening to Government Creek tumble along through the canyon below.

I felt a quiet and potent strength coming from that girl which I hadn't acknowledged before. I'd been thinking of her as a one-hundred-and-ten-pound college girl with beautiful breasts. But, man. She was steady and tough, and I saw how her grit could pull me back up our trail each morning to a clearing we had yet to make, in a stand of lodgepole pine that topped out fifty and sixty feet above us. I might have been the one who'd bench-pressed two-hundred-eighty pounds in a college gym, but day-in and day-out, Sheila was the one with the heart and the force that counted when it came to getting the work done. She might have a hitch in her walk and glasses that made her look like a librarian, but there was a strength and a toughness beneath her calm surface, as if her core had been stitched together with cat-gut strings and whang leather. All I had to do, to tap into that strength, was to sit back against a log and feel the warmth of her arm linked in mine.

SIXTEEN

Weather came to my rescue.

In that vast Cariboo country, which lies between the great mountain ranges of British Columbia, the early summer rains ride in on warm winds like a monsoon. Once we'd begun work at the actual cabin site, those rains fell in a stubborn hard downpour, sometimes for two days and nights at a stretch. We fell asleep to the hammering of rain on the tarpaper roof and woke to it still thundering down in the morning. We looked out through the wavy plastic windows, at the sodden green mess outside, where we could see the meadow grasses grow taller every day.

We had a cheap transistor radio that I'd brought from Bozeman, which let us reach beyond the bush to Prince George and Prince Rupert, even Seattle and Vancouver at night. We made our morning coffee and dialed in weather reports from the coast. "Rain can be expected in the Interior," the announcers said in their droll Canadian version of English, "and gale warnings, today, in the Georgia Strait."

There seemed to be gale warnings every day in the Georgia Strait, that long trench of rough water that lies between Vancouver Island and the mainland. But when the rains came in hard to the Cariboo, we didn't mind. We welcomed that time off to rest. We cooked slow breakfasts and cleaned the cabin and listened to the rain. I'd go to the woodshed and split kindling and small wood for the kitchen range and carry in a few armfuls to fill the woodbox beside the stove, and we'd listen to the rain. These were the mornings when the spongy sky lowered and the rains pummeled the tarpaper roof, days when there was no point in thinking the sky might clear enough to let us work. We had books, and we took turns reading to each other in the grey light that seeped through the plastic widow above the kitchen table. We listened to news at noon from Prince George on the radio. We patched our work clothes with denim and squares of red bandana. We greased our boots and cleaned our tools and listened to the rain. And we wrote letters. I sent two, one to my wife and one to my parents. I told them I planned to stay if I could, and that my mailing address was General Delivery, Hixon, British Columbia.

❖ ❖ ❖

When Sheila and I had recovered from our days of work, we'd go into the dim bedroom in the afternoons as the dark rain fell, to peel off our clothes and fall into bed, there to play like otters for hours of pure romping sex; hours when we swam together through deep green waters, otters turned to eels, articulating our way down, down, to magical depths where certain improbable dreams came true.

We'd had love affairs in college, of course, and we'd both married young. But in odd ways that mattered, we were still inexperienced, ignorant of what could happen when two like-minded people dove deeper into that murky nameless sea together. During our nights on the road we'd enjoyed sex that gave us satisfactions like those we'd each experienced with other people. But we had been shy with each other, and awkward sometimes in all our holding back. There'd been too much road and too many miles and not enough time to let us be at peace with each other. Sex on the road had been sweet but usually nervous and quick, with no moving of the earth.

But in the back room of that damp little shack on the Douglas place, in an old, sand-cast iron bed, on a mattress that sagged toward the floor in its middle, with the rhythms of rain pounding the roof above us, we took hold of each other and joined ourselves together in a sweaty, long-distance madness, a marathon of pure enjoyment that freed us from the people we'd once thought ourselves to be. Sheila made the most astonishing sounds in her throat, low, animal sub-moans of pure pleasure that hit me like God's own drug-of-choice. Her voice lifted me and drove me and made me want to own her.

The iron bed groaned and rattled and thumped as we slammed against each other. It had been painted several times during its long life, and when we gripped the iron rods of the headpiece for purchase, we could feel chips of oxidized paint falling onto our naked skin and into our hair. The paint flaked away and fell, and we surged on until pain ran through us and about us like cables made of smoke, and the pain became part of a new pleasure, which bound us together tighter and tighter, until, after hours of such lovely agony, we could go on no longer.

Then we'd lie in each other's arms and rest as the cabin grew dark, and we did not tell each other that what we'd found was love. Maybe what we found on those afternoons, in our iron bed in the back room of a cabin built of culled lumber, was not about love. But what we discovered together there was closer to love than anything we'd expected in this life to find. Whatever it was, the places we journeyed to on those best afternoons were hot and desperate, exhausting and bright. They were bottomless and green, faraway nameless places of great beauty. And when we came back to the surface, astonished and without language in the early evenings, we climbed from the bed and brushed chips of paint from each other's shoulders and hair, and we looked into each other's eyes again, and laughed.

We wanted to leave the trees on the hillside above the shelf uncut to preserve the filtered light as it had been the afternoon when we first saw the place, but there were, we guessed, enough trees, right there in the cabin's footprint and surrounding yard, to furnish the logs we'd need for our walls, gables, and purlins. Dozens of pole-sized saplings, twenty- to thirty-feet high, grew among the bigger trees. They would have to come out before we could begin building the cabin itself, but the straightest ones could be peeled and used for floor joists, and braces. These small trees were green and healthy with lush tops like little Christmas trees. Taking them out right away would give us a less cluttered workspace and later make turning and moving big logs easier, once we had them on the ground. So we spent several days cutting the pole-sized trees, limbing them, dragging away the brush, and peeling the straightest sticks to use later for joists.

We cross-ricked odd-sized poles out of the way, off in the trees beyond the edge of our clearing. We planned to saw some of them during the winter for firewood, so I simply blazed off the bark on one side with an ax to let moisture escape the green wood. We left enough space between the poles so air could circulate up and down around the green wood to help it dry. Sheila dragged off the tops and green boughs, while I lugged the poles and ricked them up, row on row, the square stacks growing taller, until they were up above my head.

Our two most important tools, besides the bow saw, were the double-bitted Kelly axes I'd brought from Montana. My great-grandfather had used the smaller of the two to cut the timber, and to trim and notch the logs that went into the cabins and barn on the Beer homestead. It was an original two-and-one-half pound W. C. Kelly with an ornate logo cast in the steel on one side that read: "Kelly Registered Ax." A line beneath the logo was intended for a registration number, to be stamped or etched into the steel and recorded by the merchant who sold it. The number on this one had long ago been worn smooth. But think of it: A hand tool, once so prized, that each one sold in the United States was meant to have its own permanent number, registered at the time of its sale, like a vehicle identification number today.

Our second ax, another double-bitted Kelly, was a pound heavier with taller cutting edges. It was meant for the heavy work of hewing big undercuts and for limbing big logs.

Both axes had thirty-two-inch white ash handles with lots of give that let them flex to absorb the shock of hard blows. I'd used them both since I was a boy, and they were as familiar to me as two old friends.

Once we had the small trees cut and cleared away, I went to work on the first of the big ones. Like the trees I'd fought on the trail, these pines leaned and hung up at first, too. But when I dropped other trees across them, the combined weight brought them crashing down. When I got those first trees on the ground, a small bit of sky opened over our heads. In the coming days, with good luck and a slight breeze at my back, I was able to get three or four trees—from twelve to twenty inches in diameter at the butt—down and limbed out each day. Before quitting time, I went back and sawed off stumps as close to the ground as I could.

I showed Sheila how to peel the bark from a log by standing on one side of it and chopping along under the bark on the opposite side with short, quick strokes of the little Kelly. By standing on one side of a log and cutting on the other, she used the log itself as a shield to protect her against accidental injuries from glancing blows. Then I showed Sheila how to chop-chop-chop away another row of bark beside the first cleared strip, and in that way to work around the log and down its length, much as I would have done if peeling fir fence posts in Montana. This method required many sharp, exact blows with the ax, which took more hand and arm strength than I realized. We needed to get the bark off our logs right away, so they could have as many days as possible to dry before we went to work building the cabin's walls. We were already several weeks late in the season. Pounding away using my method wore Sheila down quickly, and I could see I'd need to spend at least part of each day helping her peel logs.

Once I got Sheila stripping bark from the logs, I went back to work falling trees and working my way down their lengths, limbing, then topping them out, gradually converting trees into logs. Behind me as I worked, I could hear long pauses in Sheila's chopping. When she ran out of strength on that job, we joined forces carrying limbs and bark and tops away from the shelf. She was strong and doing the best she could. We were both still soft and lacked endurance, and we'd not yet found the routines and rhythms that would later speed our work. But most days, if the rain held off, that patch of sky above us opened up a little bit more.

As I took the limbs off the downed trees with my big Kelly, I could almost hear my granddad say: "Limb 'em *close!*" To leave stobs of even half-an-inch when cutting a limb from a tree trunk, was, to him, worse than poor workmanship. The way Howard Beer saw it, anyone who left knobs on a log was slovenly to the point of being trashy. A log with wooden thumbs sticking out from it made the log harder to peel and to handle, harder to slide and to pile. A log poorly limbed was not only sorry looking, it was dangerous, too, because stobs on a rolling log could catch sleeves and gloves, pants legs and boot laces. Limbing close showed that a man knew his work, could handle his tools, and respected his craft. All those things seemed important to me as Sheila and I struggled to turn trees into logs. The lodgepole pines we were cutting had very few limbs on their lower twenty feet, and not many above that, until right near the top, where bushy green branches spread out toward sunlight.

When Sheila saw that she didn't have the strength to peel logs using my method, she solved the problem with a cleverness that surprised me. The spring sap had already moved up the trees, and the very thin cambium layer, between the tree's bark and the new sapwood underneath, was wet and slick. By cutting a line through the bark, lengthwise down the top of a log, Sheila could go back, slip her ax blade under the bark on one side of that line, work the blade down as far as it would go, then pry the bark away from the wet trunk, using her ax handle as a lever. There was almost no chopping involved, except for cutting that line atop the log to get her started. Soon Sheila was prying away slabs of bark the size of her leg. It was still hard work, but it was much faster and lots easier than my method. When I looked up from an undercut I was sawing, I was surprised to see her going right along, stripping away bark in big chunks, leaving behind a slick log, all shiny and white, with almost no ax marks at all on its smooth surface. There she was, the brightest girl in my graduating class, her bib overalls black with pitch, a red bandana tied over her hair, her glasses streaked with pine sap and sweat. When she straightened and saw me watching her, she grinned and called: "We're smokin' now, big guy." And so we were, as her smile lit the day.

In early July the weather began to lift. Now and then the sun popped through the canopy of clouds for an hour or two, and we turned our faces up to it like large, begrimed plants. As the weather cleared, we went to the Mac every morning to cut trees. I'd "throw" one, as old timers would say, then measure and saw off a log thirty feet long. I'd limb out the log and whatever remained of the upper tree and roll or lever the log onto blocks to get it off the ground. Sheila usually worked on a log on the far side of our clearing, prying off her slabs of bark, piling them one atop the other, or sometimes curled inside other chunks, and carrying them away to one of our brush piles down toward the creek. In a good day, as we hardened up, we got our three or four trees down and limbed, sawed to length and peeled, with some brush carried off. I also limbed out and blazed the tops and added those poles to our ever-growing firewood ricks.

Our clothes became saturated with liquid pitch, which caught dirt and sawdust and particles of bark like glue. Whatever stuck to the pitch on our clothes during the day, became permanent parts of our pants and shirts when the pitch dried and hardened during the night. There was no good way to wash out the pitch, except with gasoline, so we each used one pair of jeans (overalls for Sheila) and a chambray shirt for working in the woods. Pitch and dirt and bug spray built up, day by day, layer upon layer. Once we undressed at the Douglas place in the afternoons, our work clothes could almost stand by themselves when leaned against a wall in the back room. We kept a gallon of gasoline and a basin well away from the cabin to clean our faces and hands. Gasoline cut pitch better than kerosene and without the lasting oily stench. In the mornings, getting dressed was like pulling on clothes made of plywood. But once we got busy at the Mac, our outfits gradually loosened up.

Getting hardened into shape took time, so we took lots of breaks, and we took them often. Every day we had new cramps, new pains; every evening we sported new blisters and bruises of various colors, from the sickly green and yellow splotches on our thighs and shins, through a spectrum of purples and blues that appeared where we'd caught a bounce-back, or from crashing downhill, ass-over-teacup, after tripping on a root with an armload of boughs piled to our chins.

We started work by mid-morning, and quit in the mid-afternoons. Bankers' hours, yes, but that was all the juice we had those first weeks. Every hour or so I'd pull an imaginary rope, attached to an invisible donkey-engine whistle, to signal my crew to gather round for a smoke. We'd find a soft spot in the moss and plop down knee to knee to talk while I rolled a Dominion cigarette and puffed away. Good times, then. Smiles on smudged faces. Sheila's voice. The joy of being there together.

As the woods warmed, a plague rose from the damp ground, from every puddle and seep, from each mat of saturated moss and standing patch of murky water; from all these places and more, in every direction for hundreds of square miles. Mosquito eggs transformed themselves into larvae and the larvae fed on bits of floating organic crud and grew to become pupae, and the pupae rested until ready to emerge as adults. The adults tested legs and wings, then rose in their countless millions, moving in clouds to search for warm, slow-moving creatures such as Sheila and me, dull earthbound bipeds filled with hot, intoxicating blood. From ten o'clock in the morning until midnight, their wings churned the air into that maddening, ever-present vibration that soon seemed to come from inside our own heads. We sprayed OFF onto our hands, necks, and faces and onto every inch of those work clothes we never washed, and still the mosquitoes came in to land on any bit of exposed skin, to dip their tiny wicks and drink.

They bit us in the middle of our backs, right through our thin chambray shirts, and they worked into our ears. They came at our eyes and hiked up our nostrils. I'd seen horseflies run deer to exhaustion in the Montana woods, and now I knew how those poor deer had felt. The mosquitoes didn't like cigarette smoke, however, so I smoked more, but there were times—and I swear this is true—that while I rolled a cigarette, so many mosquitoes settled on my exposed hands, that at times I could barely see my fingers. Sheila did not enjoy my second-hand smoke, but we developed a little ritual, when she closed her eyes and held her breath as I chuffed slow clouds of tobacco smoke around her face and into her hair. While the smoke lasted, the buzzing air quieted, and we could chat for a minute or two in peace.

Our noon break was the big event of each workday. Sheila made us a sack lunch every morning that contained peanut-butter-and-jelly-on-whole-wheat sandwiches; two of those flat cans of Norwegian sardines, that sold for ten cents a can in Prince George; and usually some kind of special treat, like home-made cookies.

We were burning serious amounts of calories in the six hours we worked each day, so we needed oil for energy and lots of it. We began lunch with a can of sardines apiece, licking our fingers and belching like lumberjacks. We drank the left-over oil right from the cans, while making happy barnyard noises. Good manners were for grandmas, we decided, and, in the woods at least, we practiced what our friend, Sam Curtis, called: "Grab-it-and-growl dining."

On rainy days, Sheila baked cookies in the wood stove's oven at the Douglas place—heavy, bendable oatmeal/raisin cookies the size of saucers and those subtle, crumbly shortbread cookies, which seemed to me to be the best cookies in the entire Free World. To complement dessert at the Mac, we usually carried along a paperback in our lunch sack, and we'd each take a turn reading a few pages aloud as we rested after eating. For a few minutes, there was *Portnoy's Complaint* and all that outrageous adolescent whacking-off, or Dan Cushman's *Stay Away Joe*, with modern Montana Indians who lived in cars. We read just about anything that came our way, except "literature," anything that could carry us off for a few minutes from the mosquitoes and the pitch and the aches of the day.

When it was over I held her in my arms, my face tucked against her cheek until we stopped shaking.

"You," Sheila said. "You take my breath away."

"Girl, when you make that sound," I said, "that's when I'm as good as gone."

"I saw something this time," Sheila said. "I had my eyes closed, and I saw flashes of iridescent green light. Then the light was gone, and I saw your face. That's the first time I've seen you with my eyes shut tight."

Sheila, it seemed to me, looked awfully good in her stiff bib-overalls and work boots, her totally grunged-out, pitch-soaked shirt and babushka-style bandana worn over her head and tied beneath her hair at the back of her neck. What really shined, though, was her laugh, her happy enthusiasm for being there in those woods with me, and the way she would say, "Oh!" and "Yes!"

I watched her, sometimes, while she worked, and I believe those were the moments when I first surrendered to the unfamiliar desire to give my heart to her.

The work was satisfying, our grub was plain but good, and we were there together. Peanut butter-and-jelly sandwiches, sardines, homemade cookies, and true companionship. Those half-hour lunch breaks touched me as if with a sense of déjà vu, and I wondered why they seemed so special, until one day I remembered how, before I'd started first grade, I spent mornings with my mother's mother, Emma Bassette, who lived right across Butte Avenue from my parents' little stucco house. There was a breakfast nook in her big sunny kitchen, a room warmed by her great Majestic wood stove. Sometimes, while Grandma did our breakfast dishes and started her busy day, I'd work on my coloring book. The pictures were illustrations of a child's ideal world in the early Fifties, in the United States, a world of innocent bounty and security where little boys and girls were happily well-behaved, and all the children were safe. The picture I liked best showed a little boy and a little girl about my age, sharing a picnic lunch on a cloth spread out in a meadow with lots of grass and wildflowers. I wanted to be that little boy. I wanted to go off with a wicker basket to a sunny spot with the little girl in the drawing, to have a lunch all our own, just the two of us. My yearning for such a perfect time kept me from ever trying to color that page with my crayons. The two children and their picnic remained untouched, except in my imagination.

Some days, on the hillside above Government Creek, the sun would peek through the clouds as we ate, and light would slice down through the timber, illuminating dark woods and waking bright swaths of color all around us. We shared a kind of happiness, then, that we had not known about before, as if, it seemed to me, my breakfast-nook daydream had been realized. We had become that little boy and that little girl, off for a while on a picnic of our own, just the two of us, with all of life ahead.

SEVENTEEN

As our freshly-peeled logs slowly added up, I began to wonder how we might go about joining them together to make walls. Right about then, I realized how little I knew about building a cabin. When I paused in my chopping to look at the spot where the cabin was to stand, I had only a vague idea of how to begin. I'd made nothing of wood beyond Boy Scout bird houses and laminated shop-class cutting boards. While I could take Sheila in my arms, look deep into her shining eyes, and whisper the first few couplets of Dryden's "Absalom and Achitophel," I had almost no knowledge of carpentry whatsoever, no skill with levels and plumb bobs, bevels or squares, no claw-hammer muscle-memory; no understanding of geometry, plane or otherwise.

It seemed I'd talked myself and Sheila into a dream requiring abilities I did not have. Now that we'd begun, I wasn't sure I had the strength, much less the skill. The green logs were heavy as iron and awkward, even dangerous, to move. How could I lift them, once the walls started going up? I didn't want to tell Sheila, but the truth was I didn't even understand myself how much I didn't know. As I worked, I thought, *the cabin needs to be level and square and plumb.* Yes. But how would I begin so things were done correctly, right from the start?

I thought about how the barn and cabin at my granddad's place were put together. In those buildings, two different corner notches had been used. The cow barn's corners were double-dovetailed, an intricate system of exact interlocking beveled cuts that joined the logs where they met at the corners. The dovetailed logs were locked together so ingeniously that nails weren't needed to keep the corners from pulling apart. Those corners were then sixty years old and still so tightly joined that a piece of paper could not be slipped between the notched logs where they met. My great-grandfather, Robert Beer, had fitted those corners with patience and extraordinary skill. I knew I could not make corners as complex as his.

My granddad's log house, though, seemed to have been built in a hurry. The corners were saddle-notched. A semi-circular portion at each end of a log was removed, so the log could sit down snugly (like a saddle around a horse's middle) to grasp the ends of the perpendicular logs below it. The saddle had to be cut at just the right depth, however, or there would be a gap, either between that log and the log below, or a gap at each notch if too much wood was removed. Cutting out the semi-circle of wood at each end let the log settle down against the log below it. The newly-notched log was then positioned so it was plumb with the logs below and spiked down at each corner. Although I'd never done it, the saddle-notch method at least seemed possible.

During our next trip to town, we applied for and received a user's card at the Prince George Public Library, and we returned to the cabin at the Douglas place with several books on log cabin building and basic carpentry. Sheila, of course, saw that I didn't know anything, but she was kind enough to pretend not to notice. Instead, she studied those "how-to" books with me in the evenings after work, until we began to get a step-by-step sense of how to go about the early stages of simple log construction. Soon I found myself asking, "What do you think about these rock pillars? Do you think we should plan for a porch, or just a front step? How are we going to keep the courses level with different-sized logs as we go up?"

We made sketches, then more detailed drawings as we read the books and worked our way toward a plan for a basic cabin with four walls and an overhanging front porch. We also tried to puzzle out how to physically lift and place those big logs with only our hand tools and muscle.

Thanks to a couple of books on wilderness log cabin construction, like Ben Hunt's *How to Build and Furnish a Log Cabin,* which had good, clear illustrations, we could see and understand necessary details that we might have otherwise overlooked. There was a drawing, for example, that showed us how to place at least two rocks, one atop the other, (instead of using just one large rock) every six feet or so along the underside of the bottom "sill" log in each wall to serve as footings. Pillars of two stacked rocks did a better job of stopping frost and moisture from wicking up from the ground to the underside of that all-important bottom log, thus helping to prevent rot.

Pretty soon Sheila and I had our heads together during our spare time, trying to plan how we would accomplish each step needed to build our walls, gables, and roof. Sometimes we discarded an idea we liked for a different approach then went back to the original plan. We simplified, discarding plans for an upstairs, then played with various ideas for sleeping lofts and room divisions. After two or three weeks of reading, sketching, and thinking, we had drawn out a plan on tablet paper with all sorts of dimensions and marginal notations. Our backwoods blueprint was just one step above a house plan drawn on the back of an envelope, but our confidence about starting actual construction was growing.

At the Douglas place, we had no electricity, no indoor plumbing, no running water. We got our water from the well Mr. and Mrs. Douglas had dug by hand. Since it was chilly just above the water level, we kept lard and margarine and partly-used cans of condensed milk down there in a lowered bucket during the days. Without frosty nights or refrigeration, we couldn't keep fresh meat or fish more than twenty-four hours. To save money, we kept our supply runs to Prince George to once every nine or ten days, and when we did go in for supplies, even hamburger and chicken were expensive treats. Sardines and peanut butter worked fine for our noon sack lunches, but in the evenings, after a day in the woods, we craved real sit-down, grab-it-and-growl suppers of meat and potatoes. We could afford potatoes, but not the meat.

Lepus americanus and *Bonasa umbellus* came to our rescue.

On our daily trips to and from the Mac, and everywhere we walked in the bush, we saw snowshoe hares and ruffed grouse in abundance. Each day, two or three snowshoes would cross the road ahead of the El Camino as we drove to and from the Mac, and we often had to stop to let them hop safely past. Ken Glaze told us that the "rabbits" were at a high point in their seven- or eight-year population cycle, and that one year soon rabbits would be scarce.

At the Douglas place and anywhere in the bush where big stands of aspen and poplar were found, the ruffed grouse (sometimes called "fool hens" because of their reluctance to fly) were in large enough numbers that we saw several every day. The male grouse had been drumming on fallen logs to attract mates when we'd rented the Douglas place, and the accelerating *bum bum bum whirrrrr* of the males' wings was usually the first thing we heard in the mornings and the last thing we heard as we fell asleep in the long twilight each evening.

I'd grown up hunting cottontail rabbits at the ranch, and my folks and I enjoyed them for supper several times each winter. We hadn't needed to eat rabbit. It was a family thing, a carry-over from the hard days of the Depression in rural Montana, when farm boys like my dad grew up using .22 rifles to help put meat on the table for their families. Shooting a cottontail rabbit anywhere other than in the eye was considered extremely crude by older men I knew, men who had learned to shoot with precision when ammunition was dear. I'd spent many hours hunting or practicing on targets with my dad's .22, and I'd even shot a few snowshoe hares up in the higher hills above the ranch, once the hares had turned their winter white. Like lots of boys in Montana then, I grew up hunting grouse on Sunday afternoons in October. The folks on Jackson Creek I grew up around, and most rural Montanans like them, were part of an honest hunting culture that had not yet been perverted by trophy seekers and hordes of well-heeled out-of-state sports. Hunting was something we learned from our fathers and took pride in doing well.

Right there, hopping across the road in front of the El Camino's bumper, and drumming across thousands of acres of bush around us, was the solution to our protein cravings. But all I had to work with was the .25-35 Winchester I'd brought from home, which was a deer rifle and far too expensive, shot for shot, to use on rabbits and grouse. It was also loud, not the best choice for poaching game birds in the summer. What we needed was an accurate, inexpensive .22 rifle.

Once again Ken Glaze helped us out while pulling a little of our cash his way. Ken and Lila were probably as short of money as we were. When I mentioned one evening, while we visited in their yard, that I'd like to find a good .22 rifle, Ken brought out an ugly old Mossberg Model 44 that looked like a length of water pipe nailed to a two-by-four that had once been on fire. The stock was grimy, blunt, and graceless; the barrel was rust-pitted along its outside; the unattractive bolt action looked clunky and over-engineered, and the bolt itself was bent down at a sharp angle for no apparent reason. The magazine was a phony little five-shot clip that snapped in place in front of a cheap-looking Bakelite trigger guard, which extended back to form an equally phony-looking plastic pistol grip with indentations for each of the shooter's fingers. The front sight was a tiny steel bead on a post; the rear sight was a very fine "V" that almost became invisible if I held the rifle out at arms length. All in all, the Mossberg looked like a pawnshop special, if I'd ever seen one.

"It don't look like much," Ken said, "but it drives tacks." He handed me a box of ten-year-old Peters .22 shells, and said "Try it out."

I couldn't think of a tactful way to turn down his offer, so I drew a circle the size of a dime on a piece of cardboard with a black lumberman's crayon, stepped off twenty paces from the hood of the El Camino, and wedged my target down in the space between a rail and the fence post it was nailed to in the corral. I rolled up my jacket and put it on the hood of the El Camino and lay the rifle across it. I noticed that the action was oily. The bolt felt tight and exact as I eased a shell into the barrel. The rear sight was just a tiny nick in a horizontal metal bar, so fine that I had to concentrate to keep the front bead visible in it. I put the safety on, tried it to make sure it would hold, then rested the Mossberg's blunt stock on my jacket again, and snuggled in behind it. Ken said, "Oily barrel. The first one will be a flier."

Lila and Sheila had been chatting behind me while I'd fooled with the rifle, but when I squeezed off the first shot they paused to see the result.

With my naked eye, I could see the bullet hole two inches high and to the right of the black dot, about what I'd expected.

Ken said, "Try another one."

So I locked in behind the rifle, put the front bead on the bottom of the black dot on the target, breathed out slowly and squeezed off a second round. I could not see any additional hole in the cardboard that time, but when old man Glaze and I walked over to look, there was the bullet hole in the bullseye.

"Mind if I run a couple more?" I asked, and Ken grinned, knowing he had me hooked. I slowly fired the remaining three shells in the clip, and when we looked at the target, four holes were clustered in the black dot, three touching each other.

"How can something that looks this bad, shoot the way this rifle does?" I asked.

"Good barrel," Glaze said. "That's what counts."

I looked at the rifle. "How much do you need for it?"

"How about twenty bucks?" Ken said.

"It's a deal," I said, even though twenty dollars was by then serious cash for Sheila and me. Ken threw in the box of shells, and the next day I shot two snowshoe hares in the head on our way down from the Mac. That evening we enjoyed the first of many suppers of fried rabbit, hash-browned spuds, and hot, baking-powder biscuits made with honest-to-God, genuine lard. After a day in the forest, the smells coming from our wood range made our bellies growl, and the meals, absolutely, were as good as any I ever ate. The next day I caught some ruffs sitting on a log in the bush north of the Douglas place. Fresh grouse, mashed potatoes, and homemade baking-powder biscuits? That's living large; I don't care who you are.

Potatoes in fifty-pound bags were then so cheap in Prince George they were almost free. We bought lard in two-pound pails for frying and baking. Pig fat and white flour, and we loved it. Today, lard has been replaced on most supermarket shelves by cooking oils because of concerns about cholesterol. But I've never tasted better biscuits or finer piecrust, before or since, than those we baked in a cast iron frying pan that summer at the Douglas place. The best things in life may not be free, but sometimes, when life is treating us just right, they don't cost a whole lot either.

EIGHTEEN

Once the clearing opened up, I was able to work around the edges, falling trees toward the center, across logs that Sheila had already skinned. Later logs rested up off the ground and were much easier for her to peel. We cut trees and peeled logs, and we dragged off bark and slash to pile as far from the cabin site as we could, and the days passed in a blur of sweat and pitch. Our hands hardened, and our grad-school flab burned away, and we settled into a rhythm and a routine.

We continued our ritual of cigarette-smoke during breaks to ward off the mosquitoes, which, in the Cariboo, were large, loud, and legion. It was sometimes hard for Sheila to endure the smoke. Like many veterans, Sheila's father had come home from the war in the Pacific with malaria and other maladies which resurfaced from time to time. He had been sick off and on as Sheila grew up, but it was probably his own cigarette smoke that killed him.

One afternoon Sheila and I were surprised to look up from our work to see a man on horseback at the edge our clearing. We put down our tools and walked over to where he had dismounted and met our neighbor, Clint Dahlstrom. He was a stocky young fella with a shock of wild blond hair and a big, honest smile. His folks, he said, had a little ranch called Hidden Meadows, which was located between the Glaze place and Harry Schmaltz's cabin on the back road to Hixon. Dahlstroms had a government grazing permit for their cows on a large tract of bush along Government Creek that included our claim. They'd grown concerned about the El Camino with Montana license plates that they saw at the old sawdust pile whenever they came up to check their cows, so they decided to find out who we were and what we were doing.

That day, when Clint saw our boot tracks going down the muddy skid trail, he followed them toward the creek until he noticed our claim tag for the Mac. Then he saw scuff marks left by our boots going up the bank into the trees. Apparently we hadn't been near as slick as we'd thought.

We told Clint about our plans to build a cabin, and he did his best to avoid seeming skeptical of our chances for success. When we'd chatted for a while and sized each other up, Clint invited us to stop by the Hidden Meadows to meet his folks.

After he'd ridden off, Sheila and I looked at each other. "What do you think?" Sheila asked.

"Looks like we're right in the middle of their deal," I said.

"But he didn't act like he was upset," Sheila said.

"I don't know, Pal. He seemed like a pretty good guy, don't you think?"

"Yes, he did," Sheila said.

We had tried to keep a low profile among the locals. This was the first time our project had been discovered by someone we hadn't approached first. "I think he was mostly just surprised," Sheila said. "But he was pretty cool about finding us here. Maybe we should swing by to meet his mom and dad, like he said."

A few evenings later, Sheila and I washed up after supper and combed our hair. We put on clean jeans and fresh work shirts, and I trimmed my beard. We took Coldbanks Road to the fork below the Glaze place and turned to the right, where we found a sign that read "Dahlstroms' Hidden Meadows." The Dahlstroms' ranch road crossed some beautiful hay ground along an unnamed creek, then climbed a small hill to their buildings. The place struck us immediately as one of those farmsteads where everything had a place and everything was in its place. There was no clutter, no unnecessary accumulation of machinery around the buildings. It was tidy, well-tended, and cared for, that much was immediately clear.

Surrounded by a yard of lawn and flower beds, the Dahlstroms' elfin cottage was so small that it almost seemed like something out of an illustrated book of fairytales. The outer walls were sided with neat, even rows of wooden shingles. A rose trellis ran up and over the front door. In the rich colors of the last direct sunlight, the place seemed enchanted. As Sheila and I walked toward the house, Clint and his folks came outside to greet us.

Helen Dahlstrom was short and square, a pleasant-featured woman who wore her white hair tied back in a bun. She wore "sensible shoes," a summer cotton dress, and an old-fashioned apron that covered her dress from her throat to her knees. She smiled and extended her hand and said, "Clint told us he'd met you. We're glad you came by."

Herb Dahlstom was a lean, hard man of medium height who looked like he'd been chiseled from a block of cured walnut. Almost gaunt, he appeared to have been pared down to essence by years of hard work outside. His leathery skin was shrunk tight against his muscle and bone, the way rawhide is stretched around a saddle tree. It was a look he wore well. His iron-grey hair was neatly combed, and he'd recently shaved. Herb had a quiet, attentive air about him; he let the rest of us chat while he listened. When we shook hands, I felt something pass through me, and I guessed that he and I would become friends.

I noticed how Herb's bib overalls and work shirt, bleached nearly white from many washings, were as clean and wrinkle free as if they'd just come off a clothesline and been lightly ironed. In fact, all three Dahlstroms looked as if they'd just spiffed up to go to town. Unlike some country people I'd known in Montana, including a few of my kin, Sheila and I learned, in the coming months, that Clint and his father not only washed up before supper but also changed into clean clothes when their work allowed. And Helen, who managed the household, their hens and garden and finances, always looked as if her dress and apron were freshly laundered and pressed. The Dahlstroms struck us immediately as people who worked hard, paid attention to details, and husbanded what they had. For a moment I thought of Scandinavian communities I'd seen years before in Iowa and Nebraska, where the white barns and outbuildings were as well maintained as the square, two-story farm houses, with their overhanging front verandas and latticework. The Dahlstrom place had that same old-world feeling of well-tended exactness.

That evening, as Sheila and I stood with the Dahlstroms in their yard and chatted, they seemed genuinely glad to meet us. Within a few minutes, we relaxed.

There might have been a "sexual revolution" in California during the Sixties, but Sheila and I were embarrassed to admit to strangers, and especially to folks like the Dahlstroms, that although we were living together, we weren't married. There was, of course, the additional horror that we *were* married but not to each other. So, while neither of us wore wedding bands, we either let the people we met assume we were married, or we introduced each other as "my friend," or "my pardner." In most cases, it didn't matter to me very much one way or the other, but I did not feel good that evening about letting the Dahlstroms assume we were married, and I've never felt right about it in all the years that have passed since then.

As such things sometimes go, I found myself standing shoulder to shoulder with Herb, looking out across his meadows while the others talked. Both of us pulled our fixings from our shirt pockets and folded our cigarette papers and poured in our tobacco, two men of the country, putting the world on hold while we rolled our smokes. We licked off our cigarettes and without being too obvious about it, compared them. Herb's cigarette looked almost as if it had been rolled by a machine; it was straight and tight and had the same amount of tobacco from one end to the other. My cigarette had a bulge in the middle with tobacco shooting from each end.

"Just getting started?" Herb asked quietly.

"I work at it, but I don't seem to get much better," I answered.

"Is your tobacco maybe a little dry?"

"Yes," I said. "It dries out fast, even in this fancy pouch," and I showed Herb my fake-leather, plastic-lined deal with the zipper on one side that I'd bought to protect my fixings while working in the rain.

"Have you tried putting in a little piece of apple?" Herb asked

"No," I answered. But I could see how that simple country remedy would help. Within a few minutes of meeting Herb Dahlstrom, he'd managed, without appearing to try, to teach me something I could use. The voices in the background were a quiet murmur, like the voices of a far-off stream deep in the woods. Herb and I stood in the soft blue evening and looked at the darkening timberline beyond his meadows as we touched fire to our cigarettes. And the fragrant smoke rose in the still air about us, and drifted off beyond a world of words and worries and cares. We both felt it, the peace of a perfect, unplanned moment that was worth savoring. So we did just that, two men, newly-acquainted and already easy with each other, enjoying a smoke in that extraordinary place in the gathering dusk.

Off to the east of the Government Creek Road, a half-mile or so below the big sawdust pile, a series of small beaver ponds followed an unnamed creek through an area where centuries of beaver ponds had made a line of bogs and meadows. Some mornings, on our way to the Mac, we would surprise a cow moose, standing up to her belly in water and pond muck, grazing on the leafy delicacies growing therein. The moose would throw up her head at the sound of the truck, then launch herself toward the dark wall of lodgepole pine on the far side of the pond. As she plowed across the pond, lifting her front legs above the water as she went, the cow seemed to hydroplane over the surface above a shining wake of flying droplets that sparked and snapped in the morning light. Sheila and I would get a jolt of adrenaline as the moose came out of the water onto dry land and cantered, suddenly huge and black in her glistening bulk, away from us to vanish among the sheltering trees. We'd sit in the idling pickup, as if holding our breath, until the surface of the water smoothed again to gentle ripples, then to glass.

Day by day in July, our growing cache of peeled logs accumulated into a jumble of sticks that rested atop one another at random angles where they'd fallen and been peeled. Except for a few, which could slide atop others while still slick from peeling, most of our logs were too heavy to move more than a few feet at a time. I was able to turn some logs now and then, but it seemed best to just leave them be, so as much air as possible could circulate around them. Others, trapped underneath, lay pressed against the damp ground. Day after day, more light came down into our clearing, until we had a patch of direct sunshine warming us while we ate lunch.

We were toughening into the work, but we still took lots of breaks. "Let's have a smoke," I'd call to Sheila, and we'd work our way toward each other over and around the drying logs. I rolled a cigarette and got it going, and we slathered on more OFF and swatted at the skirring, hovering mass of mosquitoes that grew whenever we became stationary. I took a deep drag, feeling that raw fire crackling in my lungs, then blew the smoke slowly into Sheila's hair, like a shaman's blessing. I was her personal smudge pot, faithful and true, and when the cigarette had burned down to a nub and I'd ground it out on the sole of my boot, I would kiss her forehead, then her eyes, and think to myself how much fun it was to love her.

The weather warmed; the long strips of bark that Sheila had peeled, dried and curled in on themselves, and the paths we made while toting slash and bark widened and deepened as they wove through the moss below our clearing. Sometimes, during our breaks, we talked about how we would deal with the issue of immigration, which, in our isolation, seemed to fade into a distant irritation, an insignificant problem that we'd eventually get around to solving when the time was right. We knew that in order to hold jobs in Canada we needed work visas or Landed-Immigrant status, so we knew that at some point we would have to go through the process. Not to worry, we thought. We'd get to that when we could.

We pretended, of course, that official Canada would welcome us, if not with fruit baskets and wine, then at least with big howdies and smiles. No question about it. We had degrees in the liberal arts, and we could diagram sentences. If pulpwood cutters and sawmill goons could be citizens in this vast land of bugs and bogs, this roadless swamp so recently stolen by the Crown from indigenous brown people, then of course we would go right to the head of the line, where our papers would be swiftly stamped and our privileges conferred.

Or so we maintained when the subject of our status came up. Secretly, the thought of immigration proceedings, of immigration officials in official government immigration offices, put a twist in my guts. So, planning what we needed to do to meet the requirements of immigrating to Canada, and to organize, step by step, how to accomplish that task, was a chore very easily put off. It was much simpler for me to focus on our work each day in those beatific woods; to savor the evenings and early mornings with this beautiful girl, in the cabin that so often smelled of sex, than to walk into an office in Prince George and say, "My name is Ralph Beer, aye? And I'm aboot to call your wonderful war-free country my new home. Where do I sign?" That first step seemed to me a real killer, like the last step when walking off a tall building's roof.

When the subject of immigration came up, my line to Sheila ran something like this: "You bet! Darned right, Kid. One of these first days we'll jump right on that." But to the secret part of myself that loathed going hat in hand to an unknown bureaucracy where I had every chance of failing, I said: *Forget about it, Clyde. Lay low. Cover your tracks. Disappear into the forest and learn to live on lichen and moss.*

So the brilliant days and blessed nights passed. We grew brown as berries. Calluses hardened our hands and our bellies tightened with stringy muscle and the grease of winter sloth burned away. As hungry as we were, and we seemed to be hungry all the time, we sometimes stood up, halfway through our evening meal, to rush into the backroom and the welcome embrace of a collapsing iron bed, that would soon be drumming on the floor, its headboard thundering against a wall made of two-by-fours, while showering us with pink and green and yellow chips of paint, applied in the dim long-ago by someone young and filled with yearnings, perhaps, for the same hot joys we had discovered.

NINETEEN

B ecause the mosquitoes thinned out during the hot part of the day, and because the evening light lasted so long, we often stayed up until midnight and started work late in the mornings. Some mornings I woke alone with sunshine streaming across the bed, and I rose to dress in a silent cabin. Sheila was off with her berry bucket, so I built a morning fire of small wood and made coffee and took a steaming cup into the cool sunshine outside. The meadow, once cleared, had come back into spaced poplar and aspen, and the grass, which had once made hay, stood knee-high among the trees, jeweled with dew in the early light. Those mornings, I sat on the front step, savored my coffee, and listened to the great stillness of the place, a vast calm broken only by birdsong and the quiet tapping of woodpeckers off in the trees. So many shades of green, as the brindled light spilled down through quaking leaves; so much life, green and growing, as simple and clean as a boy's first love.

At some point, Sheila would appear on the road out front, where it emerged from the bush and passed through a plank gate at the far edge of the meadow. She'd lift her berry bucket high with one hand and wave with the other, smiling madly with a jubilation that was good to see at any distance.

On such mornings, Sheila wore a cotton summer dress that looked like an old-fashioned flannel night gown. Her moccasins, I knew, would be soaked, her dress dark with moisture up to her knees. Sheila's hair, parted in the middle, fell to her shoulders and shined in the morning light as she walked toward me, swaying with the graceful adjustments her body made to counter the blunt bone in her hip. And she was beautiful. As I watched her at such times, when she was beyond the easy reach of my voice, yet close enough that I could see the wildflowers in her hair, I felt a gladness rise in me and a lightness. And I knew then what great happiness was, and how such happiness sharpened life to a keen edge.

When she was a few feet away, Sheila would say, "Hi," in that soft way of hers, that lovely, low, quiet way of hers, and when I said, "Hey, Punkin," she'd tilt her berry bucket toward me, so I could see her bounty of wild strawberries or blueberries, freshly picked, still wet with dew, all ready for our morning mush.

Reception on our transistor radio was hit or miss at the Douglas place. The radio in the El Camino had more reach and regularly played whole songs from beginning to end before fading off into the scratchy static of Canadian outer space. We lived in a world that was so quiet, except for birdsong and mosquitoes and drumming grouse, a world where days would pass with only the sounds of our voices and the clack and clatter of our living. Music, of course, became more important in the bush than it had been when the blare of humanity was with us all the time. Catching just the right song, on the way up the hill to the Mac, could accelerate a good morning into something even better, the music lifting our spirits and connecting us, if only in our imaginations, to the hip world of a youth culture that we wanted to believe we not only shared, but in the sense of Jerry Rubin's *Do It!* were actually living with great significance and force.

We might pretend to smoke huge joints, while singing along to Three Dog Night's "Mama Told Me Not to Come," or Brewer and Shipley's "One Toke Over The Line," not yet willing to admit that our make-believe land of granny glasses and love beads and beat poetry had already gone under in the shameless, bottomless pit of American commercialism. Or, we might grow quiet, as we listened to another side of the America we'd left behind. Joan Baez's "The Night They Drove Old Dixie Down," reminded us, like a nudge in the ribs, of a country at war with itself, just as our America was torn by war, which was the war we sought to escape.

One song, as popular in Canada that summer as in the United States, became *our* song. It was, during that time of angry rock 'n' roll and counter-culture anthems, an oddity, a ballad about yet another America—one that lay well beyond the blacktop, far from our Woodstock Nation and the anti-war songs spawned by the Vietnam War—in a longed-for backwoods place of old mountains and deep hollows. It became our song of exile, our mirror, in which we felt, rather than saw, the uncertainties that came with leaving a much-loved home. Our song came over the radio several times a day that summer, and we almost always paused to listen, because we shared its simple yearnings, that for us rang so true.

We had no idea who John Denver was or where he came from or what he looked like. So we made him up. We invented a lanky, hard-muscled guy in a T-shirt, who wore his black hair in a duck butt mashed down under a DeKalb seed-corn cap. Our John Denver was a coal-mine redneck from the Appalachian hill country, who had scars on his shovel-hardened hands, a dark man with a bottomless love for a place that he carried with him through the world, like a jewel in his pocket. Turns out we were wrong about the details, but dead right about the meaning of his song. "Take Me Home, Country Roads," left us feeling wistful and sad, as it opened our eyes to the beauty of the country roads we traveled together. Denver's song reminded us, too, of other back roads, the ones we'd left behind for good in Montana.

Our mail came to the Hixon Post Office/General Store. A letter from Sam and Sue Curtis, a card from Mac and Elena Watson, and a note for Sheila from her mother, our names written together on some of the envelopes. I liked that.

❖ ❖ ❖

July advanced through a dreamland of hot days that smelled of bug dope and pine sap. Our tangle of skinned logs teetered and rose; the opening in the trees advanced slowly outward; and the music of Government Creek grew faint as the country around us dried. We continued to study the "how-to" books we brought from the library, and we drew details of plans for our cabin on yellow legal pads that still contained class notes from MSU, folded up and tucked away against the cardboard in back.

Sheila's sister came to check on us a second time. Marilyn was a long-legged girl with straight blond hair, so very serious behind her big glasses. She was the kind of young woman who knew all about quasars before any-one except astronomers and astrophysicists, and she understood exactly why adverbs were to be avoided. Marilyn hadn't had much to say to me during her first visit, but when she saw our clearing at the Mac and our growing cache of logs, she seemed to warm a bit.

The next morning, Marilyn and Sheila took another of their walks. At such times, they seemed to pass through a door that gently closed behind them, leaving me and the world around me behind. They were close, and they shared an extended family and a lifetime of experiences that I could hardly guess at. After Marilyn left to drive back to Kaslo, Sheila said her sister had told her just how worried their family was about her. Marilyn wanted Sheila to drive to Montana to see their mother and step-father and reassure them that she was all right, to let them know that she was not in the clutches of a young Rasputin who had crazy powers over her, and to make them understand that she was doing something important, which she intended to finish.

"I'll be your madman, tonight," I said, letting my voice go all Boris Karloff.

"I think I should go," Sheila said without smiling. "Mom and Jim think I've slipped a cog. I need to see them and calm them down. Rest assured that I'll rustle up some goodies for us while I'm down there."

"Can you stay here until we have all our logs down and peeled and ready to go?"

"Okay," Sheila said. "Let's get that finished up first."

For the next week or so we continued tipping trees and working them into logs until we had cut what we estimated we'd need, plus ten more for good measure. Our logs were green and full of water, and they needed to dry as much as possible before we could start building the walls. Once the logs were peeled and ready to cure, we'd have a block of time open for Sheila's trip to Montana.

I had burned my draft card. As far as I could tell, my due date for the draft might have already passed. We didn't know if the Border Patrol on the American side asked about draft status or not, but it seemed safer if I stayed north of the border instead of going with her. We were down to less than a hundred dollars, and Sheila needed some of that for her trip. I would be at loose ends until she got back.

The evening before Sheila planned to leave, we found a large manila envelope addressed to me in our mail at the Hixon Post Office. My divorce papers, the lines requiring my signature conveniently marked with Xs in blue ink. I signed without bothering to read the summary of proceedings and complaints, but instead sealed the papers away in a return envelope and asked Sheila to mail them on her way home. But the court documents, with the authority the legal language conjured up, and duly signed by a judge in Helena, twisted something in me. My wife and I had known each other since before high school. She'd been my date to our junior prom. We'd had a long courtship; our families knew each other; there'd been a big church wedding. We had been friends. Half-a-dozen papers ended all that, and I felt strangely unbalanced. After supper, I took a walk and pondered how parts of our lives end, abruptly or otherwise, whether we want them to or not. Oddly enough, the sadness I felt was almost gone by the time the moon rose over our tree line, that very same evening.

TWENTY

Just after sunrise, Sheila put her arms around my waist and hugged me there in the yard at the Douglas place. I brushed her hair from her forehead, smoothing it back with my fingers to where she'd bound her ponytail with a rubber band at the base of her skull. And I wondered what it was about her that moved me so. I looked down at the top of her head and felt her warmth spreading through me, and I thought that while I could catalog her qualities, I might never be able to say what it was about her that touched me. I liked her smallness, yes, and the suggestion of vulnerability in her walk. I basked in her smiles and her laughter, and I was drawn to her intelligence and brave heart. She moved me in bed as no one had before, but I also wanted to touch her in ordinary, non-sexual ways, like holding hands when crossing a street in Prince George or touching knees, while sharing our lunch in the woods. Most of all, I was drawn to her voice, which seemed to me to knit her other aspects together like the patterns of stars in a child's picture book. What a marvelous constellation she had turned out to be.

Sheila waved from the open window of the El Camino as she drove down our lane and disappeared into the bush, headed for Montana. I stood in the meadow for a while, lost in sunshine and silence, thinking about the way her head felt in my hands.

I had a few one-dollar bills and some loose change in a jelly jar, no vehicle, and time on my hands. Sheila planned to be gone a week or more, and as I watched her dust drift into the trees beside the empty lane, a week seemed to me like a very long time.

That first morning, I hung our bedding to air on the front porch, mucked out the cabin and scrubbed the linoleum floors. I split up enough small wood for the kitchen range to last a couple weeks, and when I looked at my watch it wasn't yet noon. After lunch I tried to begin *Ulysses*. But Mr. Joyce did not speak to me. I took a little hunt in the heavy bush north of the Douglas place and shot a grouse for my supper. That evening, after I'd washed my dishes and settled on the porch to read, I still had six hours of daylight left.

The next day I took the Mossberg and walked cross-country through the bush to the Mac. The land was nearly flat for the first mile, swampy in places, with heavy stands of poplar, aspen and willow, woods broken here and there by small, grassy openings that had been bogs just a month earlier. I hadn't walked the whole three miles to the Mac before, and it seemed more than possible to get turned around in such heavy cover.

Mushrooms the size of tea cups stood at the edge of shady spots, chanterelles or slippery jacks that looked like mushroom clouds; king boletes right out of a Disney cartoon; and, of course, shaggy manes. Conks grew in abundance on the dark sides of trees in the deepest shade. In parks where sunshine reached the ground, the warming woods smelled musty and rich with decay. I went carefully through the trees, watching for critters Herb Dahlstrom had told me about, animals that were new to me, like the fisher and the pine marten. But on that trip all I saw were pine squirrels and snowshoe hares, and the little downy woodpeckers that swooped through the bush in flashes of black and white and red.

Once I got to rising ground I kept the morning sun at two o'clock. After hiking up a ridge through some pine woods, I worked my way north and east until I came out above the beaver ponds where we sometimes saw our cow moose. From there I went north through lodgepole, along another ridge west of the Government Creek road, until I could see the old mill site and the spot where we usually parked the El Camino. It was an easy hike, but not a casual stroll. Not in those woods, where grizzlies and moose used the trails, too.

At the Mac, I went to work opening a space in the center of our clearing, where the cabin would stand. I moved logs toward the outer edges of the clearing, at first sliding the ones on top along the logs below, pushing them toward the standing timber as if they were on skids. When I had moved the easy ones out of the way, I worked down through the snarl of crisscrossed logs, using a pole and blocks of wood and a length of hemp rope to pry and lift and pull more logs up and away, until I eventually got down to logs lying on the ground, some of which had turned a dull moldy green. Logs that were too heavy to move, I rolled over so the bottoms faced up. It was pick-up sticks with sticks that weighed hundreds of pounds. I moved a log then rested; skidded another out of the way and rested, re-arranging our logs to expose as many bottoms as possible to the sun.

I managed to roll four straight logs with the greatest diameter toward the center of our clearing, where I skidded them up to rest on short logs off the ground. These were to be the four "sill" logs that would make the lowest course of our walls. The butt ends of these logs were twenty inches in diameter and heavy in the way that kegs of beer are heavy. But they now lay within just a few feet of where they'd be needed when we began to build.

When I had finished, I sat with my back against one of the sill logs and ate my sandwich. Mosquitoes had been in steady decline as the country dried, and by mid-afternoon only a few settled on my hands and forearms. I sat with my back toward the creek, facing the hillside above our shelf. A faint footpath showed in the moss, where Sheila and I sometimes climbed to take our lunch breaks on higher ground, and from there gaze down at what we'd done. There was something in the folds and contours of that slope that attracted me, something that felt both inviting and safe. "Come on up," it said to me. So I stood and scrambled over our scattered logs and began climbing. From the hillside, our clearing, with the jumble of logs scattered all about, looked like a great magpie's nest made of sticks.

The hill topped out a couple hundred yards above our clearing at a narrow ridgeline, where I swung to my right and walked north along a moose trail that followed the crest of the ridge as it climbed higher above the Government Creek gorge. The steep slopes below the trail were heavily forested with lodgepole pine and white birch. In some places, there were heavy stands of the shoulder-high willows that fed the moose during the winters. After a quarter mile I stopped and caught my wind. The trail continued on north through pines and bush, running toward Government Lake and the vast, unknown country to the north and east, which appeared as blank white spaces on our maps.

Just two months before, I'd been standing beside an interstate highway near Midwest, Wyoming, with my pathetic little sign that said, *Denver*. As I looked about, I congratulated myself on such progress, for there I was, traveling now with impunity the fairways of the moose in British Columbia.

I headed back down the trail, going along quiet through the woods. On the slope above our building site I sat down in the duff and leaned back against a tree and rolled a cigarette. The sun warmed my outstretched legs through my jeans, and, as I smoked, I tried to picture our cabin standing there, the logs tanning in the sun. I looked off beyond the encircling trees at puffs of white cloud coasting across a brilliant sky. I felt how much changed the place was without Sheila. The clearing we'd made together, surrounded as it was by the greens of snowbrush and willow and moss, and the dark timber over yonder on the slopes beyond Government Creek, all seemed beautiful beyond words. Like the song said, it was almost heaven, the hillside and our clearing and the big country all around me. But it was not enough. Not nearly enough. If I had seen a future when Sheila would not come back, I knew right then that I could hike to the Cariboo Highway and stick out my thumb and be gone without much more than a backward glance.

As I sat there, smoking and resting and daydreaming, I saw that the job we'd set ourselves to do was about more than building a log cabin in the woods. Maybe because we were on our own, this quest, which in some ways had been a trial, was turning into the kind of great adventure many of our generation claimed to want—that occasion in life which would test us and prove us and leave a brightness that would not dim as the years passed. And there I was, through great good luck and much foolishness, just as I'd thought that morning of fog and geese near Revelstoke: Right in the middle of it.

I tipped the ashes from my smoke into the upturned cuff of my jeans. The woods were dry, fire of any kind a danger, and as I remembered summer fires in Montana, my daydreams turned to thoughts of home and the war. Then, without warning, I was seeing two boys who'd been in my class at Helena High School. Thomas Grose and Bruce Backeberg. I hadn't known Tom, a tall, good-looking kid, except to exchange nods as we passed in the halls between classes. Bruce, a tough, blond German-American, who could bench press more than God, had been a friend of mine. Tom had gone down in flames, I'd heard, in 1969. Bruce, only nineteen years old, was killed in Quang Tri Province, South Vietnam, by small arms fire. My mother had enclosed his obituary from the Helena newspaper in a letter to me, which I'd read as I stood in the cafeteria line at Graceland College just two weeks into my Freshman year. PFC Backeberg had been awarded the Silver Star for valor. I remembered the shock, the sense of disbelief, that the life of someone I knew could be ended so soon. And I remembered looking around the Graceland College Commons, at the beautiful girls in their nylons and helmets of lacquered hair as they carried their trays to tables where boys stood until the girls were seated, and I was stabbed by feelings I didn't understand at the time that involved being so safe, surrounded by such luxury, while boys my age were being shot to death in the far-off never-never land of Vietnam.

Was I against all war? Hell, no. I respected deeply my father's service in the Second World War and his father's service in World War I. I especially respected my dad's best friend, Elmer Wallace, an infantry sergeant who'd fought from North Africa to the Bulge and had the scars to prove it. Was I morally opposed to the Vietnam War, I wondered, as I sat there safe on that hillside in British Columbia, or was I afraid to go where my friends Crosser and Backeberg had gone? Was there something else, perhaps, some other reason besides fear? Was it sloth? Did I think I was too good, too educated, too above it all, too special, to go? I wanted to believe, then, that I had better reasons, that I was taking a stand in opposing that particular war, because it was wrong. But I wasn't sure. I wasn't sure of my reasons at all.

When I thought about it, in the stillness of those woods, I understood that the war wasn't all of it. I hadn't meant to evade just the war. I had wanted to escape the entanglements of a marriage and the pressures of two families.

One day, in the far-off future, my friend Jim Crumley would say to me, as we stood at the bar in the East Gate Liquor Store and Lounge in Missoula, Montana, "Ralph, there ain't no shit, like family shit," and I'd nod—because I'd already known for a long time—just how right he was.

I felt sweat drying on my neck and back as I looked down at the space in the woods we'd carved, and I knew that part of the reason I'd left Montana was because I didn't want to wade through any more family shit. But I also knew I was doing this hard thing, here in these woods, because I loved a woman. Leaving the States and burning my draft card and building this cabin were, more than anything else, ways to win her love. I saw that true reason for a moment, then it seemed to slip away, as it so often has over the years, a thought passing like geese flying above still waters shrouded in fog.

Below me, in the center of our magpie's nest, was the spot where the cabin would stand, and as I rested, I wondered if we could turn our logs into walls and gables. Could the two of us lift roof purlins and a ridgepole up to the tops of the gables then build a roof atop the purlins? Could we cut windows and a door that were plumb and square? Could we caulk and chink the spaces between the logs well enough to keep out the cold when temperatures fell to thirty below? Could we even find enough money to keep us going until we had it built? I didn't know and I didn't know and I didn't know. But I understood that the thing was worth trying if she was there. It was just not worth doing alone.

In our clearing, wood chips from my undercuts and sawdust littered the ground. The moss we'd trampled had tanned in the sun. Light came down through the trees on the slope behind me, and the air was filled with the bright arcs of insects in flight. What I saw and felt all around me was desirable and comforting in ways I did not completely understand, but the clearing below seemed to me a holy place, the center of something that was deeply at peace and full of possibilities. And for a moment, I could hear her voice.

I must have dozed. When the ember at the end of my cigarette burned back into my fingers, I snapped awake. I'd been dreaming, dreaming that I was walking beside Butte Avenue when it was still a dirt road, walking toward our little stucco house, and my folks were there, standing on the concrete steps outside the kitchen door, watching me as I came home.

That evening, while I was burrowing into Joyce on the front porch at the Douglas place, Ken Glaze putted up the lane on his Case tractor. We blue-skied for a while before he asked if I could help him put up some grass hay in a meadow south of Dahlstrom's. Our twenty-dollar-a-month rent was due in August, so I agreed to help Ken bring in his hay in exchange for our August rent. "It's dump-raked and ready to go. Might as well stay over to our place while your woman is gone," Ken said. "Save some shoe leather. We got lots of room and Lila feeds good."

"I appreciate it," I told him. "It's awful quiet around here."

We hitched Ken's tractor to a four-wheeled hay wagon that rolled on rubber tires. In the field, Ken stopped beside the first mound of hay, and I lifted it, one forkful at a time, onto the wagon with a long-handled pitchfork. Once we'd collected several piles, Ken climbed onto the wagon and showed me how to "build up" the corners and outside edges of the load with large "flakes" of hay. Then he tied those flakes together with others that he placed a little closer to the center of the load, binding it all together.

"Never hauled no loose hay, eh?" Ken said, brushing chaff and nettles from his whiskers.

"No, Sir. Just bales."

"Well, pay attention here 'cause you're learning from the best."

That old man was slick with a pitchfork, I had to admit. The grass was three feet long and slippery. Where my flakes wanted to slide off when the wagon moved, Ken's hay stayed right where he put it. We built up the outsides of the load, then gradually filled the center of the wagon and topped it off with a big mound in the middle that helped hold the load together. This simple-sounding task was harder to accomplish than it might seem, and I began to appreciate what was possible to accomplish with just a pitchfork. As we worked, Ken told me about haying with horses when he was young, and how it had been possible to put up big wild hay meadows for no expense beyond the mower and rake and harness. "Not like tractors and gasoline, today," Glaze said. "We ran them horses on grass and oats and creek water. Didn't cost nothin' at all."

We had to travel a mile of gravel road from the meadow to Ken's barn, so I climbed up on the load and lay on my back, resting as the wagon rumbled along, going in and out of shady spots created by road-side trees. The hay jostled under me, and I felt like a kid again, a stem of grass between my teeth, riding a buckrake-load of hay to our barn with my dad. Under the eternal sky of endless summer, we crossed our meadow to the sudden cool of cottonwoods and the deep-shade scent of mint, a young man keeping an eye on the boy atop the load, who floated along between the sweet luxury of timothy hay and a boy's best mid-summer dreams.

Pitching on a load soaked my shirt with sweat, but the breeze in shady stretches of the road cooled me back down. If I close my eyes right now, I can see the tree tops passing overhead above the back road to Hixon, and the white clouds of summer loafing along far above. Those slow rides on Ken's hay wagon were as close to childhood as I've ever come when awake, while my chauffeur, hunched over the tractor's steering wheel under a broken straw hat, had once married a nickel heiress thought to be worth millions.

At the barn, I stood on the load and pitched the hay overhead to Ken as he stood in the open mow and took the hay from my fork with his. The sun beat down against the side of the barn, and the sun pounded on the load of hay, and in no time at all, my shirt was soaked through again. Dirt and chaff fell back on me as I lifted the forkfuls of grass, and I became aware of new, as yet unknown groups of muscles burning in my arms and neck and back. Every so often I'd climb into the airless loft and help the old man carry hay to the stack he was building at the back of the barn. On our return trips to the field, I stood in the front of the wagon, holding my shirt open with one hand, already thinking about floating through the shade of passing trees, once we got the wagon loaded again.

Ken was never in a hurry to start in the mornings, when the hay was damp with dew. But once we got rolling, he did not like to stop. Hauling the hay in took several days. In the evenings I ate supper with Ken and Lila, then climbed the stairs to a spare bedroom, where the floor was littered with cardboard boxes overflowing with yellowed paperback Westerns, remnants of ten thousand winter evenings spent reading beside wood stoves. They were books that had been read in the light of kerosene lamps, volume after volume of Louis L'Amour and Zane Grey and a couple dozen writers who wanted to be Zane Grey and Louis L'Amour.

One volume, near the bottom of a box, caught my eye. *Grass Beyond the Mountains* by Richmond P. Hobson was a non-fiction story based on the exploits of three cowboys from Colorado. Hobson and his friends got permission from the Canadian government to trek into a wildhay paradise in northwestern British Columbia in the mid-1930s, to build a ranch in a region so remote that they had to take their new mowing machines and dump rakes apart and freight the pieces in on pack horses, then reassemble the machines again once they reached the vast meadowlands they had claimed. I lost quite a bit of two nights' sleep reading that book, and it fired my imagination about an area to our northwest, which had then been occupied by white people for less than forty years.

Maybe because I'd been pitching hay for a few days, maybe because I was so close to where the book's story took place, I discovered, thanks to *Grass*

Beyond the Mountains, a new sense of British Columbia as a recent frontier. Sure, there were highways and towns now, some big mills, even the shopping center up in Prince George. But here was a story about three men who rode into a country few whites had seen, a wild place where they built log cabins and horse barns to get them through the first winters, with nothing more than horses and hand tools.

Right about then I stopped thinking of myself as a drug-addled, drop-out draft-dodger. I opened my eyes one morning to find myself living and working near a place—where only thirty-five years earlier—men had come into virgin country the way my mother's people had taken up land near the headwaters of the Missouri River just after the American Civil War. British Columbia! I thought. A last chance; a place where a person could still start with little more than a good woman and some hand tools, and make a life that was a whole lot more interesting than anything I'd ever dreamed of in Helena, Montana.

I no sooner got back to the Douglas place, after Ken and I finished up his hay, when Clint Dahlstrom stopped by to ask if I could help them move some baled hay from a ranch down along the Fraser River up to their place at Hidden Meadows. I told Clint that sure, I'd be glad to, and the next day I joined several other men who had come to help. Herb Dahlstrom drove a two-ton flat-bed truck across the field, going along in low gear between two rows of bales, while three or four of us picked bales from the ground and threw them up to the men on the truck. It turned out to be a long brute of a day. We were dragging when we finished stacking the last load in near darkness. Mrs. Dahlstrom fed us supper, and Clint drove me back to the Douglas place. On the way, he asked what he owed me for my work.

"You don't owe me anything," I told him. "I had a lot of fun working with you guys."

"Well, we appreciate your help, " Clint said.

As I opened the pickup's door at the Douglas place, Clint said, "I'm working on the highway crew now during the week, and Dad is getting some years on him. I'd like to have someone help him when I can't be there. Do you think you could work for us part time? We can pay two bucks an hour, if you're interested."

I had about five dollars in my wallet, and I had no idea what Sheila would bring back from Montana in terms of money. We had liked the Dahlstroms from the first evening we'd met, and I had trusted them on a gut level right away. They were good people, and I especially liked Herb, so it didn't take more than a few seconds for me to make up my mind. "You bet," I said. "I should be able to work a day or so a week, depending on how the cabin is going."

British Columbia. Without even looking, I'd found a job working for people I liked, doing work I enjoyed, in some of the most beautiful country I would ever see.

TWENTY-ONE

I might have been feeling in shape before that long day of bucking bales for Dahlstroms, but when I got out of bed the next morning, I discovered stretched cables and bent springs, all the way from my ears to my heels. There was a blue ache in the muscles of my ass, and sparks sizzled up and down the backs of my thighs as I walked. My fingers were laced with fiery blisters from lifting the bales by their strings, and my forearms burned when I tried to make fists. But I felt pretty good, considering what we'd done the day before, and how we'd done it.

The cabin was musty and too quiet as I built my morning fire, so I opened the kitchen door to let in some light and fresh air.

I took coffee and our transistor radio into the sunshine outside and eased myself down onto the top step. Daffodils speckled the meadow on both sides of the trail to the front gate, and timothy swayed in a faint breeze, as if swept by tender hands. In the early light, I could see Sheila again, waving from the El Camino as she headed off for Montana. I watched her out of sight in my lazy-morning daydream, until I realized the radio announcer was talking about the Vietnam War and the war draft in the United States.

I fumbled with the radio, turned up the volume, and caught part of the last sentence. "Say wa?" I said, jumping off the porch to carry the radio into the meadow, where the signal completely petered out. Had the announcer just said that the draft law had *expired?* I limped down the track toward the plank gate and back, wide awake by then but certain I'd somehow heard it wrong. How could I be so out of touch about something so important to my life? Then I looked around and noticed where I was.

I caught the whole story the next hour, while washing my breakfast dishes. It was big news. In February, the Nixon Administration had requested a two-year extension of the existing draft law, even though Nixon had campaigned in '68 on a promise to end the draft. Opposition to the war in Congress had stalled efforts to renew the draft, and the existing law actually *had* expired at the end of June. It seemed a senator named Mike Gravel had led the charge to stop the draft. He then held off all efforts to renew draft legislation. Until a new law passed both houses of Congress and was signed by Nixon, no one was going to be drafted in the United States!

I had assumed all along that once MSU notified my draft board when I left school, that I would automatically be reclassified 1-A. A draft notice with my name on it should have then been sent out. I'd thought that by mid-August, I might have already missed a draft physical, in violation of the Selective Service law. Now it seemed my assumptions might be wrong, since there might not have been enough time, so late in spring quarter, for the university to contact my draft board and . . . but wait . . . I hadn't formally withdrawn from classes through the Registrar's office, before Sheila and I left Bozeman. I'd just walked away, burning my bridges and giving a giant middle finger to The Establishment. But . . . if my draft board didn't know I'd dropped out of school . . . I wouldn't have been sent a draft notice.

How strange it felt, how disorienting, to think I might be able to go back to the States right then, if . . . . But so many ifs made me dizzy. And there was one more: If I hadn't used my draft card to start that campfire, I probably wouldn't be a felon after all.

Our apple-crate pantry in the kitchen was empty, except for sardines and oatmeal and maybe a quarter-pound of coffee. I dumped the change jar on the table and unfolded the dollar bills in my wallet and decided a trip to Hixon was the order of the day—just the ticket to clear my head and work out the kinks. So I laced on my Garmisch boots, shouldered my frame pack, took my walking stick from beside the door, and set off cross-country through the bush toward Dahlstrom's Hidden Meadows, where the back road to Hixon turned south toward town.

After I left the bush for the road, I tried to sort out my situation as I hiked along. Although nothing had likely changed, my draft status had seemed much simpler before the news about the draft reached me that morning. But, there I was with a few dollars and change to my name, hiking down a dirt road in the middle of British Columbia, on a sunny morning. What the hell am I worrying about, I wondered. I didn't want to go back to the States. I was right where I wanted to be. So I decided to forget the bloody draft and enjoy my walk, which I did, swinging along the shoulder of that sweet lane, past hayfields and woods, feeling a great energy rise in me and a quickness. This was my bell, my movie. I was a free man striding through a radiant land on a warm summer's day. What more could anyone possibly want?

Harry Schmaltz, dressed in his matching green mail-order shirt and pants, was working in his garden as I came swinging down the road, so I stopped to chat. I told him about our progress at the Mac and mentioned I'd been helping the neighbors with their hay. Harry said he'd been in the bush, working a sluice box on one of his claims, high-grading black sand into coffee cans to pan out during the winter. He looked tanned and fit as we waved, one draft-dodger to another, when I headed on toward town.

At Thorp's General Store, I bought eggs, powdered milk, hotcake mix, and some apples; a few slices of bacon and a can of lard; bread, a pound of coffee, and a can of jam. I had a dollar and some change left, so I added a bottle of Tokay fortified wine and a large Fudgsicle, which I ate with great pleasure while sitting on the bench outside as logging trucks bumbled by heading for the Netherlands Overseas mill. I had two nickels left in my jeans as I carried my groceries back to the Douglas place. Life, I thought, was mighty fine.

Late that afternoon, I carried our galvanized tub out into the sun and heated enough water in dishpans on the kitchen range to fill the tub half way up. I stripped down, climbed in, and sat in the soapy water with my legs over the sides, soaking while nipping the sweet wine from a jelly jar. I luxuriated, daydreaming about notching and squaring the bottom logs of our cabin at the Mac. And I saw a way to roll those bottom logs on top the stone foundation pillars without knocking the unmortared rocks out of place in the process.

I scrubbed my hair and beard, rinsed off with a bucket of cool water, and found myself humming, "Life is old there, older than the trees . . ." as I toweled myself dry. By the time I'd dressed in clean jeans and work shirt and washed my dirty clothes in the remains of my bath water, I was feeling pretty darned good.

I took a legal pad out to the front porch, refilled my glass, and began a rambling letter about pine logs and hay and love in the Cariboo to Sam and Sue Curtis. At some point, near the bottom of page three, I glanced up from the tablet to see a low-slung white vehicle emerging from the bush on the far side of our meadow. And there was an arm, flailing away from the driver's-side window, waving to me as I rose and ran to meet her.

The El Camino sat low on its springs as Sheila hopped into my arms and wrapped her legs around my waist. She was laughing and hugging me and saying, "Oh, oh, oh! It's good to *see* you!" all in a sweet rush that seemed to me then, as it does now, to be as good as any greeting I ever got. She was weightless there in my arms as she laughed and kissed me, and the kiss lasted and lingered, until I buried my face in her hair and held her as if everything depended on her love, which of course it did.

We found ourselves on the front porch, our arms hooked together at the elbows in a mad Cossack toast of uplifted jelly jars, both of us laughing, both of us talking at the same time, while the El Camino sat forgotten in the meadow, the driver's door hanging open and still.

That evening we retrieved the El Camino and began to unpack all the things Sheila had brought from Montana, as well as some wonderful plunder from her uncle Gideon's family in Lumby, British Columbia. There was a box of my jeans and sweaters and another box with winter boots, work shirts, and jackets that I'd left in Bill Figgins' garage, which Sheila had retrieved when she detoured to Bozeman to see Mac and Elena Watson and Sam and Sue Curtis. Sheila had stopped to see her parents in St. Ignatius, and while there, she filled several boxes with clothes, cooking gear, books, and good wool blankets. And wonder of wonders, there was a beautiful kitchen cook stove for our cabin, a present from her uncle Gideon, who also sent a nifty little over/under Savage .22/410 to use for hunting grouse.

By the time we had everything inside it was dark. But Sheila had one last surprise, which was, in the long run, probably the best of all. Her grandmother had died the year before, and the old lady had set aside a small sum of money for Sheila and Marilyn. Sheila opened her pack to reveal a wad of twenty-dollar bills. "And I'll get a hundred dollars a month for a year," she said.

We lit the kitchen lamp and sat at the table, and Sheila reached across for my hand. "We can *do* this," she said. "If we're very careful, we will have enough money for lumber and nails and roofing. And maybe we can stop eating rabbits for a while."

It had been a hell of a day. There was the news that the draft law had expired; my walk to town and back; Sheila coming home; and all the great stuff she'd brought with her. It was as if we'd gone through a door into a better version of what we already had. When I mentioned the expiration of the draft, Sheila said, "I heard it on the radio, too! What do you think it means?"

"It sounds temporary," I said, and added that I just didn't know. Then, in some strange twist of optimism and bent logic I no longer remember, I said, "I think we should check with the Immigration people pretty soon. Right now I'm in between bases—you know, like being caught between second and third. Let's think about going to Prince George to get my paperwork started. We can work on that and the cabin at the same time."

We got a slow start the next morning, and it took an extra hour to unload Uncle Gideon's kitchen stove and drag it under cover in the log barn at the Douglas place. When we got to the Mac, we climbed the hill above our cabin site and ate our lunchtime sardines and talked about how, exactly, we wanted to orient the cabin in our clearing.

We saw that the closer we pulled the back wall of the cabin to the hillside below us, the larger our front yard would be. Our clearing was limited in size, because just beyond the shelf, the hillside fell away sharply toward the creek. We decided to leave four feet between the back of the cabin—room enough for a walkway and no more—and where the hillside started up.

The back wall would have no windows, but the cabin's door and front porch would face due east toward the creek and the rising sun. What better way to meet a new day than to open the front door to morning light and the music of a creek?

We had one of our log-cabin books with us, and it described in simple terms how to use four stakes and a measuring tape to "square up" a foundation. We wouldn't have a foundation, of course, but I thought we could apply the same steps to arrive at the location of the cabin's inside corners and the invisible lines where our walls would eventually stand.

I cleared my throat, a professor at last: "Since we won't know how it will look on the ground, until we've measured and staked it out at least once, we may have to repeat the process several times, until we get the cabin's footprint right where we want it. I guess . . . I think . . . " My voice trailed off, and I shrugged to suggest massive befuddlement.

"Oh, God," Sheila said. "I wish you were an engineer. Have you thought about going back to school?"

When I went blank, she pointed at me and laughed uproariously, having fun, feeling good. It always seemed so easy to join her in laughter, and I joined her then.

I sawed a small pole into four pieces, twenty inches long, then sharpened one end of each to a point with my little Kelly. We began six feet from where the hill started up, at what would be the northwest inside corner. I drove a stake there, measured eighteen feet toward the south, and drove the second stake. That gave us a line for the inside of the back wall, while allowing room for a walkway between the overhanging log-ends at our corners and the foot of the hill.

I tied a chalk line between the two stakes.

Sheila held one end of our fifty-foot cloth tape at the first stake and I walked across the shelf toward the creek until I had twenty-six feet. I placed a small stone there. We measured out from the pin at the southwest corner until we again had twenty-six feet, and I placed stone there. We measured between the two stones and moved them back and forth until we had them eighteen feet apart. Then we walked around the shelf, trying to imagine how the cabin would look in that space.

Before we drove stakes to mark the corners of the front wall, we measured diagonally, from one rear stake to a rock in front. We measured diagonally from the other rear stake to the rock marking the opposite front corner. We moved the rocks in and out until our diagonal measurements were the same distance, which, our book said, meant the layout of our building was then square. Lastly, we drove our front two stakes where the rocks lay.

We tied chalk lines all the way around and hung a few strips of white rag on the chalk lines until we could clearly see from all angles how the cabin would look in our clearing. We walked around the shelf, climbing over and around our piled logs to study our primitive layout.

"It looks good to me," Sheila said.

"Yup. I think that's just fine. Let's build this dude."

We couldn't have stakes sticking out of the ground once we began rolling those big honker logs back and forth across the cabin's footprint to notch and place them, so we stole another idea from our book: We replaced the corner stakes with twelve-inch bridge spikes that we'd found at the Douglas place. Sheila flagged the top of each spike with red cloth, and I tapped them down into the holes where the wooden stakes had been, until the spikes' tops were almost flush with the surface of the ground. The tops of those spikes marked the inside corners of our walls and wouldn't get bumped out of place as we worked.

"Enough science," I said. "Let's get tough and tote some shit!"

"Yes, Sir," Sheila said. "Time to wag it and shag it. Whatever that means."

"Indeed, Miss Pie. This way please." I took her hand, and, as if we were about to begin a polonaise, led her to the rock outcrop just beyond the north edge of our clearing.

We needed flat rocks, twelve- to sixteen-inches square, to make the pillars that would keep our sill logs off the ground. River rocks from Government

Creek were too round and too far away, but on the far side of the moss-covered stone outcrop, we found a ledge of exposed rock that we could use. We had a six-foot length of one-inch steel pipe and an old miner's pick that we'd found somewhere in our travels, possibly at the Hixon Dump, where we hauled our garbage and poked around, looking for anything we could use. That was the extent of our rock-quarry equipment. Once we dug in past the weathered stone on the outside of the ledge, we found slabs of rock that broke away in nice flat chunks four- to six-inches thick, that, once we'd cleaned the dirt away with the claws of an old carpenter's hammer and rags, looked like big, rough bricks. I lugged the largest ones through our maze of peeled logs to where the cabin's corners would stand, and Sheila carried smaller ones that would make each pillar's second course. I put the very best of the big stones at the cabin's four corners, and we piled the smaller ones at random around the outside edges of the cabin's footprint to use as needed.

Our two largest logs would be the all-important sill logs. These big guys needed flat spots cut along their bottoms to provide stable resting places where the logs met our stone pillars. We shoveled away duff where the logs would run until we were down to hard clay, then rolled the sill logs up onto ten-inch logs to get them above the top courses of our pillars.

I marked the layout for the notches with a lumberman's crayon, and, while Sheila sat on the log to steady it, I sawed half-a-dozen kerfs inside my crayon marks, then chiseled away the wood inside. When the first sill log was ready, we built our stone pillars in line with the notches and rolled the log over until it plonked down in place. We did the second sill log the same way. Both logs were wobbly on their pillars, so we spiked poles to them, nailing the loose ends to stumps inside the cabin's imaginary walls.

The next morning we measured and cut the shorter sill logs for the east- and west-ends of the cabin. Sheila again steadied each log, while I carved out the saddle notches that would let these new logs grip the logs below them at the cabin's four corners. When we had again squared our four logs—by measuring diagonally, corner to opposite corner—we spiked the short logs down to the sill logs below. This sounds simple, but it took hours of tinkering to get things square and tight.

So far so good. Those first four logs looked great standing on their pillars of stone. But one thing was clear: If we didn't find a faster way to notch and stack up logs for our walls, we wouldn't have a roof over our heads by the time snow fell.

We'd heard that cull, or D-grade lumber, was cheap at the Netherlands Overseas mill in Hixon, so the next day we drove to the mill to take a look. A "bunk" containing two to three thousand board feet of mixed length 1x4s, planed on all four sides, sold for about twenty dollars, so we bought a bunk to use for roof boards. We also bought a smaller bunk of ten-foot 2x6s for our sub-floor. I told the forklift operator that I couldn't haul all the lumber right away. He glanced at the little El Camino and nodded. "Not a problem, man," he said.

He moved our bunks of lumber to a vacant area on one side of the yard, spray painted SOLD on the ends, then told me to check with him or at the scale shack the first couple times we came back to load up. "No problem, man," I said and gave him five dollars for his trouble.

There were mountains of lumber piled in long rows in the mill's big yards, much of it good-quality stuff headed for the Pacific coast and beyond. Our two bunks of culls had just been clogging up space needed for better wood, thus the low price. But our boards seemed awfully nice to us, as we slid our first jag of 2x6s into the back of the El Camino. The lumber was dry and straight, uniform and planed silky smooth, graded down, perhaps, for just a knot or bit of bark at one end. Almost everything in our bunks looked usable. The challenge was to get it from the mill in Hixon to the cabin site. Our first load didn't make a dent in what we'd bought.

At the old sawdust pile, we worked out a system for moving our lumber down the skid trail toward the cabin. We each stacked several boards on one shoulder, Sheila taking two or three, while I lugged five or six of the ten-footers. We hiked down the skid trail, the ends of our boards jouncing with each step. We stacked most of the boards on the skid trail where our foot path cut up the hill through the trees toward our clearing, but every third or fourth trip, we continued on with our boards right up to the cabin site, where we carefully ricked the lumber on poles back out of the way.

We had a good time, marching along side-by-side under our loads and chatting, and we were surprised at how much wood we could move that way, just slogging steadily back and forth, up and down the hill from the truck to our claim marker or cabin site. Moving lumber was also a pleasant way to start our days, so most mornings we drove to Hixon for a load.

To build our sub-floor, we had to cut notch-pockets, every twenty-four inches, into the two long sill logs to hold the ends of our floor joists, which we made from peeled poles five inches in diameter. I did the layout, leveling the bottoms of the pockets with a clip-on line-level and chalkline, then marking the centers and bottoms of each notch with a lumberman's crayon. I sawed and chiseled out the pockets, each one four inches wide and four inches deep. We squared up the ends of our poles, so they were four inches wide then tapped each one down into the appropriate pockets, until our joists ran from one sill log across to the other, all the way from the rear of the cabin to the front. Once we'd nailed the joists in place, we built a rock pillar under the center of each joist to prevent sagging.

Next, we had to nail down 2x6 planks to the joists to make our sub-floor. We carried and nailed, nailed and carried, working side-by-side, all the while talking about everything from Swift to Pynchon to Steve McQueen. We were still getting to know each other, telling stories from our childhoods and talking about odd bits and pieces of our high school and college years that seemed funny or somehow important. We were revealing ourselves to each other in that strange new place. Like whistling in the dark, perhaps, we told stories that helped us connect with each other, and, in some strange way, to feel a little braver.

"Hey, Pal, do you remember when Sam and Richie Furz waved their sign around at our sit-in?" I asked, and Sheila made quotation marks with her fingers: "Fire Dayton! Rehire Meyers! Cut the Crap!" And we cracked up, remembering how wonderful it had seemed when our young instructors in their jeans and boots took on those evil old college administrators. We hadn't known, when we fought to save Jim Meyers's job, how we would end up loving some of the people involved in the fight, but we were discovering just that, as we nailed down our sub-floor. Those people had became parts of our story, melodies woven into the song of our fancy adventure.

We nailed the 2x6s to our joists with twenty-penny (20d) zinc-coated sinkers, making sure to stagger those places where two planks butted together, so that no two splices matched up on the same joist. Then one afternoon, not long after lunch, Sheila and I clasped hands and stepped onto a new floor that ran from one end of the cabin to the other. It felt absolutely solid, as we walked back and forth, our boot heels going: Pum. Pum. Pum. Drumbeats amplified by the dark space below. It was the first floor either of us had ever made, every bit of it cut from the woods right there or carried in on our backs. The new deck was clean and level, square and sound, and as we marched there side-by-side, our boot heels leaving black marks on the pine, we were surprised at what we'd done. After all the bugs and rain and sweat; after all the aches and blisters and bruises, there we were, marching from one end to the other and back, toy soldiers, swinging our arms above a parade ground of wood, one that boomed underfoot, telling us yes, we could do this thing that we'd set out from Denver to do. After the years of university abstractions, we were striding across something we had made ourselves. It might have been just a sub-floor, out there in the big woods all by itself, with no walls or roof. But it was our floor, and it made us feel giddy and clever and intrepid, all at once. We were discovering what it felt like to accomplish something on our own that we could claim as our own. Heady stuff? You bet it was, and in some important ways it beat most of things in life we'd done 'til then.

TWENTY-TWO

Early one evening, after a tough day of carrying lumber and sorting and moving logs at the cabin site, I stepped outside to pitch our dishwater and saw a vehicle bouncing along, coming from the bush on the far side of our meadow. It was a red and white International Scout, and it seemed oddly familiar, as if I'd seen it somewhere before in another life. The Scout pulled up to the cabin and stopped, and Sam Curtis leaned from his open window, pushed back his broken cowboy hat and said quietly, "Hey, Ralph."

It was one of those grand surprises, one of those best moments that would one day resurface in memory and cause me to weep. It was Sam Curtis, by God, and seeing him gave me such a sudden rush of happiness that I seemed incapable of more than a smile. I stood there, in an open-mouthed attitude of surprise, dishpan in hand, looking at my friend and the Scout I'd ridden in dozens of times, until suddenly Sam's wife, Suzie, short and blond, brassy and loud, was in my arms hugging me, and Sheila was hugging Sam, and I felt an enormous relief pass through me, and the first moments of a great happiness.

We stood in the evening light, laughing at my surprise and laughing because it felt so fine to be together. It was a put-up job, of course, a conspiracy, improvised when Sheila visited them in Bozeman ten days before, then kept secret after Sheila got back. Their arrival was carried off with such understated grace, that these many years later, I can hear their voices in the evening air, so beautiful and young, so alive and welcome; Suzie's barking laugh; Sheila's normally quiet voice, raucous with excitement. And Sam, chuckling and asking, as if we'd seen each other just the day before, if they'd missed cocktail hour.

We sipped the Old Grand-Dad they'd brought, while Sheila and Suzie rustled up something for their supper. They'd taken the scenic route, and Sam talked about the country they'd come through, the wildness of the Fraser River Gorge and the beauty of the Cariboo. We exchanged news and snacked on good cheese and sausage and crackers—such marvelous treats—that appeared with many other good things from the magic Scout.

Sam said they had come to help raise the walls of the cabin, if that was all right with me. I'd worked with Sam at the Glorieta Finishing School, and I knew he was exactly the man I needed, a steady, capable worker, who would stay alert and focused on the job at hand. I knew then that a miracle of great good luck had come our way. Real help and true friends and good American bourbon, thank goodness, right when I needed them most. I told Sam that, yes, now that he mentioned it, I might be able to use some help at that.

We lit our kerosene lamps and took them onto the porch, and while Sam and Sue ate their supper and told us about their trip from Montana, I closed my eyes and savored their voices. At some point, I turned away from the lamp-light and looked west into the violet evening sky, and I felt a strange, dream-like sensation that miracles, which cannot be real, sometimes do become just that. Only three years before, Sam had taught the first writing class I ever took. And here he was with Suzie in British Columbia, having made a long expensive drive to come be with us.

When I glanced back at my friends, I noticed how Suzie's thick glasses made her eyes appear over-large and amazed, like a demented scientist with a smoking test tube from the pages of *Mad Magazine.* But just then, and much to my delight, Suzie produced a "home-made" blueberry pie that she'd found in a cafe in Quesnel. As she put slices of pie onto paper plates, Suzie told us about that year's annual Fourth of July party in Cottonwood Canyon and the comic brouhaha it turned out to be. Robert Pirsig, of *Zen and the Art of Motorcycle Maintenance* fame, had come with artist pals, Bob and Gennie Deweese, to join a couple dozen other artists, writers and assorted friends at Norm and Sil Strung's place, there to whoop it up with burgers and beer. Lots of boozy story-telling, of course, and laughter, and, as usual, Suzie said, a good time was had by all.

For a few moments I was transported by Suzie's voice to Cottonwood Creek, south of Bozeman, where Norm and Sil Strung lived in a log house that Sam and Sue and I once shared for part of a winter while the Strungs were off in Mexico. And I thought I could once again smell the cottonwood trees and the deep-shade scents of moss and stone along the creek, as summer there turned toward fall.

"I think we've located a little piece of land across the creek from Strungs," Sam said. "The owners won't sell, but we've almost got them talked into a hundred-year lease. We thought maybe we'd learn something about building with logs while helping you."

The next morning we drove both rigs to the old sawdust pile. While Sheila and Suzie gathered tools and our lunches, Sam took me to one side behind the Scout. He seemed concerned about something, a little hesitant, oddly serious. "Ralph," he said. "I know you want to build your cabin the old-fashioned way with just hand tools. But I brought something along that I thought might help, if you get behind. You know, if you don't mind using it." Sam seemed reluctant to go on, as if he had second thoughts, or sensed he might spoil our perfect morning.

I couldn't imagine what he was driving at, until he flipped aside a tarp in the back of the Scout. There was a bright red "E-Z Model" Homelite chain-saw, complete with a full can of mixed gas and a jug of official Homelite bar oil. The little saw looked brand new. Except for a few bits of sawdust and a smudge of oil on the sixteen-inch bar, the saw was so sanitary it might have come right from the dealer.

The truth was simple: I'd had more than enough of the Swede saw. I was so tired of grunting out every cut on my knees, of pinching the blade again and again, of the push-pull, push-pull drudgery that turned my arms to rubber. I looked at Sam and began to laugh. There was a Santa Claus after all, and he stood before me in worn jeans and work shirt, his cowboy hat sporting a tear in the crown, and a sweat stain along the band. I put my arms around Sam and gave him a tremendous hug. Suzie and Sheila, who had been secretly watching, applauded when I let Sam go.

"I think Ralph likes it," Suzie said.

"Oh, bless you both," I said, about as close to tears as I could get at that green, bullet-proof age. I picked up the Homelite. It seemed to weigh almost nothing. "This little sweetheart," I said, "is going to make all the difference. All the difference in the world."

Sam and I picked one of the biggest, heaviest logs, bulled it around parallel to the south wall, rolled it up two skid poles, and across to the north wall. It took us a while to work out a way to scribe the semi-circles for the saddle notch at each end of the log, and to rough out the notches with the Homelite. We decided that since I was more skilled with a chainsaw, I'd use the Homelite while Sam held the log, then Sam would chop out the wood between the saw kerfs while I held the log. We roughed out two logs for the long walls, but did not try for exact fits until Sheila and Suzie returned from Hixon with several rolls of inch-thick, paper-backed fiberglass insulation, a bag of roofing nails, a fifty-pound box of twelve-inch spikes, and some special treats for lunch and supper.

Sheila unrolled some insulation on the floor, then she and Suzie took turns cutting long strips, two inches wide with a butcher knife. They used roofing nails to tack the insulation strips on top our sill logs. Sam and I deepened and smoothed our notches with chisels, until a log fit down flush along its full length against the sill log below. We guessed at plumb, toe-nailed the log in place at the corners, and stood back to admire our work. Pink insulation peeked out between the logs. The corner notches, however, looked crude; several saw kerfs were too deep. Clearly I'd need to take more care when making those first cuts.

At noon, Sheila and Suzie set out our lunch on the new floor, and we leaned back against the logs in one corner to eat right there in the middle of the job. Sam removed his hat, held it over his heart, and offered grace: "Bless this grub that we are about to receive. Grab it and growl, kids," he said, and we dug in. There were potato chips and ham sandwiches, fresh bananas, and for desert, Suzie produced a bag of apple turnovers. Such bounty! Such excess! After the weeks of sardines and peanut butter-and-jelly sandwiches, this lunch, and the ones that followed in the days to come, became marvels of French mustard and fresh fruit and sugary, store-bought bakery goods. Sliced Turkey! Ham! Potato Salad! And lots of everything, thanks to Sam and Sue's generosity.

"Good God," Sam said, during lunch that first day, as he swept his hand toward the peeled logs we'd cut. "How did you do all this with a five-dollar Swede saw and an ax?"

And it did seem to me, as I chewed and looked at our logs, that Sheila and I had accomplished an awful lot with very little, while living on rabbits and biscuits made with lard. "I had good help," I said. "Sheila spent every day for weeks dripping pitch and chewing bark, and she peeled every one of those logs!" I could see that Sheila was just as pleased as I was. "The truth is," I said, "I guess we just didn't know any better."

The day heated up, and during one of our breaks that afternoon, I found myself looking at Sam. I realized I was seeing him much as I had on the first day of that writing class, three years before, at Montana State University. I was newly transferred from that strange little college in Iowa, and MSU felt to me like the big leagues. But when Sam walked into the classroom that first day I'd thought: *What's this? No suit, no tie, no shiny black FBI shoes?*

No, Sir. Not Sam. He wore jeans and a blue work shirt with the sleeves rolled back and hiking boots. His hair was a trifle long, and he sported an elegantly trimmed beard that I much admired. He was quietly professional as he went through the first-day's business of explaining how the class would work and what he expected us to do, serious without being *too* serious. He seemed not nervous, but crisp; a poised, understated young guy with something of the East Coast about him. And how strange: That interesting young instructor, who was only a few years older than his students, chose, from the first moment of the class, to sit among us in a student desk instead of looking down from the shelter of a lectern.

Sam got us started; we took our first baby steps toward learning to write stories. Looking back, years later, at that Introduction to Fiction Writing class, I'd guess that Sam didn't know at the time what a good job he'd done.

In the years that followed, I learned that Sam had come from a well-to-do family in Connecticut, that he'd gone to the Berkshire School—a rich kid's prep school in Sheffield, Massachusetts—then to Trinity College in Hartford, Connecticut. He served in the United States Army before Vietnam, then taught English courses at the American School in Lugano, Switzerland, where he met Suzie. When they returned to the States together, Sam finished an MA at Johns Hopkins and was hired straightaway to teach writing courses at MSU when he was still only twenty-seven years old. He was a skilled cross-country skier and a genuine goat of a hiker, and, as his Eastern polish wore off and his life in Montana took over, he gradually turned into something of a well-read country boy. In the many years I knew Sam Curtis, he always seemed genuine, never pretentious. He told stories with great gusto and big gestures, stories like how he had once run away from the dancing school his well-meaning mother had insisted he attend, all the while embellishing and coloring his story's narrative with the kind of grand, sweeping gesticulations that a *dancer* might use. Sam liked a tall whiskey around sunset, the time of the day he called Cocktail Hour, no matter when the sun set. He was mild and funny, honest and true, a gentleman without fancy manners or false pretense. He was, without a doubt, the most graceful man I ever met.

Our friendship was to become one of the most important in my life, and a day would come, in the dim, far-off land of the future, as Sam was dying, when I would tell him how proud I was of all he had achieved; how proud of his books and magazine articles; how proud of the beautiful log house he built with his own hands; how proud I was of him and to have been his friend. I wish I could tell him all that again.

I t felt so good to Sheila and me to have Sam and Sue there on our new floor in the woods, sharing lunches and rest breaks with us in the spot we'd found and made our own, so good to hear them talk about our place and what we were doing there. That Sam and Sue were actually with us, in our clearing, made it seem that we were still connected to our friends and life in Bozeman, and that what we were doing was not just our own private adventure, but something interesting enough to be told and talked about around campfires back in Montana.

I don't think Sheila and I had realized how isolated we felt, how cut off from all we'd once known and taken for granted. And I don't think either of us had known how much we doubted what we were trying to do. But, in the company of our two friends, we felt we were still connected to life in Bozeman, which had been so important to us. With Sam and Sue there, we also felt a new confidence, a renewed vigor, a rising energy. It was the beginning of a new momentum that would propel us through the weeks ahead.

The days continued clear and dry, and the afternoon woods pulsed with heat. The music of Government Creek had faded to a distant murmur, and in the trees around our clearing, the moss had dried and tanned with the season. Sam and I smoothed out a routine for selecting and moving each log to the spot where it best fit. We taped my carpenter's level to a straight, eight-foot 2x4 and used it to check our walls for level and plumb. After a couple days we picked up speed. "Good!" Sam called from his end of a log when his notch was finished.

"Good," I answered when mine was ready, too. When we were satisfied that the log pressed down along its whole length on the log below, and that the corners were snug, we reached for spikes and sledge, and the rising hammer-on-anvil pings of spikes going home, echoed through the woods.

Sheila and Suzie kept us supplied with strips of insulation; they swept and shoveled up and carried away the chips and sawdust we made; and they freighted 1x4s from the mill in Hixon with the Scout and El Camino, carrying them down the skid trail and up our footpath to the job site, where they stacked them out of the way back in the trees. Sam and I couldn't help certain low jokes about beasts of burden, when they appeared from the bush with lumber stacked on their shoulders.

"Here come the Irish," I said, nodding toward the women as they trudged from the trees, the narrow boards on their shoulders dipping and slapping together as they walked.

"Aren't they swell?" Sam asked in an exaggerated whisper.

"Gentle but strong!" I answered. And when the women had unburdened themselves, they flexed their biceps like the girls in World War II posters, pushed out their chests, and lumbered off into the trees for another load.

Our new walls made shade as they got higher, so we gathered for our lunch breaks on the cool north side of the cabin. One noon, while cleaning her glasses on her shirttail, Suzie said, "So, Ralph, what are you two doing about getting legal up here?"

Her question surprised me. "We haven't done anything, yet," I said.

Suzie glanced at Sam then looked back at me. "Don't you think you should?" she said.

"I guess. I just don't want to stir things up right now."

"What if the Canadian authorities get wind of what you're doing and decide to play rough?" Suzie asked.

"We've talked about it, sure, but I keep putting it off." I looked over at Sam. "What do you think I should do?"

Sam seemed reluctant to offer advice, but he said, "If you're planning to stay up here for good, you'd better talk to the immigration people pretty soon, Ralph."

He was right, and I knew it. It was just so much easier to think about saddle notches and friends than regulations and application forms. "One of these first days, I'll get on it," I said. "But right now I want to concentrate on logs and pretty girls and pie!"

In the evenings we scrubbed up in tubs of warm soapy water in the yard at the Douglas place, then washed and hung our shirts and T-shirts to dry overnight on a line strung between two trees. We kept Happy Hour faithfully, and fell like savages on whatever good food Suzie and Sheila cooked for us.

We made the chips fly and the walls rose, shining in the sun. We sawed out a big window on the north side, where the kitchen would be, and we cut another large window, toward the back of the cabin, in the south wall. Our work settled into a steady pace, and at the end of each afternoon, as we stopped at the edge of our clearing to look back at what we'd done, we gloried in each other and the bright new courses of logs we'd raised that day.

Weddings and wakes, like the other great events in our lives, require witnesses and friends. Although Sheila and I would never marry, those days spent stacking up our logs, and those evenings of stories and laughter with Sam and Sue, were the ceremony and celebration that joined us. In all the years since those few days, I've never lost myself in a job or delighted in the people I worked with as I did during that short time together, when Sam and Sue and Sheila and I turned our logs into walls. Sheila and I became a couple then, just as surely as if we'd run though showers of rice down the steps of an old stone church. The four of us found, in the work and in each other, something deeper than friendship, and that love would reside in each of us for the rest of our lives.

Four feet of our sill logs ran beyond the outside front corners of the cabin to serve as the sills for our front porch. When the cabin's walls were seven feet high from the floor to the tops of eleven finished courses, we ran the last course of logs eight feet beyond the front wall, to serve as the bottom roof purlins for our porch roof.

Sam and I loaded Uncle Gideon's cook stove into the El Camino and hauled it to our parking spot at the sawdust pile. We ran two poles under the stove to serve as handles and lugged it, like coolies carrying a sedan chair, down the old skid trail then up our footpath to the cabin, where we left it at the edge of the clearing, wrapped in plastic to keep off rain and dew.

That day we carved out notches, two feet apart, in the top wall logs to hold poles that would serve as joists for our sleeping loft. Once spiked in place these poles also tied the two long walls together to keep those walls from spreading apart when the roof supported the weight of heavy snows.

The last job Sam and I did together was to build frames from 1x4s to serve as guides, one above each end wall, for the log gables that Sheila and I would build next. We settled on a 6/12 pitch for the roof, shallow enough to walk on, yet steep enough, we hoped, to let heavy snows slide off.

Sam and Sue had come to help us build the walls, and we'd done it in a week. When they said they needed to get back to Bozeman and Cottonwood Canyon, I felt like a little kid who didn't want summer to end. The last evening they were with us, we celebrated with steaks and ice cream from Thorp's store, and after the dishes were done, we sat late in the summer twilight in front of the cabin at the Douglas place, talking about Sam and Sue's plans for a future in Montana. Sam said he wanted to be an outdoor writer, like Norman Strung. Suzie thought she might teach school. We talked about Nixon and the never-ending war in Vietnam and the war protests that continued in the States. Sam mentioned again the need for me to begin the immigration process. Mostly, though, we rejoiced in our epic days of logs and chips, sawdust and sweat, and all the fun we'd had in the doing of what we accomplished together. We were tired after the pace we'd set, but the work and good company had created a high that lasted into the days and weeks ahead.

The next morning, Sam and Sue were up and away as soon as we finished a pot of coffee. Sheila and I watched the Magic Scout disappear into the bush, and we felt like waifs abandoned in a forest. We walked hand-in-hand one silent turn around the meadow, and except for birdsong and the tapping of woodpeckers, it was much too quiet.

We found ourselves standing beside the perfect log barn that Mr. and Mrs. Douglas had built. We looked across the meadow, as the sun rose through shimmering leaves of aspen and poplar, climbing until its first rays touched the tops of the tallest pines with golden light.

Sheila stepped around in front of me and took hold of my shirt with both hands and shook me. She cocked her head to one side and looked up into my eyes. "This is extraordinary," she said. "This time, this moment, this *adventure*. Do you understand?"

I looked at her there, so small and brave and pretty, and I felt something relax inside me. I felt myself open, like a clenched hand that opens to reveal a faint light, a glow like a single candle burning in the distant window of a cabin deep in winter woods at dusk. I looked at her, and I felt the warmth of that light, and I understood that I had given my heart to her.

I took her head in my hands and nodded. "I do. Let's remember this place, and the light coming through the trees the way it is right now, and the ways we've loved each other here. Let's promise each other right now to look back at this time, if we grow old, to remember how we felt about each other when we were young and full of light, and it was always morning."

"Yes," Sheila said. "I promise. I absolutely will remember it always."

"And I will remember you, my beautiful girl, as you are right now."

After a while we walked back to the cabin, and we noticed something red partly hidden in the grass beside the front steps. It was Sam's gas can. And beside the gas can was his oil jug. And next to the oil jug was the Homelite chainsaw with a note tied to the handle that read: "Return this the next time we see each other. Now finish that cabin and become real Canadians before snow flies. We love you both. Sam and Sue."

PART III

I want to look at you, Jenny, hear you
breathe, be with you. Say a word, any word.
I want to hear the sound, the timbre, of
your voice. I want to put my hand to your
neck and feel it vibrate when you speak, as
though I were a deaf-mute just learning.

—Larry Heinemann
Close Quarters

TWENTY-THREE

The day Sam and Sue left for Montana, Sheila and I cut and nailed down much of the 1x4 decking for our sleeping loft. At the last minute we decided to make the loft one joist shorter, but instead of taking out the extra pole, we left it there, floating by itself in space above the center of the floor, two feet beyond the edge of the loft. That lonesome joist just looked interesting, and it seemed likely that we'd invent uses for it later.

The late-August mornings were chilly enough to make our wool shirts feel good as we approached the cabin through the shade in the timber. In a couple hours we'd be down to T-shirts, but that first tease of autumn each morning kicked us awake like good strong coffee.

We made a ladder from poles and 2x6s, for climbing up to the loft, and we tacked down a short 1x4 to keep the ladder's feet from skidding on the slick floor boards. Standing in the loft, we could see all of our clearing and the newly-walled space below. We ate our lunch there on the loft floor, savoring the bright space inside our walls, while listening to the logs click and snap as they dried in the sun. We dangled our legs over the edge and studied the back wall, where we had used many of our green-tinged logs. We thought they'd be less conspicuous back there against the hillside, and of course they were from outside. From our new, elevated vantage point, however, we could not avoid the zebra-stripe effect of the staggered white and green logs inside. But the wall was plumb and tight and true, and that was good enough for us.

For the next two days Sheila and I worked from the loft, building the east gable wall above our loft floor. We stacked one log atop another against the guide-frame nailed above the outside wall. Sheila held a log steady while

I counter-sunk holes with a brace-and-bit, so I could drive our twelve-inch spikes deeper into the log below with a steel punch. When the gable wall was five feet above the loft floor, we ran two pole braces up from the unused joist and mortised their tops into the gable wall. These poles, once spiked in place, helped steady the gable and keep it plumb, which would help us later, we thought, when the time came to lift the ridgepole and purlin logs to rest atop the gables.

The back wall was a tougher proposition. We had no loft floor to stand on and had to straddle the wall logs or stand on ladders to put gable logs in place. It was hard, awkward work. We couldn't afford an accident and muddled about, Sheila grappling with a log then waiting as I dropped my hammer or forgot the brace-and-bit or ran out of spikes and had to climb down. It was by turns edgy and slow. When I tried to hurry, I made mistakes, which made me snap, unfairly, at Sheila. "Goddamn," I'd say. "Can't you hold that thing straight?" Sheila would grump back at me, and we'd fumble-fart around and get on each other's nerves even more. And so it went until we got the longest gable logs spiked down. Then I saw a solution. With the bottom logs in place, I could then nail up 1x4s inside and out to serve as cradles to hold logs while I worked. And hey! We needed a hole for our outhouse.

Even at first glance that excavation was a discouraging prospect. The outhouse would stand on a natural little shelf in the hill above and behind the cabin, back in the trees and mostly out of sight. We could see that tree roots and rocks, bedded in the clay-like dirt, would make for hard digging, but, I thought, it would give Sheila something to do while I concentrated on finishing the back gable. When I suggested the job, I couldn't quite pull it off without sounding like I was trying, in a truly ham-handed way, to get Sheila out of my hair while putting her to work on a job I didn't want to do myself.

To my surprise, Sheila took a spade and our dull old pick and went to work on the hole without complaint. As I worked on the gable, I could see her scratching and pounding away at the ground back there, her face smudged with grime and her jaw set. She was thinking it over, I could tell, and that might not be good. Every so often, I'd hustle up the hill, saying, "Sanitary

Inspector!" Then I'd jump into the hole with her to chew on an ear or to reach inside her overalls to tickle her ribs until she giggled and punched my chest, fighting back with a fierce strength that always surprised me.

We borrowed Herb Dahlstrom's post bar, and for the next couple days Sheila grunted and struggled with her rocks and dirt, while I went happily about my work at a slow, deliberate pace, all the while trying to pretend that I hadn't shucked off a crummy job on my little Pard. She had my number, but she was too good a sport to gripe about each and every injustice. By the time Sheila dug a hole as deep as she was tall and four feet square, I had mortised in a long pole brace, that ran down from the top of the back gable to the center of the unattached loft joist, which locked both ends of the cabin together, by way of that joist, while steadying the new gable and holding it plumb. The next day, I finished the gable and capped it with a short log, which I dished slightly on top to help cradle the big end of the ridgepole that would run from that gable to the other.

When all the gable logs were spiked in place, I fired up Sam's Homelite, and, by following the 1x4 guides, I cut away the excess length of each gable log, leaving a nice, smooth angle down from where the ridgepole would rest, to the tops of each corner, where the walls came together. With the gables trimmed and true, we were ready for the most dangerous part of the whole job: raising the ridgepole.

One evening, when we returned Herb's post bar, Herb and I went through our ritual of rolling cigarettes in the driveway, while Sheila and Helen went off to look at Dahlstrom's garden. My cigarettes, I thought, were looking better, but when I glanced at Herb's, I saw I still had room for improvement.

Herb was a keen observer of what was going on around him, especially, as I would learn, in the bush. He seldom raised his voice and never seemed to have a bad word to say about anyone. He smiled often and enjoyed a good laugh. As we lit our smokes, he said he'd like to have me work with him one day a week on certain fall projects he had coming up. "Can you come tomorrow?" Herb asked.

"You bet," I answered. "What time should I be here?"

"Eight o'clock, if that's all right."

"That works for me," I said. "Should I bring a lunch?"

"You could," Herb said. "But Missus Dahlstrom will be offended if she can't feed us."

"That's even better!" I said.

Sheila dropped me off the next morning at a quarter to eight and headed to Hixon to do laundry and get groceries and our mail.

Our job that first morning was to drive fence posts, five-and-a-half feet long and about four inches in diameter, every twenty feet, in a straight line across Herb's lower meadow. Herb had cut and pointed dozens of willow posts and had them ready on the trailer he pulled with his Ford tractor. The fence would consist of just two thin electric wires, powered by a truck battery, so the posts wouldn't need the kind of strength required for a barbed-wire fence. We began at the creek and headed west, Herb starting each hole with his post bar, punching the bar down into the black earth and working it around and around in circles until he had a pilot hole large enough to help me get a post started. Then, facing me, he held the post plumb, while I stood on a milk crate and drove the post down with a twelve-pound sledgehammer.

We didn't talk much at first, just worked along steady, but it wasn't long before my forearms were burning from the weight and impact of the hammer. If that first morning was a test, I must have passed, because when we stopped for our ten o'clock break, Herb said in his quiet way, "I see you've used a hammer before."

I'd started splitting fir log butts with a sledge and steel wedges at the ranch when I was a boy. Working for hours by myself, I'd learned to hit where I looked and to hit hard without a big wind-up. It was a job I had enjoyed as a kid, and Herb's remark, which acknowledged a simple skill that I'd learned on my own, pleased me to no end. When he offered to spell me on the hammer, we switched off. I used the bar and started posts, then let Herb drive a few on down.

That fall, I worked with Herb Dahlstrom one day, sometimes two days a week. Each morning, Herb would have his tools and materials ready to go, and we'd start right at eight o'clock. But no matter what we were doing, if we were within a mile of the house, we went in at ten o'clock sharp for coffee and Helen's homemade coffee cake. After a fifteen minute break, we'd be good to go steady until twelve-thirty, when Helen served up a bounty of home-canned moose meat, greens, and fresh-baked bread, all prepared on the wood-fired kitchen range that she polished with stove black each week until it gleamed like patent leather. It was that kind of a world, then, in the Cariboo. A world where it was possible for a well-tended kitchen stove to be a woman's pride and joy.

Herb was sixty-one years old, a sinewy little guy with forearms like rusty cables, who stood maybe five-foot-six in his boots. He was a good worker, sure and steady and economical in his movements, and because he was such good company, I looked forward to the days we spent together. Herb knew the woods and life in the bush, and I could see that he was a better man, in ways that counted there, than I would ever be. Without either of us mentioning it, Herb became a kind of mentor to me, a man who gave me straight answers to my questions, and advice, if I asked for it. Herb had been a cattle feeder and butcher in the States before he and Helen immigrated to Canada, and he had many of the old-time skills I'd admired in men my grandfather's age. I couldn't have found a better man to spend time with that fall if we'd drawn names from all the phone books in British Columbia.

The Dahlstroms were country people who turned out to be a major stroke of good luck when Sheila and I needed luck. They took us under their wing; they offered suggestions if we asked; they gave me a job; they loaned us what we needed but couldn't afford to buy; and they helped us when we needed help, which was often.

That first day, Herb and I made it to an existing fence on the far side of his meadow, where we loaded up our tools and called it good. When Sheila picked me up at five o'clock, I dramatically counted out the sixteen Canadian dollars I'd earned.

It wasn't a lot of money, Sheila pointed out, for a long day with a sledge-hammer, but I felt pretty good about those wages. I'd managed to turn a beautiful day in a gorgeous meadow with a man I enjoyed, into grocery money. That struck me as a heck of a deal.

One evening we took the backroad to Hixon to get milk, eggs, and butter, and to pick up our mail, which included a nine-by-twelve envelope from a lawyer's office in Helena.

After supper, I went off by myself in the meadow to read the court papers from my divorce. Although the marriage had been a failure, I couldn't avoid feeling a little gutshot, there in the gentle evening light, while looking at the papers resting in my lap. It was over. I'd been a lousy husband, no doubt about that. Yet I was still fond of my former wife, who had been secretive during our marriage about some awful behavior of her own, and was, as it turned out, more than willing to let the entire shit-load of blame for my leaving slide downhill onto me.

A ruffed grouse, leading a file of half-grown chicks, cut across the opening just in front of me then disappeared into tall grass on the far side. I folded the papers back into the envelope, and remembered the first time I'd seen my wife. Her grandmother had brought her to church one Sunday when Linda was about twelve years old. She had been a beautiful kid with hair so blond it was almost white. I sat for the entire length of the sermon, looking at the back of her head, filled with a feeling of great discovery. By the time I was in the eighth grade, I yearned for her. But she was already in high school in another county, a whole world away.

Be careful what you wish for, I thought, coming out of my reverie. Then I realized that the same bleak papers, which documented my failures, also set me free. When I walked into the cabin, Sheila took one look at me, touched my arm, and said, "Come on, big guy," as she led me through the kitchen to the bedroom in back.

As we stepped from the chilly shade of the pines, the diagonal pole braces, rising there in bright lines from our floating loft joist to the peak of each gable, blazed in the morning sun. I stood there, at the edge of light and shadow, feeling quite the young stud in my faithful, red-and-black wool hunting shirt and 1930's snap-brim cap. I rubbed my cold hands together and wondered—as I had often wondered while building the gables—just how we'd get the ridgepole up to where it needed to go.

We had saved the straightest and strongest logs for the ridgepole and purlins. Except for the walls' bottom logs, our ridgepole was one of the heaviest sticks we'd cut. It was a beautiful brute, true and white and smooth as milk, that we somehow had to lift to the very tops of the gables.

I planned to roll the ridge-pole up ramps to the top of the south wall. We could accomplish that with half-inch nylon ropes looped around the log at each end. The part that scared me was getting the ridgepole from the wall to the tops of the gables. The peaks of the gables were fourteen feet above our floor, seven feet above the top wall logs.

Sheila and I leaned poles against the top of the south wall at each end of the cabin to serve as ramps. With much huffing and puffing, we dragged and levered the ridgepole log into place at the bottom of the ramps, placing it so the big end of the ridgepole would extend eighteen inches beyond the back gable.

I walked up the hill behind the cabin, stalling, while pretending to study the situation. I didn't like what I saw: There was too much log and too much gable and not enough man. At best, it seemed, I'd get one shot at lifting the big end from the top of the wall to the top of the gable. But a lot could go wrong once I was leaning toward the gable, lifting the butt end of the log level with my belt, and then, if I was strong enough, pushing it above my head. Even standing safely on the ground, I could feel my movements getting jerky. I was short of breath and realized how scared I was about what we were doing.

I looped a length of nylon rope around each end of the log and threw the ends of both ropes over the wall on the north side of our cabin, where I tied off one end of each rope to logs in the cabin's corners.

"Let's try pulling our lines straight back," I said and handed Sheila the free end of the rope looped around the light end of the ridgepole. I took the heavy end, and we pulled the slack from our ropes and backed up a step. We pulled hand-over-hand a couple times and backed up again, and as we moved away from the cabin, the ridge-pole log rolled up our ramps, turning smoothly like a long wheel inside the looped ropes, just as the illustration in one of our books had promised. We pulled until the ridgepole log came to rest, kerplonk, atop the south wall. That part of the process seemed almost too easy.

After a smoke and a short rest, I looked from the ridgepole log to the tops of the gables. "Are we ready?" I asked.

"I don't know!" Sheila said, sounding spooked herself. "Let's try it."

I tied one end of a rope around the ridgepole, about four feet from the big end, climbed the rear gable and draped the rope over the cradle on top. I positioned Sheila on the hill beyond the cabin's back wall, which I thought would give her a straight pull and more leverage on her end of the rope.

"Just pull slow and steady," I said.

I stooped atop the wall in a deep squat and lifted, sliding the butt end of the ridgepole up the gable slope to my knees, then my waist. Sheila hauled on her end of the rope, and the log slid up the gable until it was level with my shoulders. She kept tension on the safety line, and after a couple deep breaths, I pushed the log farther up the slope. "Easy!" I said, gulping air. "Easy!"

My neck and shoulders and outstretched arms burned, and as I gripped the gable logs with my thighs, my knees jack-hammered under me. Then the ridgepole slid into place in the cradle I'd carved in the top log, and I could breathe again.

I climbed up the gable and tapped in a temporary spike on each side of the ridgepole then bound the tops of the spikes together with several wraps of tie wire.

I looked down at Sheila. I felt light-headed and silly, resolute and more than a little brave when Sheila shook her fist at me and grinned.

We moved the safety rope to the other end of the ridgepole, and while Sheila pulled, I stood on the loft floor and slid the light end of the ridgepole part way up; I shifted my grip and pushed the log into place atop the gable.

Again, I set two temporary spikes and wired them together for safety, then we took our lunch and climbed the hill behind the cabin for our noon break.

"I really didn't know if we could get it up there," I said, as Sheila opened our lunch sack.

"Well, you most definitely could. Just look at it now." Sheila keyed open a tin of sardines. Below, the ridgepole ran like an arrow from one end of our cabin to the other.

"I think we are going to do this thing," I said.

"Of course we are," Sheila said, dangling a sardine above my open mouth as if I were a seal needing a treat.

After lunch, I scrambled up and sat on the light end of the ridgepole, countersunk two holes part way down for spikes, and drove the spikes home.

As I worked on the ridgepole, Sheila took a snapshot with her Instamatic. I remember her standing there in the sunlight with the uplifted camera to her eye. I heard the click of the camera's lens. Of the things I've accomplished, large and small, in the years since the day we raised our ridgepole, few memories have remained as vivid as the moment when I looked along the length of that log, running as it did then, in a bright level line from one end of our cabin to the other. And I can think of no single event that has given me more confidence when I've had to face other precarious situations. It is odd, however, that in memory, I'm working at the east gable when the camera's shutter opened and closed. But in the photograph, I'm at the west end, boring a hole in the log's butt with our brace and bit.

There was glory in that ridgepole, up fourteen feet in the air, and as I squeezed the gable between my thighs and looked down at Sheila, I said, "Punkin, we ain't grad students any more."

TWENTY-FOUR

We decided to celebrate the ridgepole with a day off. The money from Sheila's grandma gave us enough cash for a long-overdue shopping trip to town, so the next day we washed up and headed north to Prince George for lumber, hardware, groceries, and fun.

At the bright new supermarket, we stocked up on sardines, cornmeal, sardines, peanut-butter and jelly, spuds, and sardines. Then we added another ten cans of sardines. We hit the hardware store for a fifty-pound box of ten-penny nails and twenty-five pounds of roofing nails, three heavy-duty strap hinges for our door, and four buckets of tar. At the lumberyard we scored some nice 2x10 planks and a big roll of construction-grade plastic sheeting.

We stopped for lunch that day at a strange burger stand called McDonalds, where a sign out front claimed millions of hamburgers sold. The hamburgers were mashed buns hiding a slab of gray meat, covered with a limp slice of cheese. A mysterious goop dripped from the burgers into our laps. We swore McDonalds would never sell us another burger, ever, but we went back inside for soft ice cream cones, the fancy ones with a swirl on top. Soft ice cream from a machine had come to Prince George, and we saw that soft ice cream from a machine was good.

In a final gesture of extravagance, we hid our supplies under our tarp and entered the theater at the new mall for an afternoon matinee of "Little Big Man." Two hours of Dustin Hoffman, Chief Dan George, and—oh, my God, Faye Dunaway, as Mrs. Pendrake—topped off with a tub of buttered popcorn, seemed about as good as any combination of drugs I could imagine. It was a glorious day of city over-kill, so intoxicating after those long, sober weeks in the bush, and not in the least diminished, when we checked our mail in Hixon on the way home that evening, by the arrival of a letter, forwarded on by my mother, from my draft board in Helena.

The board had been nice enough to send out letters to those of us in limbo, informing us that the United States Congress had, in fact, temporarily failed to renew induction festivities. The board would be in touch, the letter said, as soon as its bottleneck was eliminated, and the assembly line to boot camp could again be put in motion. In the meantime, an enclosed form requiring updated information was to be filled out and returned within ten business days.

A few days later, caught up in a moment of silliness, I posted a polite note along with the Selective Service form to my draft board, saying that I was having the time of my life up in Canada, living in sin with a family of muskrats, deep in a secret north woods bog, where the fishing was good and the living easy. I closed by offering to take board members out for trout or grouse, should they ever come our way.

We had been hearing strange news reports on Canadian radio about secret United States government documents dealing with the history of the Vietnam War. It seemed that a man named Ellsberg had copied several thousand pages of documents stamped "Top Secret (Sensitive)." Ellsberg had then given those copies to the *New York Times*, which had begun publishing them earlier that summer. These papers, it seemed, disclosed that from Truman to Nixon, each administration had publicly claimed one set of reasons for our involvement in Vietnam, ("containment" and the "Domino Theory" for example) while secretly pursuing completely different purposes related to US domestic politics, the most obvious being the Cold War fear among elected government officials, especially members of Congress, of appearing "soft" on communism.

Ike said we had to protect our rubber interests in Vietnam. That pragmatism was soon transposed into the fairytale mission of protecting the freedom of the South Vietnamese people. Even as extreme corruption in the Diem government in South Vietnam was exposed, President Kennedy allowed American involvement to escalate, saying, "We also have to participate—we may not like it—in the defense of Asia." Kennedy then looked the other way when President Diem was assassinated with the involvement of our own ambassador in Saigon and the CIA.

Lyndon Johnson told his great lie to the United States Congress—which led to the Gulf of Tonkin Resolution in 1964. The Gulf of Tonkin Resolution gave Johnson the authority to use conventional US armed forces in Vietnam without an official declaration of war from Congress. From there the American military involvement in Vietnam began its rapid escalation. Daniel Ellsberg exposed all that—or enough of it that Americans could finally get a true picture of the war they at first supported.

The Ellsberg documents revealed a credibility gap the size of the Pacific Ocean between what the United States government told us and its actual reasons for conducting the war. Hundreds of thousands of Americans my age had been sent off, many to their deaths, in the service of these lies. By 1971, most small communities across our country had at least one hometown son killed in action, and others sent home damaged beyond repair. Mr. Ellsberg had the spine and the moral wherewithal to expose the lies. And my man, Senator Mike Gravel, had the guts to enter some four thousand pages of these "Pentagon Papers" into the *Congressional Record* by way of his Sub-committee for Buildings and Grounds.

In the mornings, on our way up to the cabin, we often stopped at a radio sweet-spot near the beaver ponds where we occasionally saw our cow moose. Certain cosmic lines apparently converged there making radio reception especially clear, so we were sometimes able to catch the news coming our way from Seattle or Vancouver. It was there that we first learned of Henry Kissinger's secret negotiations with China to prepare the way for Nixon's visit to that communist nation the following year, even as Americans were still fighting Communism in Vietnam.

One morning, when we stopped to listen to the latest Pentagon Papers disclosures, we noticed fresh patties in the road ahead, recently deposited there by Dahlstroms' cows. Each green mound was covered by a hovering cloud of blue butterflies. The radio announcer explained that even after a recent US Supreme Court decision in favor of Senator Gravel's actions to make the Pentagon Papers part of our nation's permanent historical record, Daniel Ellsberg (in our view, a national hero) was going to be tried by the Justice Department for high crimes, maybe even treason. That morning's news seemed as incongruous as beautiful blue butterflies flocking to fresh cowshit. In our brave new world, it was now a high crime, perhaps treason, to reveal the truth about fraud and deception in the United States government.

But the news, as so often happened back then, seemed too awful or absurd to absorb without first hiding behind the shield of mockery.

"Sheila!" I said, thumping the steering wheel with my hand, "our government has been lying to Americans all this time about the liberty of rubber in Southeast Asia and the secret mission of blue butterflies to enslave the freedom-loving peoples of the world!"

"Sir, I'm as shocked as you yourself must be," Sheila said, transforming herself into a wide-eyed bumpkin from somewhere like Two Dot, Montana.

"Why have these butterflies decided to wage a war of aggression on fresh manure?"

"A mystery beyond the powers of a liberal-arts education," Sheila said. "We should have studied political science, or, better yet, chemistry and math. Then we could build rockets instead of silly old log cabins."

On the radio: "From Vancouver, today's weather: Clear and mild in the Interior. Gale warnings in the Georgia Strait."

The butterflies rose and resettled as I steered the El Camino around their patties.

"This much is certain," Sheila said. "I need some vanilla ice cream from a machine."

Since our day in Prince George, ice cream had come to stand for all that was most desirable in our world. Blue butterflies, on the other hand, would soon become scrambled in our minds with The Pentagon Papers. Blue butterflies, as we came to understand them, were the wee beautiful beings in America's grand myth of itself, hovering above Henry Kissinger as he grumbled in his B-movie-monster voice; they were the halo of lies and betrayals in Richard Nixon's hair, as he flashed his V-for-Victory salutes. Shit-loving butterflies became our metaphor for all that fed upon the smelly things in our native land that were not as nice as our nation's leaders might pretend. Ice cream, however, was about what was cool, sweet, and good. Ice cream from a machine just might be worth fighting for.

But news of the Pentagon Papers, while not the least bit funny, was exciting. Maybe, just maybe, the veil of lies and secrecy was being pulled aside. The history and politics of the Vietnam War were fiendishly complicated, the truth about American involvement so long obscured by the steady drip of propaganda and dissemination. If Americans chose to be informed, if they chose to be more than Fourth of July patriots, who closed their eyes to the nation's crimes even as they sent their sons and daughters off to war, they had to stand up at some point and say NO, which brought us full circle, from a chance encounter with shit-eating butterflies and the radio news, back to us. Even in another country, as we were then, the Vietnam War was still a storm of great power, a fearsome gale howling in distant straits.

In order to save the twenty dollars for another month's rent at the Douglas place, we decided to get as much roof over our heads at the Mac as possible, so we could move in before the 15th of September. In two days, we cut notches in our gables for the purlin logs—logs which would run parallel to the ridgepole from one end of the cabin to the other—to support roof boards. Working together with looped ropes, we raised the beautifully straight purlin logs into place. Four purlins ran below the ridgepole on each side of the roof and extended eight feet out beyond the cabin's front wall to support a porch roof.

Next came the roof boards. Sheila measured and cut to length odd boards and passed them up to me. And she nailed off the bottom end of each 1x4 to the lowest purlin. At one point, as I sat straddling the ridgepole, I found myself watching her as she sawed off a 1x4. Although we'd been together nearly every day, I was surprised by how much she had changed. No fat ankles now, Bucko, I thought. Just look at her! All vestiges of the baby fat she'd once carried were gone, except, of course, for her marvelous breasts. She had slimmed down and hardened up, and she was obviously stronger, clearly more sure of herself as she moved. Her rolling limp had all but disappeared. My God, I thought, we've created a monster! The new Sheila came up a rickety scrap-lumber ladder toward me, a lean young woman with dimples in her cheeks, a claw hammer in her belt, and nails on her lip.

She noticed me sitting there with my legs all adangle, and when she smiled at me, I realized with a jolt that Mac Watson had been right. She *was* beautiful, so fresh and open-faced. And right then I understood something. One of the things that had first attracted me to her—way back in Mac's Shakespeare class—was her ability to think quickly and to articulate precisely what she thought. Sheila had been precocious, true, but she also had a quick perceptive way of seeing and understanding almost simultaneously, that set her apart from the other intelligent people I knew. Sure, smart is sexy, I got that. But what surprised me then, up there on our ridgepole, was just how vulnerable I was to Sheila's brand of acuity when it was coupled with her physical radiance. She waved her hammer at me, smiled again, and tapped a nail into a 1x4. When she lowered her head to drive the nail, I noticed how the morning sun fired the highlights in her hair. From that angle, as from so many others, she seemed to me to be one of a kind, a sweet and beautiful original.

I walked down to the creek one afternoon to fill our water jug. In the fine sand left beside the creek by high water that spring, I noticed some tracks.

Dog, I thought. I bent down and placed my hand in the damp sand next to the track. The track was an inch or more longer than the palm of my hand and about the same width. Some dog, I thought.

Music helped keep us moving, so we took the transistor radio with us during the days, and we sang along with our favorite songs as we worked. Wings's "Uncle Albert/Admiral Halsey," which we did not understand, and Roy Orbison's "Pretty Woman," which we did, both kicked up our energy, especially during those sunny afternoons, when a nap on warm pine tags seemed so inviting. "Is she walking back to me? Yeah, she's walking back to me!" When Roy sang, we stopped our hammering and sawing to listen. And at the sudden ending, we shouted, "pretty woman!" along with him. We liked Roy's ardor, and we laughed every time.

There were so many good songs that fall, from the hillbilly retro of Jerry Reed's "When You're Hot, You're Hot," to Freddy Hart's "Easy Lovin'," from the ethereal magic of John Lennon and the Plastic Ono Band's "Imagine," to love ballads like "Don't Pull Your Love" by Hamilton, Joe Frank and Reynolds. We sang along with CCR's "Have You Ever Seen the Rain," and when Richie Havens ripped through " Here Comes the Sun," we felt like we could fly.

The 1x4s, once nailed down, took the limberness out of the ridgepole and purlins. When we were a third of the way across, I took to walking on the roof boards instead of the climbing the purlins. I got braver and hustled up and down the slick boards until one afternoon, while jogging down for another stick, I got tangled up in my own feet, and did some kind of forward somersault as I peeled off the roof. I landed in soft duff, jumped right up, and did a crazy little sideways dance, before my sense of balance returned. Sheila, who saw the whole thing, said I somehow managed to turn in mid-air to avoid landing on a stump that was directly in my path. We were young and limber and quick as mercury, and I wanted to believe that I had the kind of athletic ability needed to turn in mid-air to miss stumps. So I grinned and said, "Sure.

Of course," as if I'd meant to do it. We laughed, but it wasn't funny. A broken arm or dislocated shoulder would have been the end of us in Canada, and the fall spooked me. I went back to the roof determined to put more thought into what I was doing with my feet.

In early September, we caught a run of dry sunny days—days when we started out with jackets in the morning and were down to T-shirts before ten o'clock. We found a rhythm, and three-and-a-half inches at a time we narrowed the open space above the cabin's floor. We still had a big pile of 1x4s down on the old skid trail, and to take breaks from the roof and to stretch our legs, we ferried boards up through the trees and stacked them on the south side of the cabin. When we emerged from the trees into our clearing, the bright log walls and white boards of the widening roof gave us a thrill. Sometimes we stopped with stacks of lumber on our shoulders to just stand and admire our work. There it was, plumb and level and true, the log-ends beyond the corner notches, so interesting in their staggered lengths and random angles. We had made that beautiful thing together, were making it, one log and board at a time. Seeing it there, in that place we'd discovered together, gave us great joy.

Our plan was to stretch clear Visqueen construction plastic over the naked roof boards just as soon as we had the roof sheathed, to keep the inside of the cabin and our things dry when we moved up from the Douglas place. We also needed to get Uncle Gideon's cook stove—that Sam and I had carried to the cabin through the woods—inside the cabin and functioning as soon as possible. Then Sheila suggested it might be wise to get our finished floor nailed down and painted before we moved anything inside. That made sense, but as the days got shorter, we seemed to make our job list longer.

Sometimes, during our days working at the Mac, we had to jog off into the bush to answer the call. Squatting in the woods was part of our normal routines, Sheila going off in one direction, and I in another when the need arose. One afternoon I headed toward my usual area north of the cabin, around the corner of a rocky ledge on the steep slope above Government Creek. I'd pulled my jeans down and was hunkering there in my bower of bliss, thinking about Dryden, Pope, or Johnson, when I caught movement on the slope above me from the corner of my eye. Startled, I turned as much as I could, with my jeans down around my boots, and I saw a mushroom the size of a saucer coming top-first down through the trees toward me. It bumped over roots and dodged around stumps and rocks, gliding along through the moss as if with a mind of its own. I was trying to not fall over backwards down the hillside while pulling up my jeans, when I noticed the mushroom had a bushy tail lofting along above it. Reefer Madness? An acid flashback? Some awful retribution for my indulgences? As I staggered about, tugging at my pants, the mushroom turned to contour across the hill just above me, a pine squirrel zooming along behind, pushing his prize toward a secret winter cache. I took it as a sign. The little dude knew the score, which was work now or starve later.

It was true about our job list: The more we got done, the more there was to do. Besides getting a roof on the cabin, another chore on the list was "Chinking." The most common form of chinking—that is, filling the gaps between logs, both inside and out—was done with mortar. The log buildings at my grandfather's ranch had first been chinked with old-time lime-and-sand mortar, which was later covered with a much stronger mud made with washed sand, lime, and Portland cement. Portland Cement, I knew, came in ninety-pound bags. Mortar chinking for a cabin as big as ours would require a lot of ninety-pound bags and a dump truck load of clean masonry sand. That simply would not work for us. We found our solution in one of the log-cabin-building books that we continued to check out in Prince George, a solution called "quarter-round chinking," which involved sawing poles, about four inches in diameter, lengthwise into four long strips, so that from the ends, each piece looked like a fat piece of pie, a forty-five degree angle on the inside and a nice round outside. The wedge-shaped inside of each stick was then tapped snug between two wall logs and nailed in place.

When these quarter-rounds were put between wall and gable logs, inside and out, they would hide the pink fiberglass insulation and stop up the biggest spaces, acting to block off drafts. What the quarter-round solution boiled down to was the need to peel a big pile of poles, then to saw each of them into four sticks. We already had quite a few poles, which we'd cut and ricked up in lengths as we'd cleared the opening for the cabin. We sawed a couple quarter-rounds and tried fitting them between the logs in the back wall, where they seemed to work just fine. Not as airtight as mortar but good enough and close enough. Sheila agreed to peel the poles, a few at a time when she had time to spare. My job would be to saw the peeled poles lengthwise into quarters with Sam's little Homelite, then nail them in place.

TWENTY-FIVE

Sheila dropped me off at Dahlstroms' place before heading to town with her list of errands: books to return to the Prince George library, a stop at the hardware store for rolls of fifteen-pound tar paper, three gallons of primer, three gallons of enamel floor paint, plus rollers and brushes.

Herb had the wooden sides on his big truck and his tools already loaded when we pulled in, and he and I were rolling before Sheila's dust had settled. We drove to a grove of poplar, surrounded by bush, unloaded our tools and water jug, and set to.

Firewood cutting in British Columbia was an odd business, it seemed to me. For example, folks there burned green birch—the greener the better—for super-hot kitchen range fires, and they used poplar, which they cut green in the fall and aged just a month or two before using it to bank their night fires during the winter. Dry aspen and standing-dead pine were mixed in with the poplar and birch in combinations I did not begin to understand. But in country where snow piled up to the eaves of houses, I figured these folks knew what they were doing.

Herb said he wanted to thin this particular stand of poplars and explained that poplar was a low-heat fuel that worked best when mixed with dry aspen and pine. He used it, he said, because he had a lot of it that was easy to get at on flat ground. Herb's plan that morning was to fall trees with his ancient blue Homelite, then block the logs into stove-length rounds just as soon as I'd limbed the fallen trees with his single-bitted axe. I would then load the blocks he cut onto his ton-and-a-half truck. Herb said that he and Clint would later split the wood at their winter woodpile as it was needed.

Herb set to throwing trees, which were tall and almost limbless for the first twenty or thirty feet. Once he had a few on the ground I went along, lopping limbs and kicking slash out of the way, opening up a trail so we could back the big truck farther into the woods as we worked. Herb's Homelite purred along, smoking a thin blue fog, and the morning sunlight slanted down through the canopy of leaves overhead, setting the bush around us ablaze with colors. The sawdust and cut wood filled the morning air with heady spices, and I heard my bell ringing.

I found myself waiting while Herb sawed the poplar logs into blocks, so instead of just loading the rounds, I tried splitting the blocks as they lay on their sides right there on the ground. The green poplar was straight-grained and heavy, and I was surprised at how easily the rounds popped in half. I walked backwards, splitting the biggest halves down into quarters, then gathered arm-loads of halves and quarters and pitched them up into the truck. We worked without stopping until the Homelite ran out of gas. Herb's expression of surprise, when he put down his saw, straightened up, and noticed his truck filling with split wood instead of rounds was worth my extra effort. Neither of us had ever tried to split wood like that before, but with green poplar, it worked.

Herb was man enough to call a halt now and then for a smoke, whether he was paying wages by the hour or not. When we stopped to roll our cigarettes that morning I said, "Herb, I saw some awful big dog tracks in the sand beside the creek below our cabin the other day."

Herb licked off his cigarette and looked over at me. "How big was the track?" he asked.

I held the palm of my right hand up toward him and with the index finger of my left hand indicated the space between the heel of my hand and the first knuckle of my middle finger. "And about as wide as my palm," I said. The leaves on aspen and poplar tapped and fluttered above us; spruce and snow brush cast darker shades of green here and there in the bush. I lit my smoke and noticed that some shrubs in the understory had begun to turn colors, a few already gone red, others to yellow and tan.

"So he's back," Herb said. Then he told me about his nemesis, a lone male wolf that traveled a big swath of country to the north, who sometimes turned up after the first hard frosts to follow Herb's trap lines for the snacks Herb's baits provided. "He's slick," Herb said. "One year, he ran me plumb off my lines. I can't catch him, and after a while, a fella gets tired of hanging bait just to keep him fat. I sure hope he gets old before I do."

Herb had seen the wolf only once in seven years. It was in mid-winter, while Herb was crossing Government Lake on snowshoes. Herb had his lever gun with him, a 300 Savage with iron sights, and when he saw the wolf come out of the timber onto the lake, running broadside to him far out on the ice, Herb took a couple off-hand shots at him. "He was black, and he was big," Herb said. "When I checked his trail, I could see I'd hit ten yards short of him, both shots. "But I wanted to let him know that I was back there."

Herb didn't make the wolf sound evil or sinister, like the wolves in our fairy tales. If anything, it seemed to me Herb admired that rangy old scout. But there was something in the quiet way Herb described that scene, the frozen lake, the flat, gray winter light and the deep, mid-winter cold: I could hear the boom and echo of the rifle, and I could see the wolf, way out there on the ice, traveling in his easy, ground-eating lope. It made the hair on my arms stand up. Herb Dahlstrom's wolf story was, I think, as close as I ever came to the wild Yukon where Sergeant Preston called to his huskies in my mother's radio.

During our lunch break, Herb told me about his winter trapping business. He owned the fur-trapping patent to a vast chunk of hill-country bush and big-woods north of the Hidden Meadows, that he trapped full-time during the winter months. He concentrated on weasel, pine martin, beaver, otter, lynx, fisher, and wolf. "If you want," Herb said, "I'll show you how I work a line, once the weather turns off cold."

The sky that morning above the poplars was the electric blue we would see so often that fall, the early morning air snappy, yet shirt-sleeve warm by mid-day. That particular morning was one of those rare ones, a day that seems to swing, as if on great hinges, between the seasons, one of those happy, consecrated days, when work and weather, place and good company, all come together to make something a man will remember with clarity for forty years and more. Even while working hard enough to sweat through my shirt, I knew how special the day was, and how lucky I was to be there in a poplar grove, working with my friend, Herb Dahlstrom.

Day after day that fall, I would look up from my work at the Mac or from some job while working with Herb, to be spiked by the beauty around me and filled with a child-like sense of delight in that new world. I guessed, even then, that I was feeling something of what Lawrence Ferlinghetti had been saying in his great all-American poem. "And I am waiting/for linnets and planets to fall like rain . . . and I am perpetually waiting/for the fleeing lovers on the Grecian Urn/to catch each other up at last/and embrace/and I am awaiting/perpetually and forever/a renaissance of wonder." And I knew. I knew right then, as I knew other days that fall, that *my* waiting lay behind me. This was *my* time. At such moments, I'd pull a big lungful of air and open my eyes wide, certain, in the freshness of it all, that there was nowhere else on Earth filled with such wonder.

We needed 1x6 pine boards to make our finished floor, so the next morning we drove again to the Netherlands Overseas mill in Hixon, where our friend the forklift guy, sold us a partial bunk. The rest of the morning we carried our 1x6s to the cabin on our shoulders. While walking back to the truck for more boards, Sheila mentioned a girl she'd picked up hitch-hiking in Prince George the day before. The girl, who was a Canadian living with a draft dodger from the States, said she thought the government was cracking down on Americans evading the draft in Canada, or at least in BC. There had been some petty crimes—shoplifting of food, mostly, a pot bust or two—involving hapless, stoner-type dodgers, who likely would have been busted, sooner or later, for the same infractions in Iowa or Oregon. The arrests had received enough negative press to focus public attention on Americans living outside the system, including people like me—who were working illegally and paying no taxes.

Why, those American no-goods! They were stealing *jobs* from Canadians! Taking food from Canadian babies' mouths, and they were paying no taxes!

Paying no taxes? No taxes? And suddenly even the dullest apparatchik in pro-vincial government saw a threat to the treasury that wrote his paycheck. Something would have to be done to stop this invasion of American busboys, fruit pickers, and swampers! Which seemed kind of funny to Sheila and I, because almost everyone we'd met then living in BC had immigrated from the United States.

That evening we stopped to tell Ken and Lila Glaze that we planned to move out of the Douglas place, a day or two before our next month's rent was due in mid-September. We explained to them that although we still had no roof, windows, door, or finished floor, we figured being there around the clock would give us more time to work on the cabin each day. We knew bad weather could make it miserable, we said, but we were feeling lucky.

Ken was oddly quiet, not his usual, windy self. I noticed that he didn't make eye contact. At some point in our brief conversation he said, "I hear you're working for Dahlstrom, now."

I said yes, that was true. I'd been helping Herb with odds and ends.

"Before you move out over there, I want you to replace all the wood you used from the shed," Ken said, abruptly.

We had probably used a pickup load of stove wood for cooking and heat at the Douglas place while we were living there. Replacing it sounded fair to me. "Sure," I said. "Of course. But would it be all right to do that later this fall? We're trying to get a roof over our heads right now."

Ken didn't say yes and he didn't say no, but I could see it nettled him to trust me. I brushed it aside, impatient to get home to our supper, in no mood to fuss with him over a little jag of stove wood that would take me one after-noon to cut. "We'll get that wood back in the shed for you by the first snow," I told him. "For sure."

"That was very strange," Sheila said as we drove away. "Did you two have a problem while I was in Montana?"

"No. We got along fine. I guess Ken was hoping we'd rent a while longer."

"He seemed upset about something."

"Himrongs and such," I said, and Sheila snorted.

But she didn't let it go. "We shouldn't blow this off," Sheila said. "Something is out of kilter with Glaze, and we should find out what it is. We're going to be neighbors, after all."

"Except for the stove wood we used, I can't think of anything we've done that would be a problem. And I will get that wood for him, like I said."

Sheila's instincts proved right. We would never know what, exactly, was bothering Ken Glaze, but it was enough, whatever it was, to eventually have consequences for us.

We went back to work on our roof. The mid-day shadow from the new boards overhead crept across the floor until it slid onto the sleeping loft. It was a happy time for us, with lots of music and sunshine and progress we could see, Sheila cutting and passing boards to me, as I scrambled back and forth from one side of the roof to the other, to nail them in place. When our roof reached the front gable, we kept going, following the purlins for another four feet beyond the front wall. We planned to extend the porch roof even further, once we had posts and beams in place to support a bigger roof properly.

We swept up sawdust and chips from the sub-floor, and when we had it as clean as possible, we unrolled the fifteen-pound tarpaper and tacked it in place with roofing nails to the sub-floor's 2x6s. The tarpaper, our library books said, would act as a moisture and draft barrier. It would also make the upper floor a tad bit warmer in cold weather.

Once we had the tarpaper in place, we worked our way from the back wall toward the door, nailing down our 1x6 boards over the tarpaper. This new layer of boards really stiffened the floor, and made a big difference in the way it felt when we stomped back and forth in our work boots. I nailed down the boards, staggering the cut ends for added strength, and Sheila followed along beside me with a nail-set, tapping the heads of the nails down just below the surface of the wood. Our knees got tender and our backs stiffened up and our necks hurt, but our new floor seemed so clean and firm and grand that when we had it all nailed down nice and tight, we marched up and down, back and forth, swinging our arms like toy soldiers as we chanted, "Hup ho! Tickity tock! Our floor is solid as a rock!"

The forecast was for dry weather, and there was no morning dew to speak of, so while Sheila brushed on primer around the edges, where the floor met the walls, I rolled primer onto the rest of the floor. We let the paint dry for a day, then rolled on a thin first coat of pale green enamel, which dried nicely in the warm shade under our roof boards. A day later we rolled on the topcoat of enamel and decided to let it dry for forty-eight hours before moving anything indoors. The days had run together quickly while we had our heads down working on the floor. When we looked up, it was time to cart our possibles from the Douglas place to the cabin.

In two trips we moved everything we owned. We spent the last morning at the Douglas place mucking out the cabin, making an effort to leave it cleaner than when we'd moved in. We took a last quiet walk around the meadow; the flowers were gone, and the timothy had tanned. The place had been good to us in a rough-handed way. While there, our first infatuation with each other had grown into something else: a partnership blessed with a happy affection and a gladness for each other's company. As we said good-bye to Mrs. Douglas in her meadow, we sensed that things would never again be quite the same.

At the Mac, we piled our things outside and covered it all with plastic so we could stay off our new floor. There was so much to be done, so many big jobs as well as all the odds and ends, that we simply attacked whatever lay right in front of us. We carried up the last of the 1x4s from the old skid trail, and we cleared a spot along the edge of the south tree line for the woodshed we planned to build, and we put down the first courses of small, unpeeled logs for our outhouse.

We slept on the ground our first night at the Mac, spreading our bedrolls on one half of our old US Army tarp, which we then folded back over us from our feet up to our chins. As the twilight faded, we crawled into our sleeping bags to watch stars blink on above the opening we'd carved in the forest. The water in Government creek was low by then, and the stream ran quiet in the windless night. Sheila found my hand with hers and gave it a good squeeze. "It seems like such a long time since we slept under the stars our first night in Colorado," she said. And so it did. Lots of miles and lots of sweat from that night, when our journey began, to this place, where a log cabin stood luminous in the starlight, clearly visible against the darker timber beyond. We had packed a lot of living into just four months, and along the way, we'd made something big with very little. We were together there in the moment, holding hands and talking in low voices, and that strange expansive feeling flooded through me again, the feeling I'd had on the morning of the geese near Revelstoke and again the day Herb Dahlstrom told me about the wolf crossing Government Lake on the ice. I was filled with certainty, as we lay there looking into the night sky, that this particular evening was an event that we would carry with us, together or apart, as long as we lived.

We watched the stars move in the heavens, and Sheila told me about scientific discoveries her sister, Marilyn, had come across in the extensive reading she did. One phenomenon Marilyn had described to Sheila was called a "black hole." We looked into the great night of British Columbia, as Sheila explained that out there, far beyond the darkness we peered into, vast maelstroms of super-dense material inhaled all matter within their reach. Nothing escaped these pits of darkness, not even light. It was all news to me, this business of neutron stars and supernovas and gravitationally-collapsed objects, and I felt as if I had stepped into an old, hand-dug well at night, to fall with dizzying velocity until I became nothing. I was lost in a new sense of how small and inconsequential we were, in the grand scheme of things, when the first field mouse ran through Sheila's hair.

Sheila squeaked and reared up, slapping at her head. I flicked on the flashlight in time to see the little guy scooting off into the duff. We laughed and settled down again and were growing quiet when another mouse decided to build a nest in my beard. Then another zipped across Sheila's face. There suddenly seemed to be a considerable amount of activity at ground level in this one small clearing in the woods. Then it dawned on us that our carelessness over the summer, with bread crusts and such, had made us a certain number of new friends. Several times each evening the mice would seek out the warmth of our sleeping bags or my beard or Sheila's hair. During the next few nights we almost got used to them.

The mice were a tease in the great comfort we felt during those first nights in the forest, when, in our happiness and fatigue, we lay with our fingers laced together under an old army tarp, looking into a sky brilliant with stars. We talked about distance and trajectory and time, and we wondered what parabolas our lives would scribe before winking out in all that dark. So strange, that we'd first found ourselves holding hands in a theater, while watching an epic film about space travel, to feel her hand again those nights in our clearing, when she had become what I had in all the world that mattered most.

Our talk drifted off as our eyes grew heavy. A night chill passed across our faces, and small creatures rustled in the woods. I watched the autumn sky turn above the clearing we'd made and wondered if our cabin was as vast and miraculous to our friends the mice, as the Milky Way in the far-yonder was to us. And it seemed those evenings, as we pitched into the deep well of sleep, that our cabin rose like a magical craft, like a sky-voyaging clipper ship or wooden shoe under full sail, coursing, as it would forever through our best dreams, "on a river of crystal light, into a sea of dew."*

---

* "Wynken, Blynken, and Nod" by Eugene Field

TWENTY-SIX

The second floor of an appalling cinderblock-and-glass office building in Prince George, one of those Sixties-modern turquoise rectangles that architects must have once thought contemporary. In their execution, there in the Canadian north woods, such structures managed to radiate a sense of having been built by forced labor in a wasteland inhabited by convicts, somewhere in the vast taiga of Stalin's Siberia.

Through the big door, then, to the hushed ticking of typewriters in fluorescent spaces beyond a counter, where one might, after a period of shifting from one foot to the other, come face-to-face with the local Episcopal minister's wife, a grandmotherly type of vast good cheer, who, when she was quite ready, would ask how she might be of help.

I turned on the charm. "I'm interested in immigrating to Canada, Mum," I said. "Can you please give me the appropriate forms and guidelines, please?"

I assumed the lady opposite me was a worker-bee, one of millions in bureaus everywhere, doing thankless jobs while sinking to their eyeballs in bogs of ennui. She stooped with some effort—she seemed a little breathless when she straightened—to produce from under the counter a cluster of forms and instructions, even a big envelope to hold it all. When I asked for an additional set of forms to use as worksheets, she complied, rearing up before me the second time, quite pink in the jowls.

"Will there be anything *else?*" she asked.

"Oh, no. Thank you. This will be lovely."

"Tourists?" she said.

217

There I stood in logger boots, my jeans and chambray shirt stiff with pitch and OFF! bug spray. There might have been sawdust in my hair. Any fool could see I'd been sleeping in the woods and living on roots and berries.

"Visiting," I said, tensing as I felt for the trap with one foot as a coyote might. "Love your country."

"Yes," she said. "Do you have family here in British Columbia?"

"Friends, actually," I said, feeling suddenly damp and dull. I turned toward Sheila, who blinked back at me with an expression of mild alarm.

"And how long have you been in Canada?"

"Well, now, hmmm. . . . Let me see . . . ." And there it was! The steel pan between the jaws of a Victor Number Three, RIGHT THERE! partly hidden under pine needles and leaves. On one jaw, the date we crossed the border from Montana, on the other, the date of my Free Miner's Certificate. "Since June? " I said.

"I see," she said. Then she made involuntary guppy-puckers with her lips.

I couldn't look away from her mouth, which seemed to me like something I wouldn't want to observe too closely, even in an aquarium.

"I'll need to see some identification."

As I dug my Montana driver's license from my wallet, the lady slid a card across the counter. "Fill in your full name, phone number, and current address."

The clerk eyed my driver's license. "This has expired," she said.

Sweet jumping Jesus, I thought. Of course. The license had expired on my birthday in August. What had I been thinking? I would have been nailed by Canadian police at the very first traffic stop for some infraction like a broken tail light. And there was probably no way I could get a Canadian license before achieving landed immigrant status.

I glanced at Sheila. So much in her expression said, *I'm not with this guy!*

I scribbled my name, no phone, general delivery, Hixon, BC, in the appropriate spaces on the card. I was no longer quite so charming. The clerk compared my license with the name I'd written on the form, wrote "driver's license expired" at the bottom of the card and handed my license back to me.

"I have a gold mine," I said.

"I'm sure you do," she said.

Without realizing it at the time, my performance that morning put my card among others just like it in a desk drawer in an office on the second floor of that grotesque building in Prince George, there to incubate and grow.

Mid-morning in the Prince George Library: immigration forms spread across a big table, a dictionary at my elbow, Sheila and I bearing down on a draft of my application for landed immigrant status. We had nowhere else to work, with no furniture whatsoever at the Mac, so there we were, earnest hippie folk in from the bush, scratching away with our Bics. While Sheila read instructions and made a list of materials I'd need, which included high school diploma, college transcripts, birth certificate, and letters of reference, I filled in my basic information, a brief biography, work history, and education. Since Sheila was still married and neither Sheila nor her husband, Jon, seemed to be thinking about an official divorce, we had no status as a couple. I had to apply alone, as a divorced single male. It must have been about then that we began to wonder if Sheila could successfully immigrate on her own, since she had family in Canada.

But, man, didn't those forms just bring all the old raging uncertainties to a boil? Sweaty palms, acid in the belly, a pulse thudding away in my neck, as I attempted, in short simple sentences, to explain why I wanted to immigrate to The Big Frosty. My prose fell short of inspiring, and the reasons I gave for wanting to immigrate seemed simpleminded at best.

What did become clear to me, as I blundered through the forms, was that I did not feel worthy. In fact, I felt absolutely unworthy and unwelcome. And as soon as Sheila and I saw the necessity of pretending, for a bureaucracy we could not even begin to imagine, that I was there in Canada alone, our situation became so much more confusing. Right there a new level of lying began. And we both hated that.

We mailed off a transcript request to Montana State University, and an awkward letter to my folks that went something like this: "Hi, Mom and Dad. The cabin is coming right along. I'm applying for immigrant status here in Canada. Could you send up a copy of my birth certificate, my high school diploma, my brown suit, brown wingtips, and a white shirt and tie so I can dude it up for the interview?" The letter, scratched out on a yellow legal pad, felt to me like asking strangers for handouts on the street. At least we hadn't been reduced to that.

We went to BC Hardware, and our serious shopping began. The big item was a heater stove, and we knew just what we wanted. Airtight heaters were oval-shaped affairs made of rolled tin with crimped seams, about three feet long, two feet high, and eighteen inches wide, that stood ten inches off the floor on flimsy tin legs. It seemed in those days that every hunting camp, garage, calving-shed, and hermit shack had one. They were simple to operate, with a tin flip-top lid that hinged in a single bent metal rod, and a round draft in front that could be adjusted to increase or decrease air flow by turning a tin dial. Airtight heaters were so light that if a person built a fast fire, say with pitch-pine kindling, it was not unusual for the stove to gasp and gulp so hard for air that it would begin to sup-sup, then rattle, and sometimes even try to hop up and down off the floor. Those of us who had learned the finer points of airtight heaters, filled the stove's bottom with two or three inches of sand to add ballast and insulation. Airtights heated and cooled quickly and were hard to bank for all-night fires, but they were cheap, and they would burn anything. Sheila and I chose the top-of-the-line model, a Reeves Airtight by Empire, which had a "liner" inside it made of corrugated metal, that was designed to protect the stove's sides from melting when Cousin Leroy filled his airtight with chunks of railroad ties or maybe some nice creosoted bridge decking. Price: $12.00, Canadian.

To go with our airtight, we bought two 6/12-pitch roof jacks; twenty-five lengths of six-inch "blue" stovepipe; plus sandpaper, five pounds of sixteen-penny (16d) finish nails, a keyhole saw, three feet of 3/8-inch, square steel bar to use as a stove poker, and a brass, ten-ounce plumb-bob.

We also purchased a big roll of window plastic, a thick, clear sheeting designed for greenhouses and backwoods cabins like ours. It was possible to see through it fairly well, even when doubled to create an insulating air space between two sheets. In practice, window plastic kept air from blowing through a shack while giving the outdoors a wobbly, underwater look from within. We couldn't afford glass windows that fall, and besides, Clint Dahlstrom had mentioned that our cabin's half-green logs might shift and twist enough, while curing that first year, to break glass windows. Plastic would have to do until our logs had dried and we had the cash to buy glass. Last on our list was a kindling hatchet for Sheila.

A thin overcast had eased across the Cariboo that afternoon, and, as we drove south from Prince George, a wan, lemon-colored light filtered down, reminding us of November skies we'd seen in Montana. The black cottonwoods along the Fraser River had begun to turn, and a few splashes of yellow showed here and there among the old trees' darker greens. We'd had no frost yet, but clearly, summer was catching the next bus headed south.

Somewhere around the village of Woodpecker, we tuned in a song on the radio. It sounded like a garage band fronted by a wino who smoked three packs a day. "Wake up, Maggie, I think I got something to say to you," he rasped. "It's late September, and I really should be back at school."

Sheila and I glanced at each other. It *was* September, almost "*late* September." It was also the first September—when we stopped to think about it—since we were six years old, that we were at last done with school, with bells in dark hallways, and classrooms where wall clocks refused to move. No wonder we had been feeling so frisky, so fancy free.

"Wow," Sheila said. "Dig this song." And we did. Hapless youth, ensnared by a trickster with wrinkles. But we were above all that; *we* were young, our faces *smooth*, our bodies *hard* and *throbbing* with *sex, sex, sex*. Still, the song, in some unsettling way, seemed to have something to do with us. And the poor bloke singing the song even admits, that when all is said and done, he loves old Maggie anyway.

We laughed a little nervously at Rod Stewart's college boy lament as we zipped, without intending to, right past the turnoff to Coldbanks Road, both of us a little surprised to be missing school and those first weeks of fall quarter on a university campus, where most of the kids wore new shoes and hadn't yet bloated on dorm food. After a bit, we realized where we were and decided to drive on to Hixon for gas and our mail at Thorp's store.

When I'd pumped the tank full, I opened my wallet to discover that we didn't have enough cash left, after our day in Prince George, to pay for gas. Inside, Mrs. Thorp shooed away our embarrassment and asked if we'd like to start an account at the store. "The Dahlstroms speak well of you," she said. "I'm sure it will be fine."

Her gesture struck me as uncommonly generous, especially if one considered our usual pitch-begrimed appearance and bug-repellent smell. I signed the chit that started our account at Thorp's store with a flourish, and we turned back toward the north with our lumber, stove and hardware, along with a letter that had come that day from Mr. D. V. Drew, the Gold Commissioner in Quesnel.

Sheila tore the envelope open as I drove and read aloud: "With reference to your Notice of Intention and Affidavit for Placer Lease. We require three sketches on separate sheets of paper in addition to the Affidavit you submitted. Please forward these drawings to our office, as soon as possible, so we may process your application."

"Notice of intention?" I asked. "Application? Hell, we've already filed for our claim." "We'll have to ask them," Sheila said. "Next time we get down to Quesnel. It's probably just paperwork—nothing to worry about."

We could not have known that afternoon, with the wistful, sepia tone in the September sky, that the Provincial bureaucracy of British Columbia was finding its feet in the Interior, taking some baby steps toward becoming a full-fledged, Kafkaesque hall of mirrors. Had we been paying attention, we might have taken Mr. Drew's letter as a hint of what was yet to come.

I could hear a rustling in the woods—a faint movement in the leaves of the white birch overhead, a patter on the bare roof boards of the cabin. I luxuriated in Sheila's warmth under the shelter of our tarp until I understood what the sounds in the woods meant. I sat up, smelling the rain as the first drops hit my face. The pines around our clearing stood above us in black silhouette against a grey, pre-dawn sky. There was no wind, and the rain fell straight down. Sweet, sweet rain, I thought, then remembered we hadn't yet rolled out the plastic sheeting to cover our roof.

Except for lunch in town the day before, we'd been getting by on sandwiches and sardines while we waited for our floor paint to dry. We didn't mind the cold grub all that much, but we found we could not live without at least one cup of strong coffee in the morning. The woods were very dry, and we hadn't wanted to risk an open fire on the ground, so we'd gone without our morning brew. Those were some grumpy times.

I climbed from my sack, found my socks, and pulled on my jeans. "Up, up!" I said. "We've got rain."

We dressed in a rush, pulled the tarp over our sleeping bags, and attacked our first job, which was to skid Uncle Gideon's kitchen stove, a few inches at a time, up two planks, and through the door opening. It wasn't a big range, but it was heavy and awkward enough for the two of us, as mismatched in size and strength as we were, to get inside and over to the northeast corner of the cabin without scratching our beautiful floor.

The rain stopped before it had even wet our hair, but we'd had our warning. We put the stove where we wanted it, with twenty inches of clearance between it and the two walls in the corner. I climbed onto the stove and dangled our new plumb-bob on its chalk line down from the loft to the middle of the smoke-hole at the back of the stove. By keeping the plumb bob centered there, and letting out string until my hand was up against the loft boards above me, I was able to find and mark the exact center of the hole I needed to cut so the stovepipe could pass through the loft. Working fast, I cut a square sixteen-inch opening with the keyhole saw and framed its edges with 1x4s. Then, hunkered on my knees in the loft, I repeated the process, plumbing up again from the center of the stove's smoke-hole to the underside of the roof. I drove a nail up through the roof board to mark the center of the hole then climbed onto the roof and cut the second hole for our stove pipe.

The pipe came in flat pieces, which had to be rolled into a round shape so the stamped seams along each side could be snapped together. The two-foot sections of pipe could then be joined by sliding the crimped end of one length into the larger, un-crimped end of the next pipe.

Once I had several lengths fitted together into one long pipe, I slipped it up through the openings in the loft and roof and out through the roof jack, the simple tin device used to hold a stove pipe steady and centered in the hole through the roof.

I fitted the crimped end of the bottom length of pipe into the smoke hole at the back of the stove, then climbed onto the roof, placed a short piece of 2x6 across the end of the top pipe and pushed down to seat all the lengths of stovepipe together. Lastly, I centered the stove pipe and roof jack in the hole I'd cut through the roof and nailed the jack's flanges down in place.

I was stuffing balled-up newspapers into the firebox when Sheila came through our door-opening with two, military-surplus jerry cans, which she had dippered half-full of water and toted up from the creek. An empty can weighed seven or eight pounds; with three gallons of water inside, they each weighed twenty-five pounds or more. Sweet Sheila Malone, former graduate student of English Literature, had just carried fifty pounds a hundred yards up the old skid trail, then another seventy-five yards through the woods to our cabin. As I tipped one of the jerry cans to fill our galvanized water bucket, I wondered what had happened to the young lady I'd known in Bozeman. She had apparently decamped for parts unknown, and here, in her place, was this pumped up little stranger wearing a damp T-shirt with no bra underneath, flexing her biceps and grinning at me.

"Coffee, coffee, coffee!" my new friend said.

I added a handful of dry wood shavings and some twigs to the firebox. I struck a farmer match on my jeans and touched it to the paper then added sticks of kindling-sized wood until we had fire. Sheila filled our tin coffee pot and set it on the stove to heat.

We stepped outside. Smoke huffed from the pipe toward the rain clouds churning east above us. We could see fat drops slanting down against the dark timber at the edge of our clearing. "The roof," Sheila said.

"Okay. Right. Let's do it now and have our coffee in a dry cabin."

"Gnnarr!" Sheila said, as she pushed the coffee pot to the middle of the stove.

The Visqueen construction plastic had to be unrolled on the ground then unfolded to its full twenty-four-foot width. Once we had it opened out, we cut off a piece the length of the roof. I climbed up and draped it down the south side of the roof, then tacked a long 1x4 from the ridgepole down to the eve over the plastic at the back of the cabin to hold it in place. Sheila nailed the bottom end of the 1x4 to the roof boards on the eve down below. Working together, we smoothed the plastic and stretched it tight. Backing from west to east, we nailed temporary lengths of 1x4 from the roof's peak to the eve as we went, trying to keep the Visqueen snug. Even a slight breeze would have made the job a lot harder. We got lucky. The rain held off and so did the wind.

Before we started hanging plastic on the north side of the roof, Sheila stoked up the fire and slid our coffee pot back to the firebox side of the stove. I lapped the second sheet of plastic over the plastic already in place at the roof's peak. By the time we had the Visqueen tacked down tight on both sides of the roof, with a hole cut for our stove pipe, we were in need of caffeine and dry clothes. Fat drops popped on the plastic above as we looked from the open doorway to savor the rain and the rising scent of the woods around us.

As soon as we finished our coffee, we uncovered our gear in the yard and carried everything we owned inside. From various bags and boxes, Sheila produced a frying pan, potatoes, and lard, and from a grocery sack some bacon, bread, and eggs that we'd bought the day before in Prince George. Inside the oven we found a wire rack that we could use for making stovetop toast. Such bounty! Hash browns and eggs, bacon and toast with lots of hot coffee! That's the way to do it!

A soft rain fell for a while then tapered off and quit. We lowered the oven door, backed up to the stove's warmth, and stood drinking our coffee as the smells of frying bacon and browning spuds rose from our new stove.

"I love this," I said.

"Me, too," Sheila said. "This is *my* bell you hear ringing."

Although we'd been working steadily on the cabin, the rain goosed us into a higher gear. Our job list continued to get longer, even as we crossed items off. I looked around the empty open space inside of the cabin. Our things lay in a heap in the center of the floor. My God, I thought. We'll have to sit on the floor until we make something to use for a table and chairs. We will have to make *everything*.

Sheila helped me frame in the windows, and she helped stretch the stiff window plastic over 1x4s to make double-paned windows. At first, the double plastic seemed like overkill when we looked at all the pink spaces between the unchinked logs in our walls and the cracks between the roof boards overhead. The windows were slow going and they took patience. If I tried to step up the pace, I mismeasured or let slack creep in as we tried to pull the plastic tight enough to nail in place.

Once the windows were done, we dug into the ricks of poles we'd stacked around the edges of our clearing, setting aside dozens of poles eight feet long and about four inches in diameter, so we could begin the seemingly endless job of chinking.

I sawed a stump off flush with the ground and showed Sheila how to stand a pole on end atop the stump, so she could work her way down from the center, chopping away the bark and rotating the pole as she went, keeping, always, her pole-holding hand well above where the ax struck. The stump acted as an anvil, greatly increasing the hatchet's force, while protecting the cutting edge of the blade from dirt and rocks when Sheila was chopping near the bottom of a pole.

It was one of those things I'd picked up working with my granddad when we cut fence staves and rails at the ranch. I knew the job would be hard on her hatchet hand, and that it would soon get dull and tiresome. "Work up a few, then do something else," I suggested, as I put an edge on Sheila's new hatchet with my oil stone. "I'll get after them, too, a few every day."

"Do I *always* get the bummer jobs?" Sheila asked. "Like outhouse holes?"

"Now that you mention it, we are going to need postholes for our woodshed."

"Ah, you're sweet," she said and put her arms around my waist. I fell for it, of course. Before I knew it, Sheila had pulled my shorts a foot above my belt in back and was dodging off through the stumps, a woodland sprite gone horribly wrong.

Twenty-Seven

"Here it is," Sheila said as she waved a piece of paper she'd located in our files. She was seated at the new plank table we'd made, in the warm light of a kerosene lamp, swinging her feet back and forth under our new plank bench, like a schoolgirl. We'd made our table with lengths of unused cabin logs for legs, bolted to a top of joined 2x12s. It was homely and probably strong enough to support a bull moose.

Our files, mislaid during our move from the Douglas place, consisted of a beat up manila envelope containing half-a-dozen pieces of paper. I looked over Sheila's shoulder. The paper she held was a work copy of forms we'd filled out back in June for our placer-mining claim. Right at the top of the first page it said: Application for Placer Mining Lease. "Hmmmmm . . ." I said. "Application . . . bla bla bla . . . Crown Land . . . bla bla . . . Cariboo Mining District."

"Oh, look," Sheila said and handed me a receipt from "The Province of British Columbia" for $20.00 as the "deposit on an application for a placer mining lease."

Dog-eared to the back of our application work sheet was an early sketch we'd made of our claim in June, which showed the creek running through the east side, a compass heading for the claim's center line, and the overall length and width in feet. Sheila took a blank sheet of typing paper and began drawing a rough duplicate of our original.

"All this time . . ." I said. "All this time, I thought we *had* the claim once we'd filed for it. Isn't that what Harry said? This looks like we just, well, *applied* for the privilege of renting the darned thing."

"Yes, it does," Sheila said. I'll find out tomorrow when I'm down there."

"Sweet Jesus, Punkin. We did all this work and somebody in an office gets to decide—at some unknown future date—if we get to keep our claim or not?" I heard an aggrieved whine in my voice that I didn't particularly like. "Fuck!" I said as I walked to the kitchen-end of the cabin, where the red eye of the stove's draft glowed in the shadows. I raised the front lid to add a stick of wood to the dying fire. "I thought it was too damned good to be true!"

"Settle down. I'll get all the poop on how this works and any printed materials they have," Sheila said. "I'll see if I can talk to the actual Gold Commissioner himself. It'll be all right."

"Try to find out when this will get decided, would you? And how much more this "lease" will cost us than the twenty bucks of our deposit."

"Roger, Wilco," Sheila said, completely focused on her drawing.

When Sheila finished the first of the three sketches that she planned to hand-carry to the Gold Commissioner's office in Quesnel the next day, she slid it off to one side. I looked it over and noticed that below the southeast corner of the Mac, she'd drawn in a happy little squirrel holding out a mushroom at arm's length.

We had moved our sleeping bags, foam pads, blankets, and clothes to the loft as soon as we had the construction plastic on the roof, but actually sleeping up there took a some practice. The cabin made all sorts of nocturnal whale sounds, pops and groans, clicks and sighs, as the logs dried and settled and got used to each other. Our new window plastic—even though we'd stretched it as tight as we could—crackled as it moved in and out, pushed by drafts flowing through the spaces between our unchinked logs. The mice had followed us inside, of course, since there was still no door to slow them down. Boring beetles chewed noisily under the bark of the pine blocks that served as legs for our benches, and some mornings we found tiny cones of sawdust below their adits. As soon as we blew out the lamp each night, the mice would be off to the races, the scamper, scamper of tiny feet a lot louder than one would think, as our little pals did hot laps down below.

Maybe because we were burning thousands of calories during each twelve-hour workday, I couldn't seem to stay awake much past eight o'clock. Like most tasks at the cabin, just going to bed took extra effort. One of us climbed the ladder to the loft, took our sleeping bags from the diagonal pole braces—where we draped them to air during the day—fluffed them out over our foam pads, and undressed. If I went to bed first, I'd snuggle into my sack and switch on our flashlight, so Sheila could have enough light to climb up and join me after she blew out the lamp. Warm air rises, so the loft, even with no chinking and no door, was briefly the warmest place in the cabin, warm enough I soon discovered, for a young woman in her prime to undress at her leisure. I aimed the flashlight at the ridgepole and watched her as she dreamily unfastened buttons. Ah, yes, I thought: One of those little extras, a sweet marvel at the end of another jeweled day. Sometimes she smiled and cocked her head to one side with that look of hers, the one that packed the jolt. And sometimes, even in the middle of her undressing, I'd drift away and be snoring like a bear, the flashlight's beam still wavering on the roof boards above us, when Sheila crawled into bed.

Some nights, I fell into a heavy, painfully deep sleep, only to wake after half an hour or so. Then I lay in the dark and listened to Sheila's soft breathing as raindrops drummed on the plastic above. I was often surprised, as I rose from the deep well of sleep, to find us there in the big woods, snug in our down bags under the roof of the cabin we'd set out from Denver to build. With every breath I smelled the drying pine of walls and gables and roof of what had started out as just another drug-fueled drop-out's dream. But the cabin was *real*. Our adventure was *real*. We had abandoned the conventional American obedience of our parents' generation. We had gone off to *Do It!* just like Jerry Rubin's title shouted, and we *were* doing it. I was enormously proud of that, even as I felt doubts creep in about our future.

It was dark in the big woods on those cloudy, moonless nights. But sometimes, in the blackness above me in the loft, I could I see the ridgepole as it looked after we'd first raised it to the tops the gables; I could see the dead-straight line of it, all by itself up there, and I was madly proud of that ridgepole, since it was, quite obviously, the high point of the best thing I'd ever done.

There was so much good, it seemed to me, in what we were doing, and the doing had been so good to us, making us fitter, quicker, and more wide-awake to the world around us than we'd been. As I lay there looking up into the darkness, I knew I'd never been so alive, that I'd never gone through a succession of days with so much gladness. Clearly, the good things came, in one way or another, from the girl who lay sleeping beside me.

Savor this, I told myself. Hold this close and hold onto it always.

As my insomnia led me through the dark hours, my thoughts roamed on to small concerns about jobs that lay ahead. There were so many poles to peel and saw into quarters for chinking; there was the roof above me that must soon be covered with heavy tar paper, each overlapping seam sealed with tar; there was the roof jack and stove pipe for the airtight heater; and there were cords and cords of firewood to block and split for the coming winter. I knew that we'd chip away each day at those necessary tasks and get most of them done. But could we have the essentials in place before the big snows came? What if the snows came early? How could we get hundreds of pounds of winter supplies up the Government Creek Road then? The El Camino, low slung and wearing street shoes, would be useless in six inches of snow. My God, I thought: Up here they measure the snow in meters.

Gradually, my thoughts drifted on to other uncertainties. Always the American war draft, though in another country now, came to pay a visit, sometimes wearing the faces of classmates killed in action. Then the war and the draft faded away to be replaced by monsters of my own creation, like the great Canadian bureaucracy, thousands strong, lurching toward us through the bush, waving papers and moaning, "This has expired. This has expired."

I was surprised, during those nights, at how often I found myself thinking about my folks at home. My father was a good man, sometimes burdened by depression that he tried to keep at bay with work, a responsible, generous man who was always busy. Even after eight hours in his blacksmith shop at the smelter, he was forever welding up another truck bumper or cattle chute; another branding table or hay trailer; another set of iron railings or branding irons there in his shop at home. That is, when he wasn't busy helping his old dad at the ranch on Jackson Creek. And my mother, heavy, awkward, cheerful; a sweet woman obsessed with her religion, convinced that any day Jesus would walk through her kitchen door to take the hand of his good and faithful servant and escort her Home. Good people, cursed with an erratic son. I was deeply ashamed, when I thought how the members of my parents' congregation must have whispered and tittered about my running off. Dad, I supposed, would shed the talk without much damage. But my mother, I knew, would be wounded in her heart of hearts.

And now this business with the Gold Commissioner. If we lost the Mac, we were lost. We'd thrown everything into this one pot, and our cards didn't look particularly good. Our situation here in wonderland sometimes seemed so uncertain, so unreal, that I imagined us inhabiting a Disney cartoon, the Mad Hatter shuffling a deck to determine our future, an ace up each sleeve and a third tucked into the band of his hat. What would happen if things went wrong with Canadian Immigration? What would we do then, Tinker Bell? The answer was clear: I'd be grounded in Never-Never land with no fairy dust in my hair.

Worries, dreams, and visions came round and moved on, wobbling about an uncertain center there in the darkness, like an unbalanced carousel of garish wooden beasts in a peyote-eater's dream.

And from far away, I heard a faint voice crooning, "It's late September, and I really should be back at school . . . ."

We had slept in. The cabin was filled with a cold gray light as I pulled on my jeans. I tugged on a pair of wool socks and climbed tender-footed down the rickety ladder—the same rickety ladder that I vowed every morning to replace with a sound one made with wider steps that would be easier on stocking feet—and I was stunned to see through the door opening an inch of fresh snow on the ground outside.

I pulled on a jacket and built a fire in the kitchen stove, wishing I'd taken the time to plumb in the stovepipe for our airtight heater. I pulled on my boots, swept off the front porch, and headed down to the creek for our day's water. The snow had stopped falling. All was still in the woods as I carried the jerry cans and a bucket down the old skid trail. Only the tracks of a pine squirrel in a big hurry crossed the trail ahead. A few leaves fell silently from aspen and peachleaf willows to litter the snow around me.

I dippered water into our jerry cans with a bucket and lugged the cans back up the trail as far as our claim marker. I felt my arms getting longer, and I noticed a deep burning in my smoker's lungs as I trudged up the slope. Carrying water was a chore that would soon get old, but it had to be done. The trick, I saw, would be to carry water every afternoon so we'd be ready to go each morning.

We had so much to learn, so many routines and rituals to invent and work through and refine. Almost everything we touched in a day was heavy or awkward, dangerous or late in getting done. I knew I needed to work smarter and accomplish more.

I lifted the cans—over forty pounds each when topped off—kicked little steps up the slippery clay-bank slope, and went on along our trail into the trees.

Snow was sliding down the visqueen on the roof as I set the water cans on our porch. I cleaned the bottoms of my boots with a rag, stepped inside the cabin, stoked the fire, and was making coffee when Sheila hung her head over the edge of the loft. She was still in her sleeping bag, wearing a silly little stocking hat that made her look like one of Santa's elves. "Canu, ganu, Canuck?" she mumbled sleepily, in what might have been barroom Welsh.

"Mush, ganuck ganu!" I shouted. "Eat, eat, eat!"

Wakeful nights made me ravenous, hoggish for oatmeal and eggs and toast, and madly in love with our cabin and that girl, smiling so sweetly, upside down above me.

The snow was gone by mid-morning. Sheila headed off to Quesnel to visit the Gold Commissioner's office, and I set about building our cabin's door. It was a job I'd put off, concerned about getting both opening and door square and plumb, the door snug in its frame, and hung in a way that was functional and pleasing to the eye. It was wet outside in the bush, a good day to work indoors, but the cabin seemed cold and still with Sheila away.

I'd been stopping in the doorway, as I went in and out the previous few days, to study the rough opening Sam and I made when we stacked the walls. I kept two short 2x6s just beside the doorway, which I sometimes held up and tried in different combinations, looking for the best way to build jams that would make a good tight seal when the door was closed. Luckily we'd stacked our 2x8, 2x10, and 2x12 planks, and the last of our best 1x4s and 2x6s inside the cabin against the back wall to keep dry.

I replaced the doorway's temporary uprights by framing in the new vertical jambs with 2x10s, careful to get each one plumb, with an inch-and-a-half of overhang extending beyond the logs on the inside walls. I drove the five-inch nails home, listening to each one's ping rise in pitch, as the spikes dug into the logs behind the planks. I nailed our last 2x10 to the wall on the right side of the opening, flush against the overhanging jamb. Lastly, I spiked home a horizontal header inside the doorway, up tight against the log above. And there she was: A nice square opening, framed in and true.

I felt pretty good about my job, until I banged my head against the new header board, and discovered that the extra inch-and-a-half of plank made the door too low to pass through without stooping. I could have avoided that by cutting out an inch or two from the log above, but now it was too late. One more item, I thought, that I could add to the growing list of mistakes I'd made because I didn't know what I was doing. Undeterred, I guzzled coffee and moved on to build the door.

I tacked a big piece of cardboard to the cabin's floor. I carefully measured the door opening's height and width, both top and bottom, then measured everything again and wrote the numbers on the cardboard. When I was satisfied that my measurements were dead-on, I subtracted a quarter of an inch from all four sides, then used an eight-foot 1x4 as a straight edge to draw an exact outline of the door onto the cardboard. From there it was simply a matter of filling the outline on the cardboard with planks and tying them together with 1x4s.

When finished, the door turned out to be *a lot* heavier than I'd anticipated. I stood it on shim shingles in its frame, and tacked it temporarily in place with pieces of lath. I marked where each of the three big strap hinges would go on the door's right side. I used a carpenter's square to get the hinges perpendicular to the door, then scribed their outlines on both the door and wall with a carpenter's pencil. My forearms burned as I screwed the hinges to the wall and door with an old screwdriver, whose blade I had to re-true several times with a file before finishing the job.

For an inside doorknob I fastened one of Sheila's empty thread spools to the left side of the door with a woodscrew. I removed the lath at the top corners of the door, held my breath, and slowly pulled the door toward me. Our door moved evenly and without binding or scraping the floor until it stood all the way open against the wall. It closed just as nicely when I pushed it back toward the jam with one finger. Open. Closed. Open. Closed. I was beguiled by that big slab of wood, moving so smoothly in and out. The door not only worked, but seemed to me as solid when closed as the oaken barrier to some ancient castle keep.

For a latch, I used a thirty-inch piece of pole that I'd peeled and sawed in half lengthwise. I attached the latch-pole with a single quarter-inch bolt through the door, so the latch could pivot up and down. I built a cradle from 2x6 blocks, to the left of the door, that the latch-pole could drop into to lock the door closed. I drilled a hole through the door, a foot above the latch, tied a leather boot lace to the pole, and ran it out through the hole. From outside, a gentle tug on the boot lace was all that was needed to lift the latch. At night, we could pull the latch-string inside. Lastly, I screwed a cheap metal handle to the outside of the door, so we could pull the door closed on our way out.

I was playing with the door when Sheila got back from her day in town. Latch up, door open. Door closed, latch down. It was, like magic! Sheila made ooh sounds then tried the door herself. It was a Look, Ma! moment, and I was smiling so much it hurt.

"Hey, man, that's a *door!*" Sheila said. Now we can keep out the wolverines. Maybe some mice, too."

When I asked about her trip to the Gold Commissioner's office, Sheila said, "Well, some good news, and some not-real-bad news. Actually, it was a pretty good day."

As we hiked up to the El Camino for groceries, Sheila explained that yes, we had only *applied* for the placer claim and that our application was being *reviewed*. "Mr. Drew, the Gold Commissioner, was really nice," Sheila said. "He told me he was new to the job and certain things in the department had fallen behind before he took over. Some sort of paperwork log jam; lots of routine stuff not getting done. But he looked at our paperwork and the drawings I took in today, and he said everything looked all right. We should hear from them in a few weeks."

"Okay. And what's the 'not-real-bad' news?"

"We have to do $250 worth of "representation work" on the mining end every year, *including* this year. That means we can pan up and down the creek, maybe build a sluice box and work some gravel down to black sand. We call it 'exploration' and pay ourselves a few bucks an hour for the work we do. Then we send in a report. That's it."

"Not a problem, unless the creek freezes up before we get to it."

"Right," Sheila said. "But we may need to submit information to the water quality folks, stuff that involves the cubic-feet-per-minute—or gallons-per-minute—of water that we intend to use, and the way we plan to mitigate the silt we create when we disturb the creek bed and banks."

"Hmmm," I said, not much liking the sound of that.

"It could be hard to figure and work up in a way that satisfies the water-quality office, especially since we don't yet know what's acceptable. Our creek really *is* confined down there, with steep hills and boulders on each side. Settling ponds for the silt from sluicing might be a problem. You need to look at the materials I brought home. But that's it. Otherwise we should be cool."

The requirements of our placer-mining claim were more complicated than we'd thought, but in the days that followed, we focused completely on getting the cabin ready for winter. I figured we'd get to the paperwork and "that mining stuff," once we finished our chinking and roof.

TWENTY-EIGHT

We started our days early; we worked until last light; and the days passed too quickly. While Sheila dug through our wood ricks for the right-sized poles to peel with her hatchet, I used a crude sawbuck to chainsaw the poles into quarter-rounds for our chinking. When I had cut an armload, I carried them to the cabin, and, beginning at the bottom of the south wall, wedged each piece between two wall logs then nailed it in place. The quarter-rounds were still half green and limber, and the nails pulled them tight into the cracks between the logs, creating a surprisingly good seal. As soon as I used up all the poles Sheila had skinned, I took my small Kelly and went to peeling, too.

During breaks, we talked about our childhoods, how we'd lost our virginity, and our first loves. And we spoke of the coming winter and the writing projects—as yet undetermined—that were to be our winter's work. I had no idea what I would write, no ambitious project in mind, and certainly nothing on the scope of a novel. Sheila had graduated with honors and possessed good editing skills. She could have gone to work as a researcher or copy editor for a newspaper in a heartbeat. I, on the other hand, was then so naïve that I hadn't yet even begun to guess what I didn't know about writing. After all, I hadn't actually *written* anything beyond the obligatory college papers that I'd churned out, like every other English major in the land. Sheila had actual skills, while my notions about writing were still moored to moonbeams, fluffy clouds, and the marching-songs of pseudo-revolutionary rap.

There was an exuberance, though, in those rambling conversations, a pleasure in revealing the oddities of our earlier lives. But for me, the best part

of listening to her was the sound of her voice, low-pitched and lyrical and precise. Such music there was, in the graceful lilt and articulation of her speech!
That, too, was my bell ringing.

A letter for me at the Hixon Post Office, from my draft board in Helena.
The board's message was straightforward and clear: Congress had passed
legislation to continue the wartime draft. I was to appear in Butte, Montana,
for a physical examination and induction on the 17th of November, 1971.
There was no mention of my invitation to board members to join me up
north for trout fishing, and my little joke didn't seem quite so funny any more.

Although we'd moved inside, living in the cabin was still a kind of rough
camping out. At night the breezes blew through, and the plastic sheeting above us luffed and sighed. Each time I walked to the cabin dragging
green poles for Sheila to skin, I looked at the roof and its temporary sheet of
Visqueen. And every time I looked, I found another excuse for not doing the
right thing, which was to shag on up there to lay out and nail down the tarpaper, which stood waiting in rolls just inside our new door.

We finished the bottoms of our eaves with poles that we had sawed in half.
We nailed the roof boards to the cut-sides of the poles and trimmed away the
overhanging1x4s with a carpenter's saw. The pole trim was a nice touch, giving
the cabin a built-from-scratch-in-the-woods look.

I planned to put the tarpaper on the roof in long, horizontal strips, working upward from each eave to the peak above the ridgepole, lapping each new
course three inches or so over the course below and tarring the seams with
black roof-goo. But somewhere along the line I convinced myself that the two
of us couldn't drag thirty-foot lengths of tarpaper onto the roof and lay them

out in straight, even rows from one gable-end to the other, without kinking the tarpaper into all sorts of wrinkles, folds, and tears. The more I looked at the roof, the more sure I was that we couldn't do the job. We needed to finish the roof soon, but I became certain that no matter what we did, the finished job would end up looking like something right out of Li'l Abner's Dogpatch, a motley of splices, kinks, and rips, with two catawampus stovepipes and maybe a buzzard asleep on one end of the ridgepole. So I put it off, waiting for I knew not what, without even giving it a try. Avoiding the roof seemed a lot like the way I delayed facing up to Canadian immigration. Sheila saw it, too, and cut right to the quick. "You have a way of making certain things a lot harder than they need to be," she said. "Why do you *do* that?"

Herb had mentioned an old woodcutters' trail, that he said ran along the west side of Government Creek from just below our claim to his place. Dahlstroms used the old track during the summers to check cows and haul salt, and Herb walked it on snowshoes when he headed north to work his trap lines in the winter. Weary of peeling and sawing poles, Sheila and I knocked off one afternoon to walk down the creek to take a look. We found the trail downstream from where we filled our water cans, two dim tracks worn into the gravelly soil by wagon wheels and overgrown with meadow grass. But there it was, a narrow lane cleared of brush and windfalls that made for much easier going than plowing through the native bush. As we walked south, the hills drew away from the creek; the water slowed and looped back on itself, scribing lazy oxbows under old cottonwoods of great girth. In most places we could go along side-by-side, so we hiked the three miles down the creek to Dahlstrom's, just lazing along, enjoying the afternoon sunshine and the colors lighting the bush around us.

"You know, I could walk down this way when I work for Herb," I said.

"You bet," Sheila said. "Then I can use the El Camino those days to run errands and not have to worry about picking you up when you're done for the day. Instead of waiting at Dahlstrom's for you and Herb to come in, I could be back at the cabin getting supper ready."

"That's my woman!" I said, always ready to play the chauvinist running-dog lackey. But cooking at the cabin *was* a time-consuming task, as was just washing dishes. Every drop of water had to be hauled from the creek before being heated in big aluminum pans on the stove. Sheila did the lion's share of the kitchen work, cooking and cleaning up at least twice a day, but like most jobs at the cabin, I pitched in, too.

Where Dahlstrom's stock fence crossed the creek, we turned back toward the Mac. After a bit, Sheila reached over and took my hand, and we passed through a stand of lodgepole like two kids in junior high enjoying their first romance. As we left the pines, sunshine came down from the west through the canopy of leaves above us. The bush was lit with splashes of light, and not a bit of air stirred in the woods—everything around us so still we might have been the only living creatures thereabouts. Then a Pileated woodpecker swooped across the trail ahead of us and landed smack against an old aspen snag. We watched as the bird listened to the wood, then went to hammering at the aspen's papery bark with great enthusiasm. He laughed his madman's giggle, calling to us, or to an unseen mate, or to what some folks might think of as God, then he attacked the deadwood again with a vigor that suggested immense joy in being a woodpecker, on such a fine day, in woods as bountiful as those.

Each evening we went back outside after supper, evenings when the air cooled fast and the fading light in our little clearing turned blue. There was kindling to chop and stove wood to saw and split and endless chores like gathering up limbs and trash wood to tote off toward the creek. We had quite a pile of peeled logs and lumber scraps left over from the cabin, which I planned to put to good use on projects like our woodshed and outhouse, or to just saw up that first year for firewood.

Over the course of several evenings, I dug postholes for the woodshed's four uprights and notched header logs to serve as the front and rear lintels. I spiked the headers to the tops of the uprights, and with Sheila's help, stood each unit up, dropped the log butts into the postholes, and tamped them tight, creating the two headers of a simple shed roof.

We ran six, five-inch poles down from the front header to the rear and spiked them into place as rafters. Then we sheathed the roof with spaced 1x4s and Visqueen. The woodshed was a hurry-up job, true, the roof just good enough, we hoped, to keep our wood dry through those next few months.

Without Sam's Homelite, we would not have had the means to do half of what remained undone. No way could we have made our winter's wood before serious snow began to fall. Sam's thoughtfulness and generosity made what we accomplished—and what we yet needed to do—possible. What could I have been thinking, I wondered, as we stacked the first rows of stove wood in the back of the shed, to have even contemplated building a cabin without it?

When the air was heavy during those deep blue evenings, smoke from our cookstove hung in the trees around our clearing. Soon after sunset a chill flowed down the canyon from the north, and the smoke would drift off, in no great hurry, toward the south. There was a spice in that smoke, a mysterious, cidery fragrance that seemed peculiar to that place alone. We were then burning mostly pine in the cook stove, with a few pieces of birch thrown in green for extra heat. Did the birch create that delicious scent? Or did the smell come from odd bits of spruce or sub-alpine fir or peachleaf willow that occasionally ended up in our woodbox? Perhaps some strange element in the soil had found its way into the trees that made our wood? We didn't know. Whatever the cause, Sheila and I would sometimes stop what we were doing to tilt our faces up and nose that delicious air like hounds. I've never encountered that scent anywhere else, although a whisper of its fragrance has come back to me several times over the years—coming from somewhere deep inside me, I suspect—a phantom atmosphere as powerful and compelling as a recurring dream of great sexual pleasure.

Look! It's Sheila, standing among the stumps in her bibs and kerchief, pointing up at the cabin's roof then waggling an index finger at me as I walk by.

My dress clothes arrived from Montana, the brown suit and white shirt pressed and carefully folded in tissue paper; my wingtips shined, a pair of brown socks in the toe of one shoe, a necktie in the other. A note from my mother said that she and my father missed me at home but wished me luck with the interview. That evening Sheila cut my hair and trimmed my beard.

We found a photo-booth in Prince George for the photographs that were to accompany my immigration application. Three snaps for a dollar. I shed my work shirt long enough to slip into the white shirt, tie, and jacket, then waited behind the booth's drawn curtain as the machine flashed and whirred. I couldn't have felt sillier if I'd been wearing lipstick.

"Oh, yes," the lady at the Immigration office said when I handed her my application. "We thought we'd lost you."

She flipped through the pages in a desk calendar to find a time for my interview. "Everyone seems to be taking vacation all at once," she said. "Happens every year with hunting season and fall fishing trips. How would 20 October be, say right after lunch?"

I wrote down the time and date and left, feeling like I'd just made an appointment to have my front teeth pulled. But the thing was done. From then on, my future was in the hands others.

When I walked the woodcutter's trail to work for Herb, I passed, in the early mornings and again in late afternoons, through a miracle of ripening colors, always within the sound of cold water in motion, even when the creek was out of sight. During the last week of September the bush flared into bonfires of color and texture. Glorious billows of yellow flamed in the tops of cottonwoods, while alder and willow and bog-laurel smoldered in deep reds down below. And here and there, the bright flames of Douglas maple.

One morning, as I walked down the Government Creek trail, I crossed patches of that year's first frost in the grassy clearings beside the creek. That day Herb and I went back to cutting firewood, this time in a grove of standing-dead lodgepole located in the hills east of the Dahlstrom's buildings. Herb had backed his trailer in among the trees with his tractor and was gassing his saw when I walked up. We fell to, throwing the dead pines and limbing them out. Herb's trailer was a rusty homemade job, seven feet wide, by fourteen feet long, with weathered sideboards sixteen inches tall, and it carried a good jag of wood, probably close to a cord, when loaded carefully. While Herb sawed, I split the blocks in half and stacked them on the trailer. During a smoke break, I mentioned that I'd promised to replace the firewood we'd used at the Douglas place. I told Herb I had some dead lodgepole spotted near the old sawmill site, but didn't want to risk taking the low-slung El Camino back into the woods there. Besides, I said, the little pickup really couldn't haul enough in a load to make it worthwhile.

"You're welcome to use my tractor and trailer," Herb said. "Take it home tonight after we finish up and drop it off tomorrow when you're done."

"Ah, no. I can't do that," I said.

"It's fine," Herb said and smiled. "Go on and use it. Just don't scratch the paint."

The next afternoon I cut a fat load of lodgepole. I split the blocks in half and hauled it all down to the Douglas place, where I restocked the woodshed. As I worked, I realized that I missed returning there in the evenings.

The sky wore a film of high thin clouds, and the meadow was lit with a soft, buff-colored light. When I finished moving the wood, I sat down on the top step of the front porch to roll a cigarette. As I looked across the meadow, I saw again fleeting moments of the days Sheila and I had lived there together. I saw the drizzly afternoon when I had walked in the rain from the house to the front gate, punchy from sex and preoccupied with the notion that no one in the world could possibly know about the deep green waters where Sheila and

I sported with otters. I saw Sheila drive through that same plank gate when she arrived back from Montana, the El Camino's door hanging open as we ran to hug each other. Then Sam and Sue Curtis pulled up in the legendary Scout to within feet of where I sat, and Sam leaned out, tipped his hat back with his thumb, and said, "Hey, Ralph." Brief sweet moments, they had come and gone so quickly, yet they still seemed alive, shimmering there in the air before me.

A stab of regret passed through me as I saw how our days were racing by, each day's great potential sometimes smothered in our busyness. I felt again that I was passing too quickly through a blessed time, one that would linger in me and resonate always, if I could just catch hold, now and then, as the hours flashed by. And I reminded myself to pause and to look up, to focus and to listen, to absorb all that was going on in and around me, as Sheila and I moved through each day. *Stay awake,* I told myself. *Be open to this world. Savor it.*

I had learned to drive on a Model 9-N Ford tractor much like Herb's. I felt a touch of melancholy as I putted down the Douglas lane and turned up Coldbanks Road, jouncing along in the familiar fenestrated saddle of a machine right from my boyhood. The empty trailer rattled and banged behind me, the little engine backfiring—pop pop pop— as we swooped around the downhill turn above the Hidden Meadows. And I wondered, where do they go, these seasons we live through and love and leave behind? Perhaps Paradise, I thought, is the place where we revisit our very best times.

No one was home at Dahlstroms'. I parked the tractor and trailer in Herb's pole barn, left Sam's saw and my gas and oil jug in the trailer to pick up later, and cut off through the woods on foot toward the creek. I was later than usual, and I swung along fast through lengthening shadows, a young man charged with purpose, moving with all the strength and grace of a man making his way home toward his supper and someone he loved.

As I stepped from the timber into our clearing I heard voices at the cabin. The cabin's door was open, and I heard two people laugh. Since I'd walked home along the creek, I hadn't passed the old mill site where we parked the El Camino, so I had no way of knowing if another vehicle might be parked there, too. I started across our clearing and heard a man's voice from inside the cabin. Then Sheila stepped onto the porch and said, "Here he is, now!"

I took several more steps toward the cabin before Jon Malone ducked through the doorway. Jon had grown a sparse little bebop goatee, and he was taller than I remembered.

TWENTY-NINE

It was one of those ridiculous moments when a man won't accept the information his eyes are conveying to his brain, while at the same time thinking—for no reason he can later explain—*Of course. Of course he's here. Of course it would come to this.*

As I walked across the open space in front of the cabin, Jon took a Dr. Grabow Viking from his teeth, one of those futuristic pipes with the segmented metal stem that was probably advertised in *Penthouse* and *Playboy.* Jon stepped down off the porch. We shook hands and looked each other over, and I could hear Sheila's voice far off in the distance, like birdsong. For once I had no words, no glib remark. What I felt, and what I've never in all the years since that moment completely sorted out, was my desire to make him welcome.

"Jesus, Jon," I said. "It's good to see you." How strange, that I meant it.

"I was just passing through, and thought I'd stop," he said, then smiled to show that of course his arrival was no accident. "Actually, I thought maybe I could help out for a day or two. Maybe do something with that roof."

Sheila stood on the porch above us, almost close enough to touch. She must have reached out and touched us both, somehow, because the tension of the moment passed and Jon and I relaxed.

Jon struck a match to his cold pipe.

"When did you start smoking?" I asked.

"About the time you left Bozeman," he said.

And that was as close as he and I got to the heart of the matter. There was no time to think, and if there had been, I doubt I was then capable of serious thought. We got on with the business of getting through that first evening.

We toted Jon's gear down from his fire-engine-red Impala and hauled water up from the creek and shared supper. There was much talk as we ate and washed the dishes, but what we said is lost to me now. I remember only the three of us around the plank table in the lamplight—the husband and his wife and the man who had stolen the wife—and the spells of tricky silence that settled over us, then lifted, then returned as the evening went on.

Somehow, through the chaos of Sheila's departure from Bozeman, Jon had managed to hold himself together. He'd finished his final quarter at MSU and graduated with his degree in engineering. During the summer, he studied for and passed the Montana State engineering examination, and received his license. But no draft worries for Jon. He was 4-F thanks to allergies to milk or wool or some such. Since early September he had been looking for his first full-time job as an engineer, ready to begin a career in his profession.

When it was time to turn in, we climbed up to the loft, fluffed out our sleeping bags, undressed in the dark, and settled down, the three of us going quiet, Jon on one side of Sheila and I on the other. The kitchen range clinked as it cooled. Beetles chewed wood. Mice ran laps where the floor met our walls.

The situation seems unthinkable now, beyond imagining. But maybe an expression popular at the time makes some sense of how the three of us could get through even a few minutes of an arrangement like the one we accepted in the days that followed. "Just go with the flow," was the counter-culture's conventional wisdom for avoiding conflicts, which we called "hassles." Just what Sheila thought of Jon's arrival, I wasn't sure, but I was beginning to see that Sheila could hold her cards awfully close to her chest. I'd guess now that we were probably scared, each of us working hard to be cool, to go with the flow until the tangle sorted itself out. In any case, that's what we did.

That first morning, Jon and I took our coffee outside and looked up at the construction plastic on the roof, littered by now with pine needles and smudged here and there with soot from the cookstove's chimney pipe. I mentioned the reluctance I'd felt about trying to lay out the tarpaper in horizontal runs.

"How about going the other way?" Jon asked. "You know, run the paper up over the top and down to the eave on the far side, one long piece at a time. Once we get the first run nailed down square with the roof, we should be able to let gravity do the work of sorting out wrinkles. Just line up each new course parallel with the last one and pull it snug at the eaves."

As soon as Jon said it, I saw how well his solution could work, and how easy it would be to do. What I didn't understand was why something so obvious hadn't once occurred to me. Engineers, I thought: They just might be of some value to us Gypsy poets after all.

When we finished our coffee, we pulled the Visqueen off the roof, moved the rolls of tarpaper outside to warm in the morning sun, and put pans of water on the stove to heat so we could warm our buckets of roofing tar. Sheila got eggs and bacon and biscuits ready to go, and we dug in like we meant to spend a day on a roof.

After breakfast, Jon and I folded a sheet of tar paper over the full length of the roof's peak and tacked it down to protect the vertical courses of roofing paper from the sharp corners of 1x4s, where they met above the ridgepole. We cut the hole at the west end of the roof for the airtight stove's pipe and tacked the roof jack temporarily in place above the new opening. We snapped the stovepipe lengths together and ran the joined pipe up through the jack, then fitted the bottom end into the stove.

By mid-morning, we had the first long run of tarpaper up and over the roof above the west-end gable. As Jon suggested, we were extra careful to place that first run square with the roof, so later courses wouldn't get increasingly out of perpendicular as we went along.

Sheila insisted on driving down to Dahlstrom's to borrow real ladders, since the ones I'd made from poles and 2x6s kept racking and twisting until they almost fell apart.

Jon pointed out that the gray ledger lines along the edges of the roofing paper could help us keep each new run parallel with the last course we'd nailed down. We spread roof-goo on the leading edge of the last sheet with putty knives, lined up our next sheet with the ledger lines on the course below, pressed the new seam down, and smoothed it all the way from the top of the roof to the eaves with our hands. At first, it seemed to take forever to get a sheet in place, but I had to admit that roofing wasn't such a bad job, with Jon's help.

The pine roof boards were slick, but the tar paper, once nailed in place, made walking up and down on the roof a lot easier. Still, the job seemed physically hard at first, one that bred charley horses in our legs and cramps in our lower backs and hips. But once we worked out a system, we picked up the pace, and thirty-six inches at a time, we worked our way east.

The next day, Jon and I were on the roof when Herb Dahlstrom rode into our clearing on his sorrel mare. It was the first time he'd been to the cabin, and he was obviously surprised at what we'd managed to do. Sheila introduced Jon to Herb as a friend from Montana. We were ready for a break, so we invited Herb inside to have coffee with us. He said he'd been taking his cows home for the winter and was out looking for strays, but added that coffee and a smoke sounded good. As always I was glad to see Herb, but I hated that we lied to him about Jon.

We went inside the cabin for a regular sit-down cup of coffee. Herb, always quiet, seemed almost shy in the new, vaulted space of the cabin. He noticed that we'd painted our floor. And the diagonal braces—rising from the unattached loft joist to the gable tops—caught his eye. Finally he said, "I've never seen that sort of thing before, but I like it."

Herb also mentioned that he'd been hired by a farmer to trap nuisance beavers that had dammed a creek, causing it to flood a hay meadow. "It's too early in the year," Herb said, referring to the quality of the fur. "But the Province says it's all right to remove the beavers now, because of the damage they're doing. The farmer pays me for the ones I take, and maybe I can use what I catch, later on, for bait."

Before Herb left, he asked if I could work extra days for the next few weeks. He had a contract to supply beef in halves to Thorpes at the Hixon Store, but he had other jobs to finish before he started butchering later in the fall. Since Sheila and I were tapped out, and it looked like we'd get our roof done before snow fell, I said sure, I could use the extra work, absolutely.

We kept at the roof, Sheila handing up cans of warm tar and rolls of paper and helping to pull the tar paper tight at the eaves. Jon was long and lean with lots of reach; he was good, steady help, and he was pleasant. As the three of us worked together, Sheila and I were cheerful to a fault. The conviviality grew strained at times, and how could it not? As we struggled with the roof paper, I wondered what to call this curious new association that had formed around the nucleus of a woman. But I had no name for it. Conversations that seemed playful one moment, could become tense and awkward the next, then effortlessly repaired a few minutes later. Sheila was happy, beaming, playing no favorites. There were few pointed remarks and no arguments. We didn't know what we were doing, but I think each of us felt like we were swimming alone, treading deep water. We did not know how to act, and we did not know how to look each other in the eye. Sheila and I had nowhere else to go, and none of us had a plan, unless, perhaps, it was Jon. So we worked. By noon the second day we had the whole roof sealed and nailed down, the roof jacks tarred in place, and the tin Airtight stove secured with sand in the bottom and ready for fire. Once we'd finished the roof, we went right to sawing and splitting stove wood for the shed and finishing the quarter-round chinking outdoors.

We told Jon about my upcoming immigration hearing, and, of course, the question of Sheila's status came up. The question was, how could Sheila find a way, once I became "landed," to stay in Canada with me, even while she was still married to Jon.

Try to imagine the three of us in the evenings, sitting with coffee at the plank table in the light cast by our kerosene lamps. Try to imagine the log walls and board ceiling and the dark corners of our cabin all thrown into a sharp relief of light and shadow, as Sheila and Jon and I talked about finding a way for Sheila to stay in Canada. I know I could not invent such a scene if I hadn't been there. But I was there. I lived through those evenings and took part in those fantastic conversations, and I can still sometimes feel the ebb and flow of what I felt then, the chagrin and the discomfort, the tension and the annoyance, and of course the guilt, just as I can still almost feel the hot force of passion I felt then for that young woman.

A man can be without pity when he has found what he wants, and he can be cruel if what he needs to defend involves love. An old man, with his cooled blood and weaknesses, may come to regret what he did in the heat of his youth; he may even grieve for the damage he caused to be done. In my case, the truth about such feelings is not complicated; it's as simple now as it was then, and it goes like this: She was desire itself. Her presence had become the white center of my life. I needed her as I needed light and warmth, and I would have done anything short of murder to keep her. So I understood that if I had to stay calm and hang in there; if I had to be dogged and pleasant and reasonable, then I was prepared to do all that and more. And in those shadow-cast evenings, enclosed by the log walls I'd helped to build, I saw that her husband felt the same way and had chosen the same path.

Jon looked at me across the lamp-lit table and folded his hands. "I've got an idea," he said. "Why don't Sheila and I immigrate, too? As a married couple. I won't stay in Canada, of course, but that would solve your problem for now."

Did Jon's offer seem bizarre? Yes. Did it seem odd that he didn't mention divorce? Maybe. I chose to see what Jon suggested as an engineering solution, offered in much the same way he'd suggested running the tar paper up and over the roof above our heads. It did not occur to me that Jon might betray us, at some point in the future.

I looked at Sheila. "Of course," she said. "Let's do that."

The first rays of sunlight touched the yellow tops of cottonwoods as I went down the trail, my breath smoking back over my shoulders, my face tingling in the cold air. Ice had formed along the edges of Government Creek, and frost lay white on the grass in openings among the trees. The sky above the cottonwoods burned a fierce blue, a vast pleasure dome, a jewel lit from within. This was it, by God, one of those October days I lived for. I pulled up the collar of my coat, put the sling of Sheila's .410 on my shoulder, and burned up the trail.

At that moment, Sheila and Jon were on their way to Prince George to get their immigration forms and set up appointments for an interview. Jon was to return with Sheila to the Mac that afternoon, then head on alone to Montana early the next morning to round up whatever documents and transcripts they would need to complete their immigration paperwork. Jon was even going to bring back Sheila's best dresses and city shoes. It was a wonder.

I crossed a little park where the first direct sunshine of the day lit the trunk of a huge old cottonwood tree. Two rows of poles, that I hadn't noticed before, had been leaned against the side of the cottonwood to form a narrow alley. I stopped walking. Five feet above the ground, in the opening between the two lines of poles, a beaver's tail hung from a spike driven into the tree. Then I noticed that the leaves and pine needles inside the lane of poles were all churned up and there!—and there!—and there!—lay three big Newhouse wolf traps, each one sprung. And between the traps and where I stood on the trail, were several mounds of fresh wolf shit.

It took me a moment or two to understand what I was seeing. Then I got it. Herb Dahlstrom had hung one of the nuisance beavers he'd mentioned by its tail on the tree. He'd then built a wolf set under the beaver. The poles were meant to narrow the avenue of approach to the hanging meat, but the great Trickster had come along, looked the deal over, and had his fun. The wolf had fired each trap. He'd then torn a beaver that weighed maybe forty pounds from the tree, eaten much of it, and left his steaming calling cards for Herb.

My first reaction to the scene was to laugh. "Hot damn!" I said to the air around me. "Go, you old hound!"

But the sprung traps revealed what Herb was up against. I knew there would be another disappointment when Herb saw what he had seen so many times before. Yet as I stood there in a pool of sunshine, surrounded by the bush in all its wild beauty, I looked at what the wolf had done, and I felt something deep inside me yearn for the vitality, the ardor, the force of that animal, as he moved even then, his belly sagging with beaver, toward some refuge in the deep woods, there to circle and lie down and sleep, and in that sleep to dream perhaps of new jests, new pranks to play on the slow animal who wandered the forest on two legs.

I had to force myself to turn back to the trail and the day ahead. I had to make myself walk a few paces until my muscles took over and I found my stride again. I went on through the deep quiet of those frosted woods sensing a great freedom as I thought of what I'd just witnessed and of the wolf out there, alone in his curious life.

Dahlstroms' meadows were white with frost when I got to their place. Herb wasn't about, as he always was when I arrived in the mornings, and his truck was gone. At the house, Helen told me that something had come up; Herb had business in Prince George that morning, and he wouldn't be back until the afternoon. Helen said their cowshed had to be mucked out, and she pulled on her barn boots to show me what needed to be done.

The cowshed was a low, windowless, post-and-beam affair, open and bright on the east side and dark as a cave in back. Manure, mixed with bedding straw, had been stomped down two feet deep in there. It was a big shed. Gradually, my eyes adjusted to the gloom in back.

"We always let it dry out in here for a couple months once the cows are on pasture, but we just haven't got around to cleaning it yet this year. Herb wanted you to wheelbarrow the manure to the big pile down there at the edge of the lot, but he didn't feel right about asking you to do this job alone. It's too much for one man, he said, so it's all right if you don't want to tackle it today."

"Heck, Helen, I don't mind," I said. "Let me bum some rubber boots, and I'll get started on it while I'm here."

For tools I had a long-handled, six-tined manure fork, an ice bar with a chisel bit four inches wide, a mattock, and an iron-wheeled wheelbarrow. I began just inside the overhanging roof, where I pushed the fork deep into the manure with my left foot and lifted. Nothing moved. Cattle had tromped the stuff down during the winter, compacting the manure/straw mixture into a sodden interwoven mat. I could feel the handle flex as I lifted, but the manure didn't budge.

After a bit I found that I could chop out squares of manure with the ice bar. Next, I used the mattock to break up the squares into pieces small enough to load into the wheelbarrow with the manure fork. A couple feet inside the shed the stuff turned as wet and heavy as ready-mix concrete, and the rich odor of hot cowshit filled the air around me. I loaded the wheelbarrow, ran it downhill to a small mountain of old manure, tipped it up, shook out the load, then pushed the barrow back up the hill at a trot.

I was surprised at how good it felt to be off by myself for a while, to be alone with enough quiet space around me to let me ponder the absurdity of our situation, to think about Jon Malone at the Mac with Sheila and me, and what it meant. Sheila had a glow about her since Jon arrived. I'd seen it, and now, as I hacked away at the manure, I could admit her radiance for what it was. Something else that had been skittering through my thoughts the past few days came into focus. Just how, I wondered, had Jon been able to find us?

There's nothing wrong with the smell of green manure, and I didn't mind the job one bit. I soon broke a sweat, my hands and forearms burned, and if I went too fast back up the hill, I got winded. I filled the barrow in the dim shed and wheeled it down to the manure pile, as October light blazed through the willows along an unnamed spring creek in Dahlstroms' meadow. Every ten or twelve trips I'd stop and roll a smoke and stand outside to soak in the crystalline light, which seemed to become more dazzling as the morning advanced. I moved from darkness into the light, again and again, until Helen came down to fetch me for lunch.

That afternoon I chopped a channel through the manure toward the back of the shed, going down as far as the native dirt below. Then I widened the channel on each side, one wheelbarrow load at a time, thinking that might help the shed dry after I quit for the day. As I worked, I experienced a feeling of purity, a cleanness of spirit, and a delight in my physical strength. There was a pleasure in the work and a joy in the beauty of the day that I never forgot.

I was surprised to discover, that even as callused as my hands had become during the summer and fall, I had some tender new blisters by late afternoon. When the blisters broke I cleaned Herb's tools, put them away in his shed, and headed back up the Government Creek trail toward home.

"I stepped out for an armload of wood, and there he was, standing at the edge of the clearing with his shotgun and ducking coat." Jon pointed at the spot where our trail emerged from the trees beside the woodshed.

"He was looking for you," Sheila said. "'Where's Ralph Beer?' he said."

It turned out that a man from the Immigration office in Prince George had been looking for the Mac when he passed the El Camino with Montana license plates on Coldbanks Road. He'd turned around and followed Jon and Sheila to the old mill site, then on to the cabin without them noticing.

"We told him we were friends of yours from Montana, and that you'd taken off for the day to explore the country on foot," Sheila said. "But he seemed all wrong, somehow, with his gun and upland getup. Very assertive. Very much in our faces."

"He said his name was Bowman, and that he was your case officer, whatever that means, but he acted like a cop," Jon said.

"I didn't know I had a case officer," I said. "Now I feel sorta special." What I really felt was that nasty old adrenaline sparking away again in my guts. "Should I go see him?"

"That's what's funny. He didn't say," Sheila answered. "He pretended to be grouse hunting, but he might as well have been wearing your wingtip shoes. I think he was hoping for some kind of bust. But maybe he got spooked, all alone out here in the woods surrounded by us hippies from the States."

"There'll be trouble if he finds out I've been working."

"I don't think he knows," Sheila said. He did seem to relax a bit when we told him we'd been in this morning to arrange immigration interviews the same day as yours. But his bad vibes still gave us the creeping willies."

That evening Jon and Sheila made up a list of the documents needed for their application and some personal items Sheila wanted Jon to bring from Montana.

The next morning Jon was ready to go at first light, planning to drive straight through to Bozeman for transcripts and letters of reference, as well as some clothes and books. I walked up the skid trail with him to the sawdust pile, where he'd parked his Impala beside the El Camino. "How's she running?" Jon asked.

"Excuse me?" I said, then realized he was talking about the El Camino. "She's running great," I said. "You did a good job on that motor."

"Take good care of her," he said. "Clean oil always." Then he fired up the Impala and backed around and went down the road out of sight. I stood there in the gray, pre-dawn light, and as the crunch of his tires faded away, I realized how very much I resented accommodating him. I'd become stronger as we built the cabin—Sheila and I both had. But in just the few days since Jon joined us, I felt some of that strength and inner resilience slip away. Jon had helped us with the roof and with firewood, and of course I appreciated his help. He'd been pleasant in a neutral way, and I appreciated that, too. But I'd given in to an urge to appease him, to mollify him, that made me feel weak and unsure. As I walked down the old skid trail, I was just so glad he was gone.

I walked into the cabin, pulled the latch string inside, and took Sheila in my arms. "Can you explain to me just what the heck we're doing here. With Jon."

"Not in a hundred years," she said.

"Are you getting a divorce? He wants you back, you know. What are you doing?"

"I do not know. I've been getting through this one minute at a time, just like you."

"But now you two are immigrating together."

"Do you have a better idea?"

"No. But are we all right? You and I?"

"We're fine. Everything is fine. We'll get through this," Sheila said, as she unbuttoned my shirt. "But I think we've forgotten something in the loft that should be taken care of right away."

I gripped her arms, gave her a little shake. "I need you . . . to be my love. My true companion. I don't want to share you with anyone."

"And you shall have me," Sheila said, as she tugged me by my belt toward the ladder to the loft.

What waited above seemed like only part of the answer I needed. Then, within a few heartbeats, it was all that mattered.

PART IV

there
was the sparkle
        of prairie grass
in their hair
        and mountaintops
in every step
        they took.

—David E. Thomas
from "Ellie and Lindy"

THIRTY

Maybe it was the light. Because right then, as we moved through sunlight slicing down through the timber, she was perfect. She was filled with warm life and a radiance that seemed to come from within as we carried our old wash tub, overflowing with wet sawdust and chips and strips of bark, she on one handle and I on the other, making our way around the mossy outcrop of rock at the north edge of our clearing, and going on, into the timber, there to contour along the hillside above Government Creek, climbing over windfalls and dodging around snags to finally stop and cast our freight down the hill. When we paused to catch our breath before turning back, I couldn't take my eyes off her. Her cheeks were pink with effort, and the down on her skin, lit by the honeyed rays of autumn light in the trees, seemed to me like the fuzz on ripe fruit. She looked at me with those dark eyes, yes, and she smiled, alert and quick as a chickadee, and I understood that she was perfect.

We stopped at the ledge of rock on our way back, and facing into the low sunlight, we looked at the cabin, standing there proud in the clearing we had made. A few unused logs lay about among the stumps, and more logs in odd lengths were decked in front of the woodshed, ready for the saw and chopping block. Filaments of smoke rose from the stove pipe above our kitchen range, coiling upward in the still air, sometimes twining into a ghostly helix then parting to fade above the trees.

"This is it!" Sheila said.

"This *is* it." I said, "Exactly it. But does it have a name?"

"Let's call The Source," Sheila said. "Because it is."

"All right," I said. "That works for me."

But as I looked at her, standing there with the old tub dangling from her hand, I thought she was wrong. The clearing was an opening in a forest; the cabin, a pile of logs with a roof and a door and some windows; and the smoke that climbed to fade above the cabin was just smoke. It was a grand sight, yes, a beautiful place, but as I looked at it, I understood that Sheila was the spark, the ignition, the true source and spirit of all that we had done there together. Without her, the woods would have gone undisturbed, and the trees that had made the cabin would have lived out their cycle until fire or age or disease brought them down.

We stepped into the clearing and went back to work. We'd made a mess with all our sawing and hewing, and we wanted to get it cleared away before the serious snows fell. So each afternoon we made a few trips with the loaded tub, going together along the hillside north of the cabin, where we could spread the sawdust and bark and chips out of sight of our clearing. Sometimes those treks, usually in the late afternoon, were the best part of our day, a time when our working together kicked up our spirits with good talk and the best laughs.

Herb had lent us a rake and a scoop shovel, and as we gathered up the chaff of our labors, Sheila said, "Someday, in a land far from here, a gallant lad will invent the wheel, and his women folk will put down their tubs and take up the arts of needlepoint and the making of sonnets, and the people will live in great contentment."

She had a point. Who would think to do such work without a wheelbarrow?

We took up our tub handles and lifted our burden between us and walked north, turning sideways to go in tandem again around the mossy granite ledge, and when I looked back at her, I felt that little pain in my center that came each time I gave my heart to her. It was like that, as if loving her had to leave a little hurt behind. And I wondered if I lived many years, would I carry that love and that hurt together with me always, as one enduring thing, and I knew then, yes, that I would.

I thought it very fine to be there in that moment, going through shafts of afternoon light with her and loving her, knowing then what I knew about love when I was twenty-four and the way love worked, how its parts braided together like smoke rising toward the light. But it all seemed to be happening too fast, the hours and the days there rushing by. I wanted to grasp that time, to hold it, to make it last, to make it mine forever. Then a fragment of a Blake poem came into my head, something Sheila sometimes quoted, something about, "He who binds to himself a joy/Doth the winged life destroy/But he who kisses the joy as it flies/Lives in Eternity's sunrise." Of course, I thought. All that matters in life is right here in front of me in this instant, and I will live all of it right now. That's what I thought just then, and I knew I would never lose her, that I would never grow old, and that I would certainly never grow old without her, because everything that mattered was in that minute, in that hour.

As the days grew shorter at the Mac, it became clear to us that the light cast by our kerosene reflector lamps just wasn't bright enough for several hours of reading each night. We decided to purchase on credit, a plain-Jane Aladdin mantle lamp at Thorp's store for the extravagant price of $20.00. It had the same mechanism as the ornate Aladdin parlor lamp my grandfather used until he got electricity in 1962. Our Aladdin had no hand-painted porcelain base or colored glass shade around the chimney, like my grandfather's model. No, sir, our bottom-of-the-line Aladdin sat down smack on the table on its polished aluminum reservoir, which had a flat bottom for stability, while the glass chimney stood unadorned by any sort of shade whatsoever. Aladdin lamps were new to Sheila, but I'd been taught to use my granddad's lamp when I was a boy. Sometimes the men didn't come in from the woods or fields at the ranch until well after dark, so I had to light the lamp myself. Kerosene lanterns were still used then at the barns, and flashlights and spare batteries were kept in outbuildings and trucks. Each autumn, until the early Sixties, my dad picked me up after school and took me with him to the ranch several afternoons a week. It was that time of year when he turned under the grain stubble with moldboard plows, and he often plowed on after dark using the tractor lights. If my grandfather was off somewhere else, I played outdoors until the light faded, then went inside and lit the Aladdin lamp and did my homework in its white light.

I was out of practice but soon had our new lamp going. A person had to be careful during the lighting ritual, however, because if the mantle above the wick was touched, it would crumble like ash. As I turned the wick knob, the light increased to a bright, warm glow—that unlike Coleman camp lanterns—was nearly silent. I rolled a cigarette. How many times had I seen my grandfather make a cigarette with Bugler tobacco, lick it off, then light his smoke by extending the far end of his cigarette into the heat atop of the Aladdin's chimney while puffing on his end? Dozens of times. When I lit my cigarette above our lamp's chimney, I could feel that old man in my body, still young and tough as latigo leather, smoking up a storm.

Sheila and I worked outdoors as long as possible those October afternoons; then, as the evening's chill slid down the blue canyon around us, we went inside to cook our supper. It was full dark by the time we did our dishes in the light of the Aladdin, which for safety's sake we kept in the center of our plank table. The Aladdin cast a soft white light that filled up even the darkest corners of the cabin without creating a glare. It was a good light to read by, and, it seemed to me, that everything looked better in its mellow radiance, including our log walls and the roof purlins overhead, and especially sweet Sheila Malone, as she dried and put away our cups and plates.

The night winds had been picking up, and some evenings, as weather moved through, the forest roared with wind. The shallow-rooted pines around our clearing swayed in that wind like tall grain at the edge of a windswept field, and we worried that blow-downs might land on our cabin. Sometimes, for no reason we could fathom, the wind would back off, quiet, and stop.

One evening, as we sat at the table eating Sheila's shortbread cookies and taking turns reading aloud from Alvin Toffler's *Future Shock*, the wind flared up, and the pines above the cabin began to dance. The future shock in Toffler's title referred to a condition modern people face when too much change happens in too short a period of time, overwhelming both individuals and their culture. The book made a dark kind of sense to us. We understood that millions of people in undeveloped Third World countries had watched on television as a man walked on the surface of our moon. Millions of Americans were leaving farms and small towns for life in post-industrial mega-cities. Anyone could fly vast distances in a morning that had taken our great-grandparents months to cover with their oxen and mules. And Toffler said that not only were there too many changes coming too fast, but the *rate* at which the world around us changed was accelerating and would continue to do so. Sheila and I found these ideas unsettling perhaps because we were going—as hard as we could and more or less alone, it seemed—in the opposite direction. Sheila and I were hewers of wood and drawers of water at a time when the United States was using nuclear powered aircraft carriers to launch bombing missions against an agrarian people who still farmed their paddies with buffalo.

Sheila read, and I ate shortbread cookies, until, on the dying wind, there came another sound. We both heard it. We looked at each other. The call, primal and low, came to us there in our snug, well-lit cabin, from the outer dark of the great beyond. Neither of us had ever heard a wolf before, but we knew at once what it was. We eased across the floor in our stocking feet, and I lifted the latch as quietly as I could. I slipped out onto the porch, and Sheila followed, pulling the door closed behind her.

It came again, as if from a great woodwind instrument, one fluted note, rising from the forest to the infinite firmament above, the slow, pure sound of lonesome solitude and longing. He was over across the creek on the steep slope east of our cabin. He might have smelled our wood smoke or our cooking in the wind. Perhaps he'd seen light from our windows. I took Sheila's hand. The last time he called, his voice quavered right at the end.

We weren't afraid. But we were terribly excited and alert, as if a curtain had been drawn back and for a few moments we'd witnessed a recital of the highest order, a voice and music from a time before man was, coming from the edge of a northern forest, where mastodons grazed past herds of ancient bison. Yes, it was an old wolf, traveling the great woods on his own hook, who had paused in his wandering to call across the distances between us. We waited, a gentle wind playing in the tops of the trees, a slice of moon showing through the timber to the east. But there was only the soft movement of air around us and the faint sound of the creek far below and the warm hand of the girl I loved. Herb's wolf had moved on.

"It's too darned dark in here," Sheila said. "We need another window!"

We were building our writing table in front of the south-facing window in the southwest corner of the cabin. Like our kitchen table, we used leftover cabin logs for legs and 2x6s to frame the outside edges at the top. We screwed the table to the wall in back for added stability, and for the lid, we used a 4x8-foot sheet of three-quarter-inch particleboard that made a nice smooth surface for writing.

"I don't want to cut any more holes in this cabin until we see how it rides frost," I said.

Sheila had heard that before, but, as usual, she pressed her point. The southeast corner of the cabin, under the sleeping loft, was dim even on a sunny day. In overcast weather it was too dark to read there, and it was easy to see how that would be a problem for the person who wasn't working at the writing table in the winter days ahead. I agreed with Sheila that the shadowed corner was a problem, but I wanted the cabin to be as strong as possible until the logs had cured and the first winter's frost had lifted and resettled the cabin. So we finished our writing table in a grumpy stalemate about the much-needed but absent window.

Because most of the scrap cabin logs I'd been sawing up for stove wood had still not seasoned, I took Sam's Homelite and a Kelly up the hill above our cabin and cut standing-dead pines, which I carried down the slope on my shoulder in eight- and ten-foot lengths. When Sheila came to help, I limbed out dead tops and cut them into lengths for her to carry home.

We enjoyed going up that hill together, although it got slippery after each light snow. When we took short breaks, we could look down on the roof of the cabin, and from that elevation see again not only our successes, but also our summer of rain and mosquitoes, of bruises and blisters, of labor and pain that had sometimes, in our fatigue and uncertainty, caused us to flare up and rage at each other at the tops of our voices. But that was then. The brutal summer was over and done. Wood-cutting in mid-October was a welcome respite and a great relief. Oh, we worked when we cut wood, but we took time, too, to sit side-by-side on a log and have those circular conversations that looped back on themselves again and again, talks about where we were in our heads, about what we had to do in the next few days, about the ongoing war in Vietnam, and about what lay ahead after our immigration interviews. There were always lots of unanswered questions.

"So, you think we'll pass the immigration thing?"

"Sure," Sheila said. "Just look at us. Young. Pliable. Ready to enter the Canadian workforce and succeed! They'll love us."

"I sure hope so, cause 'I don't want any damn Dinbinfoo,'" I drawled, imitating former President Johnson, who had famously uttered the remark when the defense of the American combat base at Khe Sanh was in doubt during the Tet Offensive in 1968. "But even if we're accepted at our interviews, we still have to sort out what happens where Jon is concerned."

"Listen to me. I'll stay with you, no matter what happens. *That's* what's going to happen. Jon will go home to Montana, and you and I will continue to march up here. Could we talk about something else, please?"

"Well, there's always this: What will we do—you and I—if I don't get landed status?"

"Ralph, you'll get in. If you don't, there's always living underground, off the grid."

"But that immigration dude already knows right where the Mac is. How can we possibly go underground?"

"If you won't go back to the States, we'll have to try living somewhere else without status."

"I can't see us doing that here. Sweatshop labor in some off-the-books deal? Forever? That would be like what we had in Denver, only worse. I won't do it. We'll go home, instead."

"But you work for Herb for almost nothing right now."

"That's different. That's for Herb. And it's enough, right now."

"But back home the war goes on. The war is still a real danger."

"It seems so strange to me now, how back in Bozeman I was always a little suspicious of my 'Hell no, I won't go' bullshit. As if I *knew*, even then, that I was trying to sound like more of an anti-war activist than I actually was. But the longer the war goes on, and especially since our summer up here and the release of the Pentagon Papers, the more I know how much I mean it, when I say I am not going to fight in Vietnam."

"Let's not get ahead of ourselves. You'll get status and I'll get status. I will make Jon see how things stand, and he and I will divorce. You and I will work a few months each year, until the writing starts to pay the bills, and we will live happily—at least part time—in our cabin in the woods."

"If you say so, I'll gladly take your word, Punkin. I suppose at some point we'll need to buy a typewriter, if we're going to make money playing with words."

"We'll call her Cordelia," Sheila said, "the faithful daughter."

"Cordelia Corona," I said and laughed. "Wasn't she Mike Hammer's girl-friend? The redhead with the big torpedoes?"

"Men," Sheila said, and pushed my shoulder with her hand. "They belch and fart; they hustle their privates in public; they talk about sex as if obsessed, but start to snore as soon as they get lucky. Always, it is the women who 'must bear the burden of being considerate.'" *

"I may be rough about the edges, sweet girl, but my heart is yours."

"Such a deal," Sheila said as she put her arm around my waist. "I'll accept if I can have you and the cabin and the wolf, too. *Those* are my conditions, and I'm sticking with them."

---

* *Romans 15:1-2*

We went in together to pay our tab at the Hixon Store, and Sheila asked Mrs. Thorp how she and her husband would feel about letting us have our winter supplies on credit.

"I don't see a problem with that," Mrs. Thorp said. "Make up a list for us. We may have to order what we don't usually carry. You're talking hundreds of pounds of flour and spuds, yes?"

Sheila took a sheet of yellow legal-pad paper from her pocket and unfolded it. "I just happen to have our list with me. We can pay you about eighty dollars a month through the winter," Sheila said. "We don't expect you to wait until spring for your money."

"That will be fine," Mrs. Thorpe said. "But you'd better get your things home before it snows."

That day we made the first of several runs starting with two hundred pounds of white flour and fifty pounds of whole-wheat flour. In the days that followed we hauled four hundred pounds of potatoes and onions, and various quantities of baking soda, baking powder, and corn starch; lard, salt and pepper and a dozen cans of spices; vanilla extract and molasses, powdered milk and powdered eggs, and fifty pounds of bacon, plus a case of sardines. There were five-pound bags of raisins and dried apricots; dried apples, figs, and prunes. The last big item on our list was a twenty-five-pound case of Cadbury Fruit-and-Nut bars. The tab came to over $400.00.

I don't think I'd ever tried to carry a hundred pounds on my shoulder any distance before that October. Our flour came in one-hundred-pound, white-cotton bags, and the spuds were sewn up in one-hundred-pound burlap potato sacks. I thought I should maybe practice a bit, so I picked up an unsuspecting Sheila, threw her onto my shoulder, and carried her down the Government Creek Road a few yards—a cartoon caveman making off with some Saturday-night love. Sheila wriggled like an eel and slapped my ass. When I put her down, she was red in the face and laughing. "You're so strong!" she said, pretending to worship me.

"Me, Man," I said. "You, womans. Yum, yum."

The best way to move cargo in hundred pound sacks turned out to be just that simple. I lifted a sack of flour from the El Camino's tailgate onto my right shoulder and lumbered off toward the Mac. The old skid trail was a gradual downhill run, so that stretch wasn't a problem. The true grunt began at the clay bank up from the skid trail to our path through the woods. I did it, huffing on through the timber to the cabin, there to drop each sack in the center of the floor until we could sort out where each item would best be stored.

In the coming days, we carried the odds and ends home in bags and buckets, and when we had the last of it put away in corners or up in the loft, we opened the case of Cadbury bars and broke off a few squares from the first one. We felt the way Saxon lords must have felt when their yeomen farmers had laid in a good harvest, and the sheep and swine were fat.

So much goodness meant we would soon have company. One night we set four mousetraps before we climbed up to the loft, and all four fired before we'd fallen asleep.

"We need cats," Sheila said in the darkness.

"Dahlstroms have kittens at the barn that are tame as puppies."

"Oh, let's do get two of them. Kittens are just what we need to keep us happy."

So I asked Herb for two kittens, and he said, "Of course. Take the ones you want."

At the cabin, the kittens divided their time between sleeping in a box behind the kitchen range and attempting to climb the ladder up to the loft. The mice, undeterred at first, raced along that space where the floor met the walls, to the great amusement of the kittens, who romped after them, two stubby fat-bodies, skidding on the slick enamel floor paint, hopelessly in love with mice and motion.

After a few laps around the cabin, the kittens' pace would slow until it was once again time to head for the quiet space behind the stove, there to lap warm milk and purr until overcome by sleep, sleep filled not with dreams of mice, but of great beasts grazing in tall grass, far out in an endless savanna.

THIRTY-ONE

The days turned overcast, the nights cold, with sometimes an inch or two of fresh snow in the mornings. Herb asked me to help with the butchering, and I agreed to work two short days a week until the job was done. I hiked down the Government Creek trail and helped with farm chores from nine in the morning until noon, then right after lunch Herb killed a steer.

Herb had been a professional butcher for decades in the States, and it was immediately clear that his methods of gutting, skinning, and halving a beef were a lot more exact than those my dad and I used on wild game.

Because Herb sold his beef in halves to Thorpes, who processed the meat in the store's butcher shop, he wanted the job done right: no knife nicks in the fat, all saw cuts straight, not one hair on the meat, head and forelegs removed without using a saw. Herb did all the knife work, which needed to be precise, while I helped with the heavy work and watched and learned.

Herb split the hocks and we ran a heavy pipe gambrel between the tendon and bone of each hind leg. I ratcheted the steer upward, a few inches at a time with a chain hoist that hung from a beam above the barn's mow, as Herb skinned the carcass. When the head and feet and hide were off, we gutted the animal, easing the offal and organs down into a wheelbarrow. Then we split the beef in half with a butcher's saw. A beef's backbone is hard, and it's a long way down through one. We took turns sawing from the front then from the back. And we were both breathing hard when the beef separated, the two halves swinging apart, nicely balanced on the gambrel beam.

We wrapped the halves in cheese cloth and lowered them onto a plastic sheet in the back of Herb's pickup. Herb nodded as he wiped down his knives with cold water. "Good job," he said and smiled. "Do you and Sheila like liver?"

"Of course," I said.

Herb placed the steer's liver on a butcher's board and sliced off a lobe. He wrapped the meat in wax paper, then put the package in the center of a clean rag, folded up the four corners, and tied them into a neat hobo bundle. "If you eat lots of good liver, you'll get big and strong like me," Herb said with a wink.

We looked at each other in the fading light and laughed. "You did fine," Herb said. I'll show you a little more each time we hang one up."

The morning was still, the creek frozen along the edges. A week before, I'd dug a hole out in the middle of the creek and piled big rocks around its downstream edges to create a sort of well where I could scoop up full buckets of water when I came down to fill the jerry cans. I'd just finished filling the second can, when I saw him standing on the old skid trail at our claim marker, watching me. I levered the lid closed on the can, hung the bucket by its lanyard around my neck, lifted a can with each hand, and kicked my way through ice as I waded ashore.

Jon stood with a rucksack on one shoulder, a long rifle cradled in the crook of his left arm in an old-timey mountain-man pose. I trudged up the trail toward him, the jerry cans sloshing and getting a little heavier with each step I took. When I stopped beside him I saw that the rifle was a cap-and-ball muzzleloader with an octagon barrel.

We shook hands, and Jon gave me the kind of appraising look that men who once fought in chain mail must have exchanged while gathering their strength to rise from their knees in the mud of some forsaken bog in the hinterland to give killing each other another try. Jon smiled, but he didn't put much into it.

"We'd about given up on you," I said.

"Getting everything together took longer than I thought."

"Go ahead then," I said and tilted my head in the direction of the cabin.

Jon climbed the bank quickly and went off into the trees, while I floundered up the slope with my jerry cans and bucket. When I got to the edge of our clearing, Sheila and Jon were locked in an embrace on our porch.

I put the cans down and waited. Jon, encumbered with pack and rifle, touched his wife's forehead with his lips, a tableau, which, from where I stood, looked like Liver-Eating Johnson kissing a young Queen Victoria.

Our interviews were in three days. Jon had their paperwork ready, and he'd brought a couple of Sheila's best dresses, her black Mary Janes, and a cloth coat I remembered from winter quarters past. In the evenings, we tried out and rehearsed different versions of a story that we hoped would explain why Sheila had been with me for several months when Sheila and Jon were immigrating as a married couple.

It wasn't much of a story. We were old friends . . . from school, don't you know? But our account sounded so lame and vague, no matter how we came at it, that each time we tried to start, we stumbled to a stop. We guessed that we'd be interviewed separately and wanted our narratives to jibe, if possible. But we finally decided that if Sheila's months alone with me did come up during the interview, we'd just brazen it out with "The Times They Are a-Changin'," don't-be-so-square attitude. That was our master plan.

The next morning I left on foot to help Herb butcher the second steer, and Sheila and Jon drove off to deliver their packets to the immigration office in Prince George.

When I got back to the Mac late that afternoon, the first thing I saw was the brand new window in the southeast corner of our cabin, the logs that Jon had sawed away to make the opening still lying on the ground, right where they had fallen.

I felt a nastiness rise up in me as I felt something like ownership begin to slip away.

"You just had to do it, didn't you?" I said to Sheila as soon as I walked through the door.

Sheila's smile faded away. She looked down and said something I didn't catch. Sheila had the habit of lowering her voice, when it suited her, so that although she was speaking, her actual words were hard to understand. Her soft murmur-mumble caused the person she was addressing to become more attentive, to actually lean toward her in order to catch what she was saying. It was a manipulation grand in its subtlety. I fell for it myself. Every time. And I fell for it that afternoon, too, bending lower to better hear her explanation for the hole I hadn't wanted to saw in that perfect log wall. Jon stood with his back to the warmth of the kitchen range, grinning like a coyote standing on a gut pile, but at least he didn't have anything to say.

I stopped listening to Sheila's muttering and stepped over to the window. Jon had done a good job of sawing out the big rectangular space, four-logs-deep in the wall, and he'd framed it in square and plumb with planks we'd stored inside to keep dry. The window plastic was stretched nice and snug around 1x4s. Jon and Sheila had also built a plank bench from 2x12s, along the bottom edge of the new opening to serve as a window seat. It looked like a good place to prop up a pillow or two to read in the afternoons. All in all, it was a job well done with rough materials.

"It looks good," I said, and it did; the corner that had been so dark was brighter, much more useable and inviting than before. Once I admitted to myself that the new window was a much-needed improvement, I felt my annoyance melt away.

The next morning I got up at first light and went down the ladder in my long johns, my jeans and shirt over my shoulder. The cabin was cold, as it was by then every morning. I lit a kerosene reflector lamp and built a fire in the airtight stove. As soon as I had that fire going, I balled up newspaper and stuffed it into the firebox of the kitchen range, added a few pieces of pitch-pine kindling and some small wood, then struck fire to the paper with a farmer match. I left the front lid off the stove, filled the teakettle half-full, and set it down over the open flames. I put my loggers on the lowered oven door to warm, then spooned a double-shot of instant coffee into my mug and waited by the stove for the water to boil.

I was drinking my second cup when Jon said from above, "Any chance we could have some privacy, here?"

The silence in our cabin was profound, broken around the edges only by the fires snapping in our woodstoves.

"Of course," I heard myself say, as if from some distance. "Sure thing. Absolutely."

I closed the drafts and dampers on both stoves part way, laced on my boots, and pulled my old field jacket over my hunting shirt. I took my Winchester off the pegs in the back wall, put an apple in my jacket pocket, and said, "I'll be back in a couple hours."

It was another gray morning, windless and cold. I climbed the slope behind the cabin to the top of the ridge and picked up the moose trail that ran north toward Government Lake. I walked dully along the trail, gaining altitude without being much aware of the woods around me. There were patches of snow in shady spots, the trail littered along its length with leaves from the overhanging willows, mostly bare by then after the big winds the week before. I wandered on north past the spot where I usually turned back, not thinking about love nor privacy nor her warm, flat belly slick with sweat.

At some point, I noticed a thinning in the brush and timber off to my right, and when I looked down through the opening, I saw some big cotton-wood trees far below, growing beside Government Creek, where a flat sheen of water lay behind the unmistakable line of a beaver dam.

A beaver dam. After a bit, I seemed to come back to myself and began searching the hillside for a game trail going down toward the water. When I found one, I followed the diagonal path moose had worn across the slope until I came out just above a meadow where berms of gravel marked the high-waters of long-ago floods. The cottonwoods had lost most of their leaves, and the leaves, some the size of saucers, littered the gravelly strand as others floated in motley on the still waters of the pond. Aspen stumps, some bearing the fresh chisel-cuts of beaver teeth, stood scattered across an acre of marshy ground beyond the creek.

As I stood there beside a young spruce tree, a beaver entered the water on the far side of the pond, dragging an aspen limb that still bore a few yellow leaves. He swam steadily, holding one of the aspen's branches in his teeth, until he reached the jumble of sticks and poles that marked the roof of his lodge, where he climbed from the water and set to work making a breakfast of the tender cambium and bark on his twig. When he was satisfied, he wedged the remainder of the branch into the side of his mud-and-stick house then sat on his tail to study the new day. A rainbow trout broke the surface of the water. Then another.

Perhaps it was the water that brought it back . . . something about the quality of the dark water in the pond or the angle of light upon it or the sunshine trying to break through the masses of cloud above the horizon . . . something in that view reminded me of an incident the year before. As I stood there, looking across the water toward the beaver resting atop his house, I remembered catching a ride from Bozeman to Helena with Jon and Sheila. We had been going down that dangerously narrow stretch of Highway 287 between Toston and Townsend, where the road had been built across spring-fed sloughs. The highway had no shoulders whatsoever, the roadside fill just wide enough to accommodate the white crosses that marked spots where highway fatalities had occurred. There were several of those crosses along our westbound side of the road, and it was easy to imagine that they marked places were people had driven off the highway at night, rolled upside-down into the water, and drowned.

Sheila noticed the heads of cattails that grew in the cold sloughs just off the edge of the pavement, and she became instantly enthused about them.

"Oh, stop!" she said to Jon, waving at the cattails from where she sat on my lap, there in the El Camino's bucket seat. "Stop so I can cut some!"

"We can't stop here," Jon said, "in the middle of the highway."

"Stop!" Sheila said.

"No can do. Don't be silly."

"Just stop for a minute!"

"Not a chance," Jon said as he drove on without slowing.

There was a spell of angry silence, and I remembered thinking in those moments, as the cattails flashed by beyond my window, that if she were my woman, I'd damned well stop for her. I'd stop, and I'd get out and hold up traffic in both directions, cars and trucks and busses, too, so she could cut her cattails. I'd do that and more to please her. How vivid and strange and unresolved the cattail incident seemed to me then, as I stood there at the beaver pond.

I felt I'd failed to understand something that afternoon on the highway near Townsend. Why did that small, misplaced incident come back into my mind, now that we three were together again, on another road with no shoulders? As I thought about it, I realized that I had wanted her for much longer than just these past few months. But I had not admitted that wanting to myself, or very much of it. No matter when the yearning started, I'd been turning toward her like the rooster on a weathervane, and I was quite astonished at how poorly I understood myself.

Movement is what animals usually see first, and because I hadn't stirred, the beaver failed to notice me. After a while, he slipped into the water and made for the near shore, pulling a gentle V of ripples that widened behind him as he came on. He was about halfway when I surprised us both by stepping away from the spruce and saying, "Hey! How 'bout some privacy here?"

The beaver yawed around and smacked the water with his tail then dove to swim beneath the surface back toward his lodge. The pond's surface smoothed again, and I stood there, thinking about distant roads and sloughs filled with cattails.

Jon had brought the muzzle-loader, for no other reason, I thought, than because he'd built the long rifle himself. The barrel was bored to .357, and if powder was measured exactly the same for each shot, the rifle at short distances was quite accurate. One evening, we nailed a paper target to a tree on the far side of our clearing, and the black-powder smoke hung in the air after each shot.

That last evening we took turns washing in pans of hot, soapy water, doing our best to scrub away at least the outer layers of soot and pitch, sweat and grime that accumulated so easily and clung so stubbornly there at the Mac. Jon had a small bottle of shampoo in his kit, which we shared, each in our turn.

When I had dried myself off, I chopped my beard way back, and Sheila cut my hair. I slipped into my only pair of clean long johns, then for no reason pulled on my brown dress socks and wingtips. I could see my reflection in the plastic of Jon and Sheila's window. I waved, then clicked my heels and saluted the brand new me.

Helen had lent Sheila two flat irons with a detachable wooden handle, and we pushed the irons, which we heated atop the kitchen range, back and forth on the clothes we planned to wear for our interviews the next day. Maybe it did some good. It was hard to tell.

In the morning we dressed in our regular jeans and work shirts for the drive up to Prince George. We smoothed out our good clothes on hangers as best we could. I handed our clothes to Sheila to hold as she sat on Jon's lap in the much-crowded cab of the El Camino. I had skipped breakfast, and the morning's coffee left me skittish and green as I drove up the Cariboo Highway through the bilious light of late morning.

We changed clothes at a laundromat, stopped at a drug store so Sheila and Jon could get their photos taken by the three-for-a-dollar machine, then went to a café for lunch. My head felt all puffy and wrong after my big shampoo the night before. As we sat in the café, waiting for our burgers and watching people walk past the plate-glass windows in front, I felt as if I were twelve years old again, about to step into the strange zinc fount in the quaint little church in Deer Lodge, Montana, where I had been baptized. I did, I realized, feel strangely adolescent in my proper white shirt and brown tie with its diagonal gold slash. But Sheila and Jon seemed all grown-up, so calm and complete, as they sipped their coffee and spoke earnestly about things that mattered.

After ignoring my cheeseburger for a few minutes, I cut it down the middle, gave half to Sheila and the other half to Jon, then pushed my plate of fries to the center of the table. I didn't want anything to do with food or wingtips, town or the afternoon ahead. I wanted to feel like a grown-up person again; to be my own man, back in the bush, standing with a rifle on my shoulder beside a pond where no one ever ventured except beavers and moose, and where nothing moved for hours and hours, except the dimpled waters where rainbows fed.

THIRTY-TWO

They had been waiting for us, it seemed, and they separated us as soon as we walked in. Jon and Sheila were led off down a hallway and around a corner and out of sight. A young woman introduced me to Mr. Bowman, the immigration official who would be conducting my interview.

I buttoned my suit jacket. Mr. Bowman hadn't bothered to wear his coat at all. He stood in the door to his office, a big, ruddy-faced man in his forties with sandy hair and blond eyebrows, a great sloppy tube of man-fat hanging over his belt. He waved me in, then went behind his desk. He sat down, and opened a file folder. I stood until he motioned to the single chair in front of his desk.

"Let me explain how this process works," Mr. Bowman said. "We use a points system to determine the suitability of applicants for Landed Immigrant status. There are many people who would love to live here in Canada, but who would bring little or nothing to contribute to our culture and economy. You will be awarded points based on documented evidence of your education, job skills, work experience, job-in-hand, financial situation, and my impression of you and how you conduct yourself during this interview. You must score a minimum of fifty points to be accepted. Now then, I have your application, transcripts, and references in front of me and this score sheet, which I will fill out as we go along. I will ask you questions. Take your time. Answer truthfully and to the best of your ability. Do you understand?"

"Yes," I answered, vaguely aware, as if watching the proceedings from somewhere outside the room, that Mr. Bowman had not once smiled. From that distance, he seemed brusque, even impatient, and I realized that in my great nervousness he intimidated me.

"So, tell me about your drug use, Mr. Beer," Mr. Bowman said.

I had expected some sort of banter to break the ice, a question or two about my farm-boy background or my education, perhaps. I was caught completely by surprise by what I sensed was more than Bowman demonstrating that for the next hour or so, he was the Man and I was the boy. Even as naïve as I was at the time, I understood that he had cut right to the chase with the kind of cop question meant to get a punk like me to blurt out some admission of drug use that would end the proceedings right there and then.

Bowman watched me. He tapped his pen on the table. I'd been caught flat-footed, and I was rattled. I guessed that an experienced interviewer could spot physical signs of shiftiness in body language, in eye movements, in facial expressions. Still, I might have been born at night, it just wasn't the night before my interview. *Keep it simple*, I thought.

"I don't do drugs," I said.

"Come on, Mr. Beer. It's 1971. We have nudity in our movies and free love. Girls don't wear bras or shave their legs anymore, even here in Canada. You spent what? Five years in university during the culture wars and the radical upheaval in your country caused by drug-addled hippies, and you claim to have not even experimented with controlled substances? Come on, Mr. Beer, everybody these days smokes something, yes?"

"I smoke cigarettes, yes. Do you do drugs, Sir?"

"You will answer my questions. I ask, you answer. Are we clear?"

"I do not use drugs. I do drink beer and I enjoy an occasional whiskey." *Shut the fuck up*, I thought. *Keep it simple.*

"That's not what we have been told. This office has been led to believe that you not only use marijuana, but have cultivated it here, in this country, as well."

I was back on my heels again. *Who had these people talked to? What's this about growing pot? What the hell is up with that?*

"I do not use drugs, Sir," I said, suddenly very conscious of my hands twisting the arm rests on the standard-issue gray office chair that I occupied.

Slow down, I told myself. *Slow way down and keep thinking.* "And I do not grow or manufacture drugs."

"But you obviously identify with the counter-culture—your beard, your lifestyle."

"Excuse me?" I said, praying that we wouldn't get around to Sheila.

"I'm talking about dropping out of graduate school to come up here to live in the bush. Let's see. Your last term at Montana State University . . . your transcript shows four failing grades. You failed all your course work last spring, except for a C in Pastoral Literature. You just walked away, didn't you? You dropped out."

"I worked my way through college, Mr. Bowman, and I worked hard in school, until it was time to go."

"Speaking of work, I've been told that you've been working illegally while you've been in our country."

"Of course not. You've been to the cabin I built. That's what I've been doing since I've been in your country."

"We have information that you have traded work for rent and worked for wages with no work permit."

The mention of working for rent meant Bowman or someone from the immigration office had talked with Ken Glaze. But why would Ken rat me out? I had no idea.

"Your information is incorrect," I said, hoping this was a my-word-against-his-word-type situation.

The interview went on like that, Bowman sometimes being the good-cop before doubling back to accusations about drugs, which were false, or accusing me of working illegally, which, of course, was true. And I continued to deny anything that might cost me the whole game, trying to avoid any slip that would get me kicked out of the country. After a while, though, I felt myself relax. I could see that Bowman had shot his bolt, that the outcome of my interview had already been decided. *Of course,* I thought, *I fucking did drugs; and you're fuckin'-A right, you moron, I worked for wages, so Sheila and I could buy grub. Sure, I was parasite on the balls of your precious society, but at least I hadn't gotten around to living on welfare, yet, like several million Canadians.*

Questions about an applicant's draft status in the States were apparently off-limits, but Bowman's condescending attitude toward me, and the interview itself, suggested that he guessed my situation and considered me a draft-dodging coward. *Oh, yeah,* I thought. *I'm a low-life,* and I could plainly see that Mr. Bowman thought so, too.

Eventually Bowman got around to the worksheet he was supposed to use to determine my points. By this stage of the interview he didn't seem interested in my answers. All that remained was to do the math.

The Canadian points system had been set up to objectively separate those applicants who would make good, productive Canadian citizens, from others, who would, in all likelihood, prove to be failures—the kind of people who would become an economic burden on Canadian society. Fifty points were required to get Landed Immigrant status. As Bowman had explained the points worksheet at the beginning of my interview, it was clear to me that a considerable amount of leeway was left up to the interviewer's discretion.

Points were awarded for degree of education; for language ability—fluency in French got an applicant extra points; work experience (a big point category); age between twenty-one and fifty helped; arranged employment—a job waiting for the applicant (another big point-getter); and something called "adaptability," which included having family in Canada or a well-educated, employed spouse who was already a Canadian citizen or a Canadian immigrant.

So, we went down the list. I had seventeen continuous years of education and was part way to a Montana teaching certificate, which maxed that category at twenty-five points. Under work experience, I had worked three summers in heavy industry at the ASARCO smelter in East Helena, including work as a mill hand and heavy equipment operator. And I had eight years of part-time work experience on the family ranch, so I got some points there, too. Plus, I was in the right age group. More points for that.

But I *didn't* speak French.

I *didn't* have a job lined up, guaranteeing employment.

I *didn't* have job skills that the Canadian government deemed especially beneficial to the Canadian economy at that time. (Apparently a lot of frost-backs could shovel cow shit and run front-end loaders, and there seemed to be no shortage of guys with sloped shoulders who could cut pulpwood and work in sawmills.)

I *didn't* have a wife who was a Canadian citizen, a heart surgeon, or the daughter of a British Columbia timber tycoon.

And I *didn't* get any of the interviewer's discretionary bonus points. Instead, I got forty-seven total points, and that was that.

Bowman smiled.

I didn't even try to argue with him.

Outside Bowman's office I saw Jon and Sheila chatting with some people at the far end of the corridor. Bowman waved me down to the front counter near the office's entrance, where he indicated a pretty young clerk.

"Jane will type up a form for you," Bowman said. "You will have, let's see, until the 10th of November to leave the country. You must leave Jane's form with the Canadian officials at the border crossing when you depart. Any questions?"

I noticed that Bowman had the beginnings of man-breasts under his white shirt. I didn't feel intimidated any more. "Just one," I said. "I wonder how many points you'd score if you had to go through a process like the one I just experienced. Do you think you're worth fifty points?"

"I'll never have to worry about that one, now will I, smart guy?" Bowman said. Then he turned his back on me and walked off down the hall.

I got my form from Jane and waited for Sheila and Jon in the hallway by the stairs.

For once Sheila seemed flummoxed, completely at a loss for words when I told her I'd failed. She stood flat-footed, her jaw down and mouth open. "Oh," she finally said. "Oh, damn!"

"We didn't have any problem at all," Jon said. "Sailed right through."

O n the street, Jon and I turned in at the men's entrance to a pub, and Sheila made for a pay phone at the end of the block. We sat down and looked at each other until the waiter brought six schooners.

"Serves you fucking right," Jon said.

"I guess," I said, feeling as far from myself as an owl from the moon.

I was already on my second beaker of swill when Sheila returned. The vagueness I'd felt during the interview grew into a fog. Sheila appeared from the fog to say she'd just spoken with her sister. "Marilyn is going to try to find out what you can do," she said. "You know, what other draft resisters have done in situations like this."

"That's great," I said. "Thank you."

In the fog I found a dull sense of relief. At least there would be no more fretting about what could go wrong with Canadian officials. It was a termination of anxiety, an end to worrying, like maybe the way a man would feel when his test results indicated that the cause of his headaches, which had grown steadily worse in the past few weeks, actually *was* the worst possible kind of news. He didn't have to fear the worst any more, because the worst had come for a nice long stay.

I remember unfolding the Canadian ten-dollar bill that I'd kept in a "secret compartment" of my wallet. My mad money. I don't know where I promoted the bottle of whiskey, but I went for it the way failures and cowards drink. The rest of that hideous afternoon is gone, lost in a puking, knee-walking blackout, except for this: It seemed very important to tell Sheila and Jon about an old man named Bill Hirsch, who had lived back in the hills between my grandfather's place and Helena when my father was a boy. Bill liked his whiskey, and when a little money came his way, Bill and his dog Pete would walk into town and tie one on. One winter night, so the story went, he passed out, dead drunk, walking home in sub-zero weather. He flopped over into a snow bank and survived, but he froze his feet. When some of his toes became gangrenous, old Bill, instead of going in to see a doctor, cut off what was left with his pocket knife and a tri-cornered file right there in his shack. It was a story I'd heard when I was a kid. For some reason it seemed necessary to retell the saga of Wild Bill Hirsch, again and again, to Sheila and Jon that night.

They managed, with some difficulty, to get me back to the cabin, and I slept it off. The next morning I still had my wingtips, but my brown suit was beyond repair.

Sheila called her sister again from Hixon, and as Marilyn talked, Sheila took notes. It was possible, theoretically, to challenge the results of an immigration hearing. Marilyn had the name of a lawyer in Vancouver, who, someone in Kaslo had heard, handled such cases. Marilyn had the lawyer's name and phone number, as well as the address of a Unitarian church in Vancouver that had a reputation for helping Americans who were in British Columbia to avoid the draft. And there were hostels in Vancouver, word had it, that provided cheap lodging to those who were trying to stay in country while keeping a low profile.

Sheila and I talked it over on the way to the creek the next day, and it did seem like there might be something in what Marilyn suggested which might lead to something else that might eventually lead to a solution. All those possibilities, however, seemed to be located in Vancouver, which was almost five-hundred miles away. But at least there was hope, even if hope was only a way of postponing the inevitable.

We had less than twenty days to find a legal challenge to the results of my interview, or to find some other solution that would let me stay in Canada legally, while pending a review of my immigration status. The other route, which seemed far-fetched and unappealing at best, was to stay in Canada and hide out.

Back in Hixon, Sheila called the lawyer's office and made an appointment for me to see him in a few days. Then I called my old high school orchestra teacher, Don Stagg, who was then teaching and living in West Vancouver. Don said I was more than welcome to stay with him and his mother, "Queenie," when I got to town.

The next day I helped Herb butcher another steer, and that afternoon I drew my pay, which, like always, was in cash. Herb couldn't believe it when I told him that I'd come up short on points at my interview. "But why?" he said.

"It seemed to me that the interviewer had made up his mind before I even walked into his office," I said. "Mostly he wanted to talk about my drug use and working illegally."

"I don't understand," Herb said.

"I don't either, Herb. I haven't used drugs in Canada and except for working off the books for you and Glaze, I haven't broken any laws."

"Can we help you in some way?" Herb asked.

"I don't see how," I said. "You and your family have already helped us so much. I don't want to get you folks in trouble. I guess we'll just blunder on through and see how it works out." And Herb and I let it go at that.

THIRTY-THREE

The wind howled overhead as we followed our flashlight beams up the old skid trail, four hours before daybreak the next morning. Jon had agreed to watch the cabin while Sheila and I were in Vancouver. He planned to head back to Montana when we returned.

We blew past Williams Lake in the dark, and by the time the sun cleared the horizon, the country had opened out into grassy hills and scattered bull pine. We left Highway 97 at Cache Creek and took Highway 99 west to Pavilion, so we could see the Fraser River Canyon that Sam and Sue had told us about that summer. At Lillooet we drove straight south on Highway 12, stopping again and again at scenic turnouts to gaze down into chasms where rainbows floated below us. At one point we could see a silent train, toy-like in the distance, moving along an impossible grade cut into a cliff face just above the river. And as we pushed on, we passed places with names we'd heard on our radio all summer: Hope! Chilliwack! Abbots Ford! Port Moody!

We had been in the bush a long time. Even the sky seemed new.

"I like the idea of a town named Hope," Sheila said, "since that's what this trip is all about."

"A last hope would be my guess," I said. "It's my fault. I should have jumped on the immigration thing about a week after we filed on the Mac. I wasn't thinking straight. Why did I think we had to hide out? I don't know. Hell, I'm still not thinking straight. What are we doing? This trip isn't going to solve anything. When we get back, we'll be broke again, we'll still owe Thorpes' for our food cache, and I'm supposed to cross the border on the 10th."

If Herb can keep me busy for a few days, we might be able to afford enough gas to get us to Montana."

"We should keep ourselves open to possibilities," Sheila said. "Maybe we can still salvage a life together in our cabin in the woods. Come on, Leroy. Get tough."

The sky cleared as we drove south. The world seemed a little kinder in the mid-day sunshine, but I felt a queer mix of anger and relief and self-loathing. Failure was failure, and mine seemed epic to me. The big draft protestor, I thought, making a stand for his principles, at least until a fat man in an office called his bluff. Thanks to that fat man, it would soon be a trip back across the border for the failed revolutionary, who was, in truth, just another craven boy who'd made a poor showing.

"Vietnam? Hell yes! Be proud to serve, Sir. Whatever you people in charge think is fair, that's fine with me. Here, Sire, let me please kiss your ring! Oh, haven't we just come a long way from old Devon, where, when the Duke said we must fight the French or the Dutch or the Brandenburgs we sent our sons and paid higher taxes to fund the wars, too. Anything to soothe the lords and ladies on the hill. And we called it love of king and country."

Sheila scooted around in her seat and stared at me.

"Did I just say that out loud?" I asked.

"Oh, yes. Loud and clear."

"Sorry," I said. "I was just thinking about war and how the wars never seem to end."

"So I gather," Sheila said. She sat back and after a while reached across the console and put her hand on my thigh. "We have today," she said. "I want to enjoy it. Tomorrow's wars will just have to wait."

The miles flashed by on the road to Vancouver, and after a while I got tired of raging at myself. Like Sheila, I wanted fun, any sort of fun, anywhere we could find it.

Somewhere near Surrey I called Don Stagg's home and spoke with his mother, reminding her that a friend and I were coming that evening for the night. She asked if we could be there for dinner at six, and I assured her that we could. Back at the El Camino, I opened the door, leaned down and said, "We're all set!"

I slid behind the wheel and started the engine. "Sheila, let me tell you the saga of Don Stagg, and how he came to be so important to a bunch of us kids."

"Okay." Sheila said. "Tell me your tale."

"Well, you see, the Helena School System's orchestra program had been moribund for years—you know, one kid with a viola, drooling on himself, another one with a bass drum; that was about the sum total of the program when Don was hired. He started teaching with not much more than a room full of broken violins and crapped-out cellos, this wild young cat with a big beard who was built like a stork—all arms and legs, you know—but with an irreverent, juvenile-delinquent sense of humor and a big honest laugh you could hear a block away. Nobody wore a beard back then, but Don did! And he had more energy than any adult we'd ever seen. He was competent and wide-awake and loud, and he woke us up and inspired us to make music!

Sheila had turned in her seat again to face me. "But how did you get to know him?" she asked. "Did you play an instrument?"

"It's a good story, Sheila. Early in my eighth-grade year at the Helena Junior High, I heard kids talking about "this crazy guy," who practiced the piano early in the mornings in the school's auditorium. You see, Don had rented a garage apartment his first year in town and didn't have room for a piano. So, he came to school a couple hours before first period to practice.

"My mother was a gifted soprano, who sang in local chorales and church choirs, and I was just crazy about music when I was a kid. I'd been interested in classical music since grade school, and I put what little money came my way into a modest collection of classical LPs. So, out of curiosity, I got to school early one morning, and, as I opened a rear door to the dark auditorium, I heard all this music! And there, seated under the spotlights on the stage, was Abe Lincoln, Amish beard and all, wringing music, such grand music, from the school's much-abused Steinway.

"I went in and closed the door quietly behind me. Then I groped my way down an aisle and took a seat. Straight-backed and elegant, the man on stage played from memory, and he played furiously, with great energy and exactness.

He did scales and Hanon Exercises, then switched to Bach Inventions and Chopin nocturnes, counterpoint flowing seamlessly into familiar themes of the Romantics, a fugue by Telemann swirling into the melodic dash of Schubert's "The Trout." Sometimes he stopped to work on a passage, then played on, one man alone, filling that dark hall with music.

"I was stunned. I'd never seen an accomplished pianist before, and it began to dawn on me, there in the auditorium, that I had just made a great discovery. I walked to school early, morning after morning, to sit in the dark and listen to Don Stagg warm up for his day.

"One morning, when he'd finished, he stood away from the piano and looked out into the empty rows of seats. Then he shaded his eyes with one hand and looked right at me."

"'Can I help you?'" Mr. Stagg called.

"I walked down to the front of the stage, and told him that I liked to listen to him practice. We talked for a bit, he asked me if I played an instrument, and I admitted that I did not."

"'We could use another bass player in the orchestra,'" he said. "'Would you be interested in that?'"

"I didn't know what to say," I told Sheila. "I could read music in a rudimentary way, I knew a few chords on my mother's piano, but I couldn't dance or sing a lick. It had never occurred to me to try to join a school band or orchestra. I guess I thought it was already too late to start. But that morning I told Mr. Stagg I'd give it a try. Within days I was standing at the rear of the auditorium's stage, right behind the row of cellos, sawing away on the open strings of an old wreck that resembled a string bass under those very same lights that lit the stage and nothing more.

"Don was a kid magnet. They kept showing up with instruments, and after a while we were sounding pretty good. At first, a lot of folks didn't know what to make of Don as he roared around town in his GMC pickup loaded with music stands, instruments, and kids, but he soon became a regular guest in the homes of those kids, on a first-name basis with parents all over town. In the early Sixties, which in Montana, as you well know, often seemed like the gray and stifling Fifties, Don Stagg was our guide to a palette of rich colors.

We had some talented kids like the Rougle boys, Eric Lundborg, even a kid named Rick Wine. Heck, we had a girl who later became Miss Montana—imagine that! And we pushed each other. By our Junior year, we owned our own instruments and were playing in the Helena Symphony, even traveling on concert Sundays to play in Bozeman and Butte. Orchestra gave us a way to participate in something that had value. But mostly, orchestra was just a lot of fun.

"I had some good teachers, but except for my Sixth Grade teacher, Mr. Nelson, no other teacher in my years in public schools gave me the stimulation, the sense of accomplishment, and the confidence that Don Stagg gave to me. My grades in all my classes improved, and I found the wherewithal to enjoy my very first girlfriend, a lass named Sharon Bozman, whose blazing red hair lit the brass section. Wow. Sharon Bozman. She was so great. Anyway, Sheila, you're in for a treat. You're going to like our Mr. Stagg."

We exited Highway 1 near Burnaby, picked up Kingsway, which took us into the city to East Broadway. In spite of our stops during the day to gawk at the Fraser Gorge, we'd made good time. With Sheila navigating, we located the building in downtown Vancouver where the lawyer I was to see the next morning kept his office, and, after driving around a bit, we began to get a sense of the city on the mainland. Before long we found ourselves driving along West Georgia Street, which happily took us into Stanley Park. We had a couple hours to find Don's house, over in West Vancouver; we were buzzing with highway miles and the shock of the city we'd just passed through, so we decided to stretch our legs and explore the seaward side of Stanley Park.

To our amazement, we entered an Eden where peacocks moved with stately ease across manicured lawns, pulling their trains of iridescent feathers with slow elegance, calling, "Ee-ow! Ee-ow! Look at me! Ee-ow."

Guinea fowl moved in tight knots here and there, creaking, clucking, and whistling, and, as afternoon shadows crept across sunlit lawns, the calling of sea birds floated toward us from the waters of the bay. With so much life to be found in such a magical garden, we would not have been much surprised to come upon a herd of Irish elk grazing out from cover, maybe a unicorn or two.

After ambling a good distance, we found ourselves going along a paved walk atop the edge of a seawall that faced west toward the Burrard Inlet and the Salish Sea, waters that then merged with those of the infamous Georgia Strait that we'd heard about so often on our radio during the summer. The tide boomed in and crashed against the seawall, throwing jets of froth high into the air, which then fell to earth in heavy clots. A group of people ahead of us were timing the waves so they could sprint under the arching spray of salt water as it rained down beyond the sidewalk. When they had moved on, Sheila and I joined hands and ran along the length of sidewalk, too, not quite timing it well enough to avoid getting a little wet.

I had never seen or heard an ocean before, and I was thrilled beyond all saying by the thudding waves and the scent of the brine from which we had come so long ago. Sheila and I looked west, and we could not believe, after our months in the bush, just how far we could see in the direction of the lowering sun, for we could see in that golden hour where the rolling edge of the Earth curved away toward the Orient and Southeast Asia. We were carried out of ourselves as the big waves rolled in to whump and smash against concrete and stone, and as we stood there, amazed at the size and beauty of the world, our concerns with Canadian bureaucracy bled away and vanished. We could smell the primal soup rolling toward us from the depths of the Pacific, and it seemed to us that we could breathe again.

When we could stay no longer, we entered the rush-hour traffic over the Lions Gate Suspension Bridge to Highway 99 in West Vancouver, which took us north to Highway 1. Highway 1 led us west to Ottaburn Road, where Don and his mother lived on a hill overlooking the bay. While I'd kept in touch with Don, I hadn't seen him in several years. When he opened the door and waved us in, he seemed unchanged, still an exuberant, gangly extrovert with his big laugh and irreverent views on all those people and institutions who thought they were in charge of the world.

Queenie was short and stout, a foster mother, really, who had taken Don in and raised him as her own. It was Queenie who bought Don's first piano and plunked him down on the bench and told him: "I've paid good money for this piano, and now you're going to learn how to play it. Get to work, young man." What a shock Don's talent must have been to the folks in Butte, as he quickly passed beyond what local teachers could give him.

I explained during dinner that I was trying to avoid Vietnam, but that my immigration interview hadn't gone well. I mentioned the lawyer I was to see the next day and our hope for an appeal. Don, of course, was against the war, and I realized, as we ate dessert, that my tendency to question official authority, even to rabble-rouse a bit, had begun right there, with Don Stagg and various comments he'd made about Montana politicians and even presidents Kennedy and Johnson when he had been our teacher. Come to think of it, Don was the reason I'd wanted to wear a beard just as soon as I could grow one.

"What do you think I should do?" I asked Stagg.

"I think you should consider the impact your decision will have—no matter what it is—on your folks. Bob and Ellen are both wonderful people, and you'll want to give them as little cause for worry or grief as possible. That would include, of course, getting killed or maimed in Vietnam."

After dinner, Don seated himself at his custom grand and began to play, first Bach's Fugue in G minor, getting playful as the third voice entered in bass octaves, then settling down again to complete the piece with that machine-like Bach counterpoint that can be so moving when phrased properly; then the Chopin Nocturne in E flat major, both pieces played from memory. Sheila and I were bowled over, delighted after our months of scratchy radio pop up north in the big woods. When we begged for more, Don finished up with one of Schubert's amazing German Dances.

Before we turned in for the night, Don insisted that after we finished what we needed to do in the city the next day, we come back and stay the next night, too, and we were very happy to accept.

Sheila waited in the El Camino. As soon as I spoke with the receptionist, she took me in to meet the immigration lawyer. He was about my age with black hair that looked wet. He seemed to be rushed, as if he should have already been somewhere else.

I quickly explained my situation: I'd built a cabin on a placer claim. After five months in country I had an immigration hearing and came up short on points. I felt that something was out of line in the way the interview had been conducted. It seemed, I told the lawyer, that the interviewer had made up his mind before I'd even arrived.

I was nervous, true, and perhaps because the young attorney seemed harried, I was probably talking too fast. But when I mentioned that Mr. Bowman had come to my cabin while I was away, and that visiting friends told me he was carrying a shotgun, the attorney threw up his hands and said, "Hold it! Hold it right there!"

I stopped talking and we looked at each other.

"You expect me to believe that a Canadian immigration officer came looking for you in the bush armed with a shotgun?"

"Yes," I said. "I was at a neighbor's place, but two friends of mine were at the cabin when Bowman showed up asking for me."

"I don't believe it for a second. There is no way that would happen. No way."

"But it did happen. Why would you think otherwise?"

"Because that's not how we do things in this country. Our immigration officials don't go chasing after people armed with goose guns. Why would you come in here with a cock-up story like that and waste my time?"

"Wait. Wait. Bowman did come to the cabin with a shotgun, but that seems beside the point to me. The point is that I'm a college graduate just like you, and I bring some job skills with me to this country. I have no criminal record, I haven't broken any laws in Canada, except for some working off the books. And, I'm actually a pretty good guy. But this particular immigration official—for reasons I do not know—acted as if he was looking for excuses to fail me as soon as I walked in. He started by asking me about my drug use and *kept* asking me about drugs all the way through the interview. I haven't been anywhere near drugs in Canada. The point is not the shotgun. The point is that I did not get a fair hearing."

"No, no, no. I wouldn't even think of representing you after that story. You're barking up the wrong tree here, friend." The attorney stood up behind his desk. "That's all," he said and pointed toward the door. "No charge. Now good-bye."

The whole thing had taken just a couple minutes. As I walked down the street toward the El Camino, I wondered, am I awake? Or is this one of those times, when I'll open my eyes and think: Thank you, Lord, it was only a dream. Then I began to wonder if there was something so obviously wrong with me that anyone with a desk and a name plate on his door could immediately see—even if I did speak in complete sentences—some mark or blemish or disfigurement that made clear just how shifty and unfit and feral I truly was. Only then did it occur to me that the young lawyer had probably taken one look and saw that I couldn't afford to hire counsel, at his rates or any other.

I explained what had happened to Sheila, who sat stunned in the little pickup. We waited there a while, as the downtown swirl of traffic churned past, until I had time to let the adrenaline wash out of my system. We didn't know what to do. We had enough gas money to get us back to Hixon with maybe a meal on the way if we were careful.

Sheila wanted to check the Unitarian church and the hostels Marilyn had mentioned, so we blundered forth into the new day, disoriented in the rush of traffic that surged around us through the corridors of the town.

We found two very sweet old ladies in the office at the Unitarian church, who seemed completely bewildered when we asked about their policy of aiding young men from the States who were avoiding the draft. "Oh, dear," one said. "Is that legal?"

The one hostel we visited seemed like a good place to very quickly have our sleeping bags and possibles stolen. After talking with a couple of burned-out street people, who were loitering around outside, we decided to give it up as a bad job. So, by a little after noon, we'd struck out.

We bought some apples and day-old cinnamon rolls and drove back to Stanley Park, where we spent the afternoon walking and enjoying each other in the sunshine and warmth. Vancouver was a month or more behind Prince George in the season, and it was a welcome relief to have a luxurious day of

September weather with no job list of work that must be done. We were again beguiled and distracted by the beauty all around us and by the waters of the Pacific battering the coast. As we explored the park's many paths, I experienced again a strange, two-hearted surge of emotion like the one I'd felt that radiant afternoon when we carried sawdust and chips in our tub. How fine Sheila seemed, there in Stanley Park, how perfect, as the spheres beyond the blue above us slowed in their courses, and time throttled back to a slow walk.

It would later seem strange to us both that while we should have been distressed by our circumstances; freaked, as we used to say, by being so obviously out of options, Sheila and I were instead lost in the beauty around us. We walked arm-in-arm along the shore, gazing in high spirits out to sea, when we might have been worrying instead about what to do next to salvage our situation on dry land there in Canada.

The Staggs fed us dinner that evening, and Don filled us up again with music.

The next morning, after Don gave us a tour of the studio he'd built to house the pipe organ he was restoring, I felt his infectious esprit again lift my spirits. His brio and dash woke me up, and I could feel an old confidence seep back. At some point, Don and I and Queenie posed on the lawn for Sheila, and the photograph she took caught something in that moment, which all these years later, I can still feel. Stagg goofed with an umbrella and derby hat for the photo, standing on one leg like a stork. It reminded me of how he not only met the world head-on but embraced it, and that seemed to me then like an example I must follow. Canadian officials and their decisions didn't seem to distress me as much just then, and I didn't feel like hiding out any more.

From Stagg's residence, Sheila and I picked up the Trans-Canada Highway in West Vancouver and followed it through the morning sunshine as it cut across North Vancouver toward the harbor, and as we soared above the water on the Iron Works Bridge, our spirits rocketed skyward, too. All that we could see of our world lay just beyond the arc of the span's parabola, and we laughed aloud together, caught up in the unreasonable joy of our flight. We had nothing actual to celebrate, true, but the high spirits of Don and Queenie's sendoff, and the astonishing day before us, gave us wings.

Somewhere later that morning, we stopped to savor the glory of fall colors through which the road passed that day, mile after brilliant mile. Snapshots: Sheila fronting a splash of red, framed by evergreens; Ralph sporting a cod-piece of Douglas maple and a grin. Two young people at the very zenith of health and youth, celebrating a grand day, filled with the joy of each other's company, as we found ourselves back on the road again.

THIRTY-FOUR

While we were gone, Jon finished the roof on our outhouse, and he built a set of bookshelves beside Sheila's window seat. Once we filled a couple shelves with books, there was a much-needed partition between the window seat and the writing table. Jon stayed a day or two after we returned from Vancouver, then abruptly said he needed to go. This time I waited at the cabin while Sheila walked Jon to his car.

Although we'd assumed, during our drive back to Hixon, that we'd sober up and find a solution, Sheila and I still hadn't come to a decision about what we would try next. We were floating, it seemed, down the Fraser without oars. Jon at least knew what he was going to do. He was heading back to Missoula to look for work. He'd send an address and phone number, he said, when he could.

As I washed the breakfast dishes and waited for Sheila to come back to the cabin, our adventure in Canada seemed to me a jumble of pain and pleasure, of anxiety and unimaginable sweetness. There were, in all those pitch-soaked days of hard labor, of rabbit and biscuit dinners, and evenings that lasted until midnight, flashes of the greatest happiness I'd ever known. I couldn't justify the running off to avoid the draft with another man's wife. Try as I might to explain or defend what I'd done, I knew I couldn't. I had been craven at first and lax, and I'd lied to people who were my friends. But I knew, absolutely knew, I would make the same choices where Sheila was concerned. I would ask her to go with me again and again, no matter the consequences. I didn't want to consider what that said about me. I didn't want to think about any of it, except about her and the way I felt about her. I dried our cups and plates and pitched our dishwater outside. Almost lost in the morning's static on our transistor radio, I caught the weather report from Vancouver—from the greater world far beyond the bush—which ended with our mantra, "And gale warnings for the Georgia Strait."

A night or two after Jon left for Missoula we got our first real snow. In the gray light of morning I measured fourteen inches in the yard just beyond our porch. The temperature fell during the day to ten degrees above zero and a strange thing happened. The snow on our roof melted off right away, except for the overhanging eaves on each side of the cabin and the gable eaves, front and back, where the snow settled but did not melt. Clearly, heat was escaping up and out through our roof as fast as we could stuff wood into our stoves. That evening, we moved a bench up close to the airtight, so we could read in the one warm spot in the cabin. When I woke at midnight, it was freezing cold in the loft, probably within a few degrees of the temperature outside, and I understood that wintering in the cabin would be like wintering in a tent.

To keep busy, we finished the pole chinking inside, all the way up to the tops of the gables. Drafts flowed in at the cabin's four corners, where we used rope to chink the semi-circular saddle notches. We sawed and split wood together several hours each morning, the rows of split wood rising higher and higher in our woodshed. As soon as the weather broke, I hiked down to Dahlstroms' to see what Herb had going.

Working together, Herb and I butchered several more steers, and we built a windbreak fence on the north side of his feed yard to shelter his cows. Days when Herb was out in the bush, setting up his trap lines, I went back to wheeling manure from the cow shed or splitting stove wood at Dahlstroms' big woodpile. The days were cold, the sky gray, and I was surprised, as I hiked back and forth between the Mac and Dahlstroms', just how far I could see in the bush, now that all the leaves were down. One morning I crossed a fresh moose track in the snow. The hoof prints were wider than my bare hand

and almost as long, and I guessed they belonged to a mature bull. Herb had warned me about grizzly bears at that time of the year, when they were larding up for their winter sleep, and he said the moose could be just as unpredictable and every bit as dangerous. I carried three .410 shotgun slugs for Sheila's little Savage in my hip pocket, and as I walked, I kept my eyes moving.

As the hours of November daylight grew shorter, the days seemed to get longer. Sheila and I usually got busy with wood or small projects outside the cabin in the mornings, then took the afternoons to read or to think about writing projects. When we looked out at the forest beyond our clearing on overcast afternoons, all we could see through the wavy plastic was a world of black and white and gray.

We talked for hours about what we were going to do . . . about what we *could* do. By then we had less than a week until I was supposed to leave the country, but we still didn't know if we would go or not. Sheila didn't want to give up. She had status. She was in. And she was brave and bullheaded enough to think that if we made a fuss there might still be a chance, some recourse or appeal that could get me in. But there was always this: People in the area knew I'd worked for rent and wages. Immigration officers wouldn't have to work very hard to document that. And if I appealed my failed immigration interview, the Dahlstroms would likely discover from immigration officials that Sheila and Jon were married. I would not let that happen.

It was during these few days in early November, as I thought about writing and doodled on legal pads in the afternoons, that I was forced to admit that I knew—really knew—almost nothing about writing, let alone about writing fiction. I certainly had no knowledge of the fundamentals of journalism. And my writing mechanics, my spelling, punctuation, and grammar were—when I admitted it—not very far advanced above that of a mediocre college freshman. How, I asked myself, had I ever managed to graduate with a degree in English Literature?

Sheila, meanwhile, immersed herself in books by Joseph Campbell, working to understand how the ingredients of our myths and legends helped shape the various elements in modern fiction. Her concentration was fierce. For hours each afternoon all I heard on the other side of Jon's bookshelves was the turning of pages and an occasional muttering. She pushed on, even as I lost traction.

I spent my time, while Sheila studied, reading and re-reading Boris Pasternak's novel, *Doctor Zhivago*. In spite of the movie version, which I'd seen too many times, it seemed to me then that *Doctor Zhivago* was an excellent model for a novel about *our* country during the Vietnam War, a book that could include dissidents in the United States who fought against the war, as well as soldiers who had been there, actually fighting it. I wondered if someone was then writing such a novel, although I was so naïve that I only slowly realized that while I had the skills required to build an outhouse, I was thinking in terms of erecting a cathedral.

At some point, in all that brooding and day dreaming, I realized the impossibility of writing such a book, or any book about war, without the actual military experience gained in going to war. As I gazed at our woodshed through the undulating distortions of the plastic window above our writing desk, I saw that I was in the process, had been in the process all these past five years, of missing *the* event of my generation, the event that would *define* that generation and the years from 1964 until the war ended.

Some afternoons I suited up and took long hikes through the boggy country to the east of Government Creek. As the ground froze, I was able to cross long stretches of muskeg-like terrain, that even when partly frozen, flexed underfoot as if I was walking on bed springs. I shot a few grouse and snowshoe hares for our suppers, and I tried to imagine what six months of winter would be like, just the two of us, trying to stay warm in our cabin.

We felt the strain of our uncertainty and the force of oncoming winter. Sheila and I treated each other with increasing seriousness during those long evenings when we read aloud or talked about what we would do. We still hadn't received word about our placer claim lease, and we only had a few days left until I was supposed to cross the border. The date set for my draft physical in Butte was the 17th of November. But, of course, I had no draft card.

In the evenings, I found myself watching Sheila as she read, and as I looked at her there in the lamplight and listened to her voice, I knew that she was more than a prize. When I pared it all down, cabin, claim, immigration, the war, she was not only the most important piece of the puzzle, she mattered more than all the rest of it jammed together. So strange, then, that even while living with her in our log cabin, as winter came down from the north and our time ran out, the certain-sure knowing sank in, that as much as she mattered to me, I was going to war.

One bright morning there was a knock on our door. I swung the door open to find Herb Dahlstrom standing on the porch.

"Come in, come in," I said.

As Herb came through the door he turned to me and smiled. "I got him," he said. "I got him."

And so he had. The wolf had finally, after several years, made a mistake. He had stepped in a trap then pulled the pole drag up a steep hillside into heavy timber where the drag got tangled in downfalls.

"When I came up on him, he didn't growl or fight the trap. He just stood his ground and looked dead straight at me until I put him down. A man has to respect that," Herb said.

Herb led Sheila and I down to where the wolf lay in snow beside the old skid trail. He was black, and he was big, just as Herb had said. Of course we had to take a snapshot or two of Herb and the wolf. Because Herb was so relieved that the long contest was ended, and that he had finally prevailed, Sheila and I celebrated with him with much praise for both the animal and the man.

When a quiet man like Herb Dahlstrom is beaming, it is impossible to not to share his gladness. It would never have occurred to us not to.

I carried the wolf to Herb's tractor at the wagon track beside the creek. We placed him in the wooden trap box on the three-point hitch in back, shook hands, and I watched that good old man go off through the bush with the wolf, the tractor's four-cylinder motor popping along steady, until, finally, the only sound left was a soft wind in the tops of the trees. The sky was very blue and the snow sparkled in the first warm sunshine we'd had in days. I headed back toward our cabin, but after a few yards I felt something twist in me. I stopped and hugged myself, quite close to tears. But the tears would not come.

I may not have understood it then, or perhaps I did. But I felt it in my center. There are things in this world that should not be stilled, no matter what the reasons. I had just seen one of those things, had carried it on my shoulders. And I was sorry for that, because I, too, was caught at last. There would be no more running off, not for a good long while.

Sheila and I invited Clint Dahlstrom to come for dinner at the cabin. We didn't think we should ask Helen to walk the old skid trail at night, so we asked Clint to come alone instead. He was maybe ten years older than Sheila and I, and he seemed to us like the kind of non-judgmental grown-up who could offer us straight, no bullshit advice. So that evening Clint walked in with his flashlight, and while we ate I told him for the first time that I had meant to dodge the draft in the States, that I'd failed to get the immigration points I needed for landed status, and that I only had a few days left before I was supposed to leave Canada. We were out of time. We had to make a decision. Sheila and I did not say anything about Jon.

"What would you do, if you were in my boots?" I asked Clint.

He took his time before answering. Then he looked me right in the eye and said, "I'd pull the two years in the army, then come right back up here and try it again, if that's what you still wanted to do."

We ate in silence for a while in the lamplight. I caught Sheila's eye, and she looked away. I looked at Clint. "Thank you," I said.

"Dad will hate to see you go," Clint said to me. He looked at Sheila. "We will miss you both. But I think heading back is your only real choice at this point."

The morning after Clint Dahlstrom came to dinner, I walked up to the sawdust pile at the old mill site. The sky was obscured by low clouds, and what snow remained in shaded areas was as gray as the sky overhead. I looked at the El Camino, which had been so good to us, and in that moment I made up my mind.

At the cabin, I told Sheila that we had to go.

"There are no good choices, now, Pal. There's only one trail, and it runs right from here to the front doors of the Army Induction Center in Butte, Montana."

"No!" Sheila said and punched my chest with the edge of her balled fist. "Don't quit on me now!"

I caught her hand. "I'm not going to jail, if I can help it, just to make a point. We have to go back, but I promise you I won't cop out. I will not go to Vietnam. I'll find a way—I'll work it somehow, from inside the damned army if I have to—so that we can be together. You'll see more of me if I'm in the army than if I'm in jail, and we'll have a lot more fun, too. Sheila, I promise. I will make it work."

"Damn it, no!" Sheila said. She pushed away and turned her back on me.

"Come on, Pard," I said.

"What will happen to us? Do you see us breaking up?"

"Of course not. Maybe you can join me as soon as training is over. I don't know how that works. Maybe we'll have to get married. Will you marry me? Will you please marry me?"

"I don't want to marry you. I'm already fucking married! And look how that has turned out. Shall I go running around the world chasing after you and the army? Will we get together for hot weekends? Is that it? Is that what's left for us?" Her shoulders trembled, and when I saw she was about to cry, I realized that I'd never seen Sheila Malone anywhere close to tears. She was too strong for tears.

And finally, at last, I saw that this entire adventure, right up to the decision I'd just made, affected her every bit as much as it affected me. How slow I was, indeed. How could I have focused so intensely on myself all this time, without understanding how totally her life had been jacked around and reshaped by my desires, my lust, my dreams? It had always been about me, hadn't it? About what I wanted, about my convoluted logic, my bullshit? But it wasn't all bad. The running off, the weeks on the road, building the cabin, and the mythology two people in seclusion create about their lives together; all those things had turned our days and nights into a larger-than-life undertaking that had changed both our lives for the better.

Sheila made a strangled noise in her throat. "No," she said.

"We'll make it. The war has been pulling young couples like us apart since it started, but we'll be together again, sooner than you think. If you and I can't make that happen, who could? We'll have to bounce around some, but we'll find a way. Don't let go of me now.

I put my arms around her from behind, covering her hands, which she had folded across her breasts, with my own, and I held her as if she were the most precious thing in the world, because I knew she was. I could feel her heartbeats shuddering through my arms and chest, and there was such power and rhythm in her pulse that I knew again that she was perfect, and that no one would ever love her as I did then.

After a bit she turned in my arms to face me, her eyes shining with tears. "All right then, Love," she said. "If we're going to go, then let's get organized."

THIRTY-FIVE

Herb and Helen agreed to buy all our winter supplies, and they said we could store anything we needed to leave behind with them. In the next couple of days, Sheila and I boxed our books and filled the steamer trunk with clothes, dishes, and cookware then ferried it all to the attic in one of the Dahlstroms' outbuildings. We lugged the flour and potatoes and miscellaneous bags and boxes of food back up the old skid trail to the El Camino and hauled it to the Hidden Meadows.

The days ticked by. We tried to slow time however we could, to make the time together last, but we were distracted and overwhelmed, uncertain, or, as Sheila said, "conflicted." What saved us, finally, was momentum. We had a lot to get done to batten down the cabin and remove anything that would draw woodrats or mice. I planned to take my Kelly axes and Sam's saw and my father's tools back to Montana, but except for a couple changes of clothes, and our coats and boots, we left everything else at Dahlstroms'. Then we cleaned the cabin top to bottom and scrubbed the floor. We took the kittens back to Dahlstroms' barn and laughed as they arched their backs and crabbed about with bushed tails when they saw their old littermates. And it seemed to me that Sheila and I were going sideways just then, too, trying for traction so we could move on.

I shaved off my beard in the light of the Aladdin lamp. The Blue Blade in our Gillette safety razor wasn't very sharp and not very safe, but, after I'd cut

307

off all I could with Sheila's sewing-kit scissors, I hacked my way through the stubble that remained, to the pale, tender skin below. I left a drooping bandito mustache and took off all the rest, stopping after each pass to rinse the razor in our basin. I nicked myself again and again, and after I scraped off the last of the lather one final time, my face felt quite cold. In the mirror, I thought I looked like a whitefish that had been attacked by a bobcat.

The last morning, we hung our foam pads from the pole braces overhead with baler twine and made a final pot of coffee. When all was squared away, we washed the coffee pot and our cups and left them on the open oven door for Herb to use in our absence. We carried our rifles and sleeping bags and thermos up to the El Camino and drove to Dahlstroms' where Helen counted out the money for our supplies on the kitchen table. We left the Mossberg .22 and the Aladdin lamp with those good people. "Use them until we come back to stay," I said. "And, Herb, stop and warm up at the cabin every chance you get."

"Please," Sheila said, as she gave our friends a quick hug. "Please do that."

The ache I felt as Herb and I shook hands, was likely the same cruel hurt so many Americans have endured during all our nation's wars. So many young men, who had no idea where they'd be in a year; so many fathers, who had no idea if their boys would come home alive or in sealed coffins or not at all.

I stopped when we reached Coldbanks Road, got out, and looked back at Dahlstrom's farmstead, there on its little hill beyond the Hidden Meadows, everything tidy, each single thing in its proper place. That's what Peace looks like, I thought. That's Peace, right there.

When we stopped to pay Thorps for our winter supplies, the sun was shining, the sky, a brilliant blue dome above the village of Hixon.

Sheila counted out the bills on the counter, and Mrs. Thorp gave us a receipt marked Paid in Full. We didn't say anything about leaving. In fact, we spoke as little as possible, just trying to finish that last chore without adding to the gloom of our past few days.

It must say something about the way Sheila and I turned inward as we headed for the border, because other than the sunshine and a blur of leafless countryside through the El Camino's windshield, I remember nothing of the drive until the next morning, when we coasted to a stop on the American side of the border at Grand Forks, British Columbia. Once we cleared US Customs, I pulled over and parked. I walked across the highway to the Canadian border station to hand over the form I'd been given in Prince George. So extraordinary, it seemed to me then, how much the world had changed in just a few months. I felt not one bit of trepidation as I crossed the road, entered the office, and handed my exit form to the Canadian official, who looked a little surprised and somewhat silly in his bellhop uniform.

"Peace!" I said, which seemed like the only thing left to say. But as I pushed the glass door open, I turned back. "I love your country," I said.

During my undergraduate days in Bozeman, Coors beer had been—probably because it was unavailable in Montana at the time—quite the big deal. So, of course, although we were nearly broke and gasoline was eating up what little money we had left, I insisted we stop in Kellogg, Idaho, for a six-pack of that golden, watered-down slush. We pulled off the road east of Wallace and carried the cold cans to some boulders, where we sat beside a flashing stream in the afternoon sunshine and sipped our beer.

It seemed so strange to be back in the States, and the distance I felt then, between myself and the girl I loved, so sudden and unexpected. It was one of those warm November days that can make the oncoming winter seem even more cruel. We sat on our rock and watched the waters tumble past below our feet. It would have been a flawless afternoon if we hadn't both been facing such turbulence in the days ahead. Sunlight jeweled the water; the river played its song; and the Idaho mountains vaulted up from the river, mountains where elk lay bedded in the shade on north slopes, looking down on their back-trails as they belched and chewed, ruminating, perhaps, on the great mystery of their lives.

Sheila looked over. "What about me," she said. "What am I going to do?"

"Can you stay with your folks for a bit?"

"Let's hope it doesn't come to that," Sheila said.

"Your friend, Vickie?"

"Not right away."

"Shall we call Jon?"

"You'd hand me off, just like that?"

"Then tell me, what do you want to do when we get to Montana?"

"Let me think. I'll know when we get to Missoula, so let's just go. This beer is giving me a headache, and I feel like I'm being pulled in half by all our uncertainty and brooding."

"Sheila, I don't have a draft card. It could be I'll go straight to jail after all. You're not the only one—what was that word you used earlier?—who is feeling 'conflicted'."

"None of this makes any sense!"

"No, it doesn't made sense. But we have to move forward to get to whatever place it is where we can be together again."

Sheila reached out and put her hand on my leg, the gesture that usually closed the distances between us. She cocked her head to one side and studied me. "We're going to have to write letters," she said.

"I will write you such letters. Letters about war and big bad love. Letters that will make you ache and squirm."

"Oh, you fast-talking man," Sheila said. "But maybe letters will work. Maybe letters, honest, thoughtful letters that are true, will be enough for a while."

"I love you," I said. "You're my true love, and I'll love you for a long, long time."

Sheila looked at the waters rushing past, water in motion fired with light, and I could see that she was crying. Then she turned back to me and said, "I know. I know you do."

"We will get past this war, Pal," I said, "if we go it together."

Sheila wiped her eyes with the tail of her shirt. "I hope you're right, RB. Please be right. Now let's go face 'em and get it over."

I pulled on the headlights a few miles west of Missoula, and by the time we got to the Van Buren Street exit, it was dark. Sheila suggested we head to the University of Montana campus, where we parked at the University Center and went in to the Copper Commons to get coffee. The can-lights overhead were turned down low, and it was pleasant there at our table in the semi-darkness. The beer had worn off, and we were both feeling the miles of the past two days. We'd slept in the El Camino for a few hours the night before, and we hadn't eaten an actual meal since our last supper at the cabin. Apples and oranges and Cadbury chocolate bars can only do so much. We didn't have a whole lot left in reserve that evening, when we decided to splurge on some Copper Common's beef Stroganoff.

We ate like a couple of coyotes, more ravenous when we finished than when we'd begun.

"I'll call Jon," Sheila said when we pushed back our plates.

"Okay," I said. "He's probably expecting us."

She seemed so small as she made her way across the room, headed for the pay phones in the mezzanine on the floor below. She swayed again at the hip, the catch more obvious than usual in her stride, a young woman, weary and vulnerable and maybe a little scared just then. *Look at what you've done*, I thought. *Look at the damage you've caused.* I stood so I could see her as she pushed through the heavy glass doors to the landing outside, before going down some stairs and out of sight. In that moment I understood, again, that the world was a completely different place without her. Somehow, in all my vacuity and folly, I had won her for a little while, and that seemed to me a marvelous thing, a tremendous if unearned blessing.

I didn't know why she had let it happen, but for a brief sweet time she had loved me with a love that was wanton and fierce. I closed my eyes and saw her again as she walked away from our table, so small, swinging along with that dip and sway, and I knew that no matter what happened in the weeks and months ahead, I had to keep her in my life. She was absolutely worth the bugs and the sweat, the blisters and the pitch, the gloomiest days of rain and uncertainty that we'd shared in the summer, and she was worth what I'd have to do, no matter what it was, in the months and years ahead. She was worth everything, and I knew that was true.

Jon found us there in the Copper Commons. He pulled out a chair and sat down. I explained my decision to come back. There was no small talk; there were no lengthy speeches.

Jon turned to Sheila. "You can stay with me for a while," he said. "Until, well . . . when ever."

We decided that I would take the El Camino to Helena that evening, because it carried my tools and pack and Sam's little Homelite saw. We exchanged phone numbers. When we stood, I held out my hand, and Jon, after thinking it over, shook it. Sheila hugged me. "I'll be over for the El Camino in a few days," she said. "Hang on tight."

It was late afternoon when I walked into the Selective Service Office in the Power Block on Last Chance Gulch. Except for a pretty young woman about my age, the place seemed to be empty. When I gave her my name, she smiled and waved me toward a chair beside her desk.

"Hi, Ralph!" she said. "We've been wondering if we'd all have to go fishing in Canada to meet you!" She laughed, but there was no malice in it.

I looked at her with some considerable amazement as she explained that I needed to provide my own transportation to Butte on or before the morning of the 17th, and that she would provide me with meal tickets and a chit for one night in a hotel, in Butte. I'd forgotten about young ladies who wore skirts and white blouses, nylons and not quite sensible shoes. She was a tall girl with long chestnut hair; she seemed relaxed and efficient and friendly. I was surprised to wonder if she was flirting with me.

"Do you have any questions?" she asked.

"I lost my draft card," I answered.

"Not a problem," she said. She pulled a blank Selective Service form from a desk drawer, inserted it in her IBM, and typed out a brand new card with my current information. When she was finished, she handed me the card along with meal tickets and the hotel pass.

I stood up. I didn't know what to say. "Is that it?" I asked.

She stood, too. "I want to wish you the very best of luck, Ralph Beer," she said with great seriousness. "Please come home safe and sound."

"Thank you for your help," I said. "And for being so nice."

On the street outside, I realized it had only been a year since I'd walked all bushy-tailed and full of jive from those very doors behind me, with a brand new deferment that I really didn't deserve. Fair enough, I thought. I've been to the dance, and now its time to pay the band.

THIRTY-SIX

My mother had been overjoyed when I'd stopped at our white stucco house on Butte Avenue; tears streamed down her face even as she laughed and hugged me. My dad, who always seemed to be lining up more work for himself than any normal man could handle, had taken some vacation days from the smelter to work on a shop he was building in the Helena Valley. We shook hands, and he asked me if I wanted a job for a few days. I was broke and at loose ends, so I said sure, fine, let's get to it.

The shop was concrete block on a slab. I worked three long days, carrying hod with our Jackson Creek neighbor Laramie Wallace, both of us hustling to keep up with two bricklayers who were always in a hurry because they got paid by the block, not by the hour. Dad helped move scaffolding, carried sacks of cement and lime from the truck, whatever it took to keep things moving ahead of the masons. At the end of the job, Dad paid me thirty dollars, and I was flush again.

Sheila rode the Dog to Helena. I filled a cardboard box with elk steaks from the folks' freezer and picked up Sheila at the Greyhound Station. It seemed we'd been apart longer than just a few days. We were quiet with each other as we drove to Bozeman, where we were embraced by Mac and Elena Watson and the Toad at their new place, an old farm house on some acres off the Hyalite Road, just around the hill from Cottonwood Canyon. They turned on all the lights in the house that evening, broke out some wine and smoke, and put the first Cheech and Chong record we'd ever heard on their stereo. We laughed until we hurt. And it hurt so good, that laughter with those people we needed so much.

Sam and Sue Curtis were house-sitting again at Norm and Sil Strung's cabin in Cottonwood Canyon, where they had signed a one-hundred-year lease on a cabin site just across the creek. They had also signed contracts for teaching jobs at the Rocky Mountain School in Carbondale, Colorado, for the following two years—jobs to help pay for the first stages in building a log house of their own. Sam and Sue came to dinner at Watsons' the next night and we filled that old farm house with the bright noise of friends reunited.

At one point, I brought the little red Homelite into the living room and returned the saw to Sam with great ceremony. "This made the cabin possible," I told him. "I owe you one. A big one."

The next day, while Mac was at the University, I walked around the mountain into the Cottonwood Canyon drainage to Norm and Sil Strungs' cabin. Suzie was just leaving to pick up Sheila for a trip into Bozeman, so Sam and I splashed across the creek to see the land they had leased. The cabin site was in a low spot beside the creek, on ground overgrown with dogwood and brush and some big old hawthorn bushes that sported thorns two inches long. It felt good there, situated as it was in a grove of overspreading cotton-wood trees.

"No road, " Sam said. "And we like that. It might be a problem getting our cabin logs to the building site, but Strungs are going to let us park over there by the Screw Shack, and we'll build a foot bridge across the creek for every-day access." The Screw Shack Sam mentioned was a small cabin where Norman tied fishing flies and stored outdoor gear. There was a bunk and a woodstove, and young rakes, who had nowhere else to go, were known to sometimes bring girls out there for an evening.

The morning sun had cleared the timbered ridge east of Sam's cabin site, so we climbed a cutbank to a hayfield that lay between the creek and the hillside above. We walked through stubble to the center of the field, where an old apple tree stood all by itself. Sam gathered some apple-wood branches that had fallen to the ground under the tree. He wanted to use them to flavor the smoke when we bar-b-qued steaks that evening.

"Ralph, can I talk to you about your decision to come back?" Sam asked.

"Sure, Sam. Of course."

"I've noticed a tone in your conversation, since you've come back, that really doesn't have to be there. A tone that suggests a kind of apology. But the fact that you're going into the army doesn't do a darned thing to alter what we've done or said or what we love in common; those things still exist. They still count, and you're still the same person!"

"I'm not sure I follow, Sam," I said.

"Do you remember that day at your cabin when the gals were off hauling lumber or something, and I said that I thought you were doing the right thing—that Hixon was a place where you could get your shit together?"

"Yes. I remember that."

"Well, I think your decision to go into the army now is the result of getting it together. I don't see you copping out on anyone or anything! And as far as the dream is concerned—the dream of a woman and a cabin in the woods, well, that northland is still there. Sheila is with you a hundred percent, and your cabin is real! That ain't no dream, man."

I looked at Sam, so lean and earnest there in his red down jacket and tattered cowboy hat. I could see that he was trying hard to reach me, to break through my alternating glibness and gloom. He was trying to tell me something important that I needed to hear.

"One of the things I remember about how you seemed, as we put up the walls of your cabin last summer, was your feeling of homelessness. I could really sense that in you," Sam said. "And that feeling alone is enough reason, in my mind, to make you decide to come back home to your people—to us— because after all is said and done that's all there is: home and people. And very few people at that. So, welcome back, my friend. We are very glad to see you both, on this side of the border."

I didn't know what to say, but I was a tad uneasy with Sam's intensity.

"Look at it this way, Ralph. We're in for a two-year hitch. You and Sheila in the army, Sue and I teaching to pay for the cabin we'll build in the summers.

Not two years we want, true, but we'll make it. And we'll have our friends, we'll have each other, when we finish this part of our lives."

"You're right," I said.

Sam reached out and touched the apple tree, a remnant, most likely, of a long-gone homestead, and he said, "You know, this tree grows the best darned apples around."

I can see him standing there yet, some apple-wood branches resting in the crook of one arm, and behind him a steep slope timbered with slow-growth Douglas fir, trees that cast shadows down toward us in the field where we stood. Maybe because I respected Sam, or maybe because Sam alone made the effort to speak to me about my decision, I was then able, in the coming days, to gradually feel better about returning to Montana to go into the army. And I sensed, as we stood in the shadows cast by that apple tree, fruitless then in November and bare, that if I survived the coming two years, I would return to that sacred spot between a cold water stream and the hillside above, for many years, until the years played out, and we were no more.

The Montana Hotel was an exhausted remnant of Butte's mining boom, those years when saloons and whorehouses ran twenty-four-hours a day, fueled by wages the miners earned underground. And it was the only place where I ever saw a drunk projectile vomit from a third-floor landing into an open stairwell. There were other young men in that sad hotel that night, scared and drunk; boys, really, who would be going for draft physicals with me the next morning. I found my room, undressed, and turned off the light as the monkey-house bedlam in the hallway echoed with the hoots and shouts of those made loud by whiskey.

There was a tough-looking young pug from Butte, who showed up that morning sporting roughed-out leather jeans and a couple of broken teeth. *Keep your eye on that one.* And, of course, the Bohunk smoothie, also from Butte, who showed up in mod bellbottoms, paisley shirt and tie, even an expensive-looking overcoat. Let's call him Nick. *Really keep your eye on him.*

I looked at my fellow draftees, standing in their shorts in the line ahead of me. There were maybe forty of us, the fat and the lean, farm boys and townies, a few actual men. We were poked, inspected, prodded, and submitted to humiliations that few of us understood. We were given eye tests and hearing exams. Our hearts were listened to, our backs thumped, our throats examined as we said ahhhh. We turned our heads and coughed. And we filled out forms, putting down the same information again and again in black ballpoint ink. On one form we were told to read a three-page list of subversive organizations, then confirm with our signatures that we did not belong to The American Communist Party, nor The Polish Defamation League, nor The Sacred Knights of the Burning Cross—or was it The Burning Knights of the Sacred Cross? Did it matter? We signed every form that came our way. Some of the guys, I noticed, had suitcases. Suitcases. I had my lucky red-and-black wool hunting shirt and a few one dollar bills in my wallet, which was all I figured I'd need.

It had been a gray November morning in Butte, Montana, with clouds tumbling overhead out of the southwest. After a grim lunch at the counter in the Greyhound Bus Terminal, we returned to the Induction Center for final processing. A few of the boys were clearly scared, others put on a grave face. Most of us were from small towns in Montana, although there was a Utah contingent and a few lads from the Dakotas. We waited, then waited some more, until we were finally herded upstairs to a large room, where we milled about and waited for something to happen. A sergeant walked through and told us to "Smoke 'em if you got 'em," and we did.

I struck up a conversation with the man in the leather jeans. His name was Larry Cotter. He was taciturn and gruff. He spoke very quietly as he lit a cigarette on the butt of his last one. His old man, he said, worked the mines. He did, too. Didn't know much else. I told him my dad ran the blacksmith shop at the smelter in East Helena, and that I'd worked there in the summers. Larry looked me in the eye for the first time then nodded, and I saw that we'd be friends.

An officer in dress greens entered the room. The sergeant organized us into four lines of about ten men each, one row behind the other, each rank standing behind a yellow line painted on the floor. The officer, a major, someone said later, walked to a podium in front. The sergeant called us to attention, and there was some disorganized shuffling. Most of us stood up straight and looked toward the front of the room, where the officer said, "Good afternoon, gentlemen. You are about to be inducted into the United States Armed Forces. This ceremony takes place in two parts. I will first ask you to take one step forward, across the yellow line in front of you, which signifies that you have volunteered to serve. I will then administer the oath that officially places you into military service in the United States Army.

"Before we begin, I would call your attention to that building across the street, which most of you can see through this window." The officer walked to one side of the room and indicated a floor-to-ceiling window with one hand.

We looked outside, and I noticed that the clouds had parted. A weak November sunshine lit the top two stories of a square, concrete or stone building with a smokestack on one end.

"That building, gentlemen, is the Silver Bow County Jail," the major told us. "If any of you are going to refuse induction, that will be your next stop. Is there anyone here who plans to refuse induction?"

To my surprise, two men raised their hands.

"Please go to the back of the room and wait until we're finished here," the major said.

We were supposed to be at attention, but most of us turned to watch the two men, one a Native American, the other Asian—Japanese, perhaps—walk to a dim corner at the rear of the room.

I had not considered the possibility of refusing to be drafted at the last minute, when I was right there, standing in the open jaws of the United States military. I felt a faint tug in the direction of the jail. It still wasn't too late, it seemed.

The officer walked from the window back to the podium, but I continued to look outside at the sunshine warming the walls of the jail. The major was talking to us. But I yearned toward that light outside, where, for a moment, I saw sweet Sheila Malone, as she walked down those stairs toward me, from the glass doors above and behind her, there in the Student Union building at MSU. She carried her funny purse, the one that looked like a miniature picnic basket. As we passed at the foot of the stairs, she gave me just the brightest smile, and after I'd gone a step or two, I turned to watch her go down the hallway, past the bookstore windows, walking with her blend of friendly determination and physical grace, which in my eyes at that moment seemed perfect. Then I faced about, and as I felt a wonderful new thing come alive in my center, I went up those steps two at a time, heading for the glass doors above and the afternoon light outside.

The moment passed, and I looked back toward the front of the room.

"Take one step forward," the major said.

And I did.

a rush
of green
boiling
over stones
a sweet kiss
of liquid cool
in the quickly
warming
air.

—David E. Thomas
from "Almost Summer"

"Building the cabin made everything that followed, possible."

—Doctor Sheila Roberts
in conversation

EPILOGUE

I t's September up in Montana, and the creek runs cold past a tidy log house
and woodshed, shaded yet by old cottonwoods. Creek-side brush has commenced turning red and a few big leaves spiral down to land in quick waters,
there to voyage north and west toward the Gallatin River. Sam's house, which
he built himself, fitting every log precisely with his own hands, seems as
appealing to me as it always has. The woodshed, which often stands empty
now, calls to me. Work here, the woodshed says. Fill me up again.

To the east of Sam's house, an apple tree stands by itself in the stubble of
a hayfield. Beyond the field, a hillside timbered with slow-growth fir leaps
steeply up as it climbs toward the first ridges of the Gallatin Divide. Such a
slope is too abrupt for a man my age, so I cheat. I find a game trail that angles
gradually up through the firs to a grassy opening, where a hawthorn bush as
tall as a man bends under the weight of its own red fruit. This little park is my
destination. It's where Sam's children, Patrick, Molly, and Will, brought his
ashes and spread them over ground he loved.

At the upper edge of the opening, I lean my stick against a fir and clear a
spot of cones and rocks where I can sit and lean back to rest against the tree's
rough bark. From this vantage point I can look across the canyon and listen to
the great stillness all around me. I believe the purpose of sacred places such as
this is to free our hearts from the present so they can roam the past.

So strange it seems to me, to sit on a sun-warmed hillside in Montana and
remember the military I'd tried so hard to avoid. The army was almost too

easy. I added a year to avoid Vietnam and settled into a cadre slot at Fort Sill, Oklahoma, where Sheila joined me for a year and a half. Then a year at the super-secret complex at Nakhon Phanom, Thailand, and I was out. True to her word, Sheila was my faithful companion and correspondent during those three years. She should have received a Good Conduct Medal, too.

The Vietnam War *was* the event of my generation, whether we think much about it now or not. The suffering it caused the Vietnamese and American people was biblical in scope and hellish in its lasting pain. On our side 47,378 Americans lost their lives in Vietnam. No one knows how many Vietnamese, military and civilian, died during the years of our involvement there. The war can only be seen as a tragic and senseless waste for us all.

Sheila and I were together, off and on, for nearly fourteen years, years when I worked for almost nothing on my grandfather's ranch, worked for wages in the woods, and did a little writing. Sheila went back to graduate school, blazed through master's and PhD programs, then moved on to careers in petroleum geology and as a university professor.

Suzie Curtis died young. Sam remarried and started raising kids. He built a log addition on the north side of his cabin to serve as his office, and he became an outdoor writer and photographer just as he'd planned. Over the years he wrote dozens and dozens of articles as well as three fine books there in that room, where his work still lines one wall.

Mac Watson, our friend and teacher and favorite rabble-rouser, went home to Santa Fe, where he prospered as a building contractor and restorer of historic properties. One year he saved my bacon by offering me work on an adobe crew when Sheila remarried. I miss him, but I can turn my head and close my eyes and hear his laughter still.

A black-capped chickadee lands on a twig in a bough that swoops down from above me.

"Hey, Punkin," I say.

But the chickadee has no time to spare. "Too busy! Too busy!" she says and flits off down the slope to vanish among the trees.

If I stay too long, my rump goes numb, and my legs cramp up and ache. When I stand and walk toward the mighty hawthorn in the park's center, I think about Sam's ashes being scattered here, and about other things once loved, which have been reduced to ashes over the years. The spot where my father built our stucco house in Helena is now a vacant lot, as is the property on Lee Boulevard in Lawton, Oklahoma, where Sheila and I once lived.

Much loss, yes; yet over the years, so much happiness, so much good luck. The great luck of living through times of shared convergence, when adventures and friends, good books and love braided together into the best times of our lives—times when it seemed we'd be young forever, times when, to our amazement, our hopes were realized. What greater cause for celebration could there have been than to discover myself again and again with that perfect girl —the one who once stood with me on a seawall as the sun plunged into the Pacific, and the in-running tide thrummed through the earth beneath our feet with the resonance of a Welsh men's choir a thousand voices strong?

There have been, too, those many nights, when she has emerged from darkness to visit me in dreams, brief flirtations when we almost, but not quite, speak of those days and nights we shared in the woods when we were young. I see her in all her loveliness in those dreams, and I hear the littoral undertow of her voice. Sometimes she lingers in me like a prayer, after I've come awake.

Sheila and I kept up the required work on our Government Creek placer claim for several years. We stayed at the cabin one last time together in 1975. I sent in the annual payment a few days late in January 1977, and the Gold Commissioner, apparently fed up with us, refused the late payment. Sheila visited the cabin once during the Nineties; she found it in good condition and in use by persons unknown to us. I have not been back.

But that's not true. I go back often in memory, to walk the wagon road north from Dahlstroms' farmstead, passing through the bonfires of autumn in the paradise of the bush. I turn from the old skid trail to the path at our claim marker and ease through the timber to our clearing, where I stop beside our woodshed in the blue evening light to nose the air like a hound, trying to scent that rare smoke that I've never found anywhere else. And sometimes I go back to look at the white new logs in the walls, before the roof purlins and ridgepole went up, and I see people in the window openings, people who wave and smile as I take a photograph from too far away, people I will cherish until I, too, am ashes.

And sometimes I see her with our washtub, her cheeks flushed with effort as she smiles at me there in the autumn light slanting down through the trees above our cabin. And when I see her there, I'm glad, even when I feel that pain in my center, the one that always finds me, when I love her.

Made in the USA
San Bernardino, CA
03 August 2017